ANOTHER SHOT

Other Books by Joe Kita
Wisdom of Our Fathers
The Father's Guide to the Meaning of Life

ANOTHER SHOT

BY

JOE KITA

How I Relived My Life in Less Than a Year

RODALE®

Printed in the United States of America

Abridged versions of some chapters of *Another Shot* originally appeared in
Men's Health magazine.

Jacket and Interior Designer: Christopher Rhoads
Jacket Photographer: Mitch Mandel/Rodale Images

ISBN 1–57954–267–0

Distributed to the book trade by St. Martin's Press

RODALE

WE **INSPIRE** AND **ENABLE** PEOPLE TO IMPROVE
THEIR LIVES AND THE WORLD AROUND THEM

To all those who have messed up. To anybody who has ever failed. To every single person who has ever wished he could take another shot. Guess what?

You can.

contents

The Regrets

introduction

Before we begin this journey, this adventure into our possibilities, let me tell you a couple of stories. Consider it our basecamp briefing. Our inspiration.

The first one involves Jeff Bezos, the founder of Amazon.com and *Time* magazine's Person of the Year for 1999. When he was at his career crossroads, trying to decide whether to leave his existing job and head off into the Internet, he used for his personal analysis something he calls regret-minimization framework. Don't be intimidated. It's pretty basic logic.

He imagined himself at 80 years old, reflecting back on his life and career. What would he regret more? Attempting to start an online business and failing? Or never having the courage to start one at all? His decision suddenly became simple.

"I realized I'd be proud of myself for having taken that risk," he told *Time*. "It was like the Wild West, a new frontier. And I knew that if I didn't try this, I would regret it. And that would be inescapable."

The second story is a bit less straightforward. It involves bats in New Mexico. Terry McDonell, the former editor of *Men's Journal* magazine, and author George Plimpton were out birding one evening. They were searching for an elusive species of owl and not having much luck, when they noticed some bats flying overhead. Suddenly, Plimpton stripped off his T-shirt, balled it up, and flung it as high as he could. He did it repeatedly until he had attracted so many of them that the sky was a fluttering black curtain. The bats' sonar evidently interpreted the T-shirt as a giant moth, and they came in droves to inspect it.

Later, after the bats had departed, McDonell noticed that Plimpton's T-shirt was two sizes too small and probably not his at all. This unforgettable experience had not been miraculous happenstance, but the result of careful forethought.

McDonell learned a lesson that night, which he later shared with the readers of his magazine. "Good times should be orchestrated and not left to the uncertainties of chance," he wrote. "It's an idea that should have great purchase in every thinking person's strategy to avoid the accidental life as lived by its so-called victim. There is no sadder story than a life of small regrets."

I recently turned 40, and while I have much to be proud of, it's the time of life when you naturally question yourself. I've been a journalist for 2 decades, and I've had many great opportunities. I've traveled to exotic places, met famous people, had adventures many people just dream of. (And what's best, I didn't have to pay for any of it.) I've loved just one woman, and she me, and we've had two great kids to complete our destiny. I've been healthy all my years and have lost just one person who was very dear. Yes, I have indeed been blessed.

Yet there's a part of me that refuses to be fat and satisfied. It is forever unsettled. It looks at my life to this point and deems it largely accidental. The majority of my adventures have been job assignments—even my love, the result of a blind date. I have not set off on my own to explore any new frontiers, nor have I impulsively stripped off my T-shirt on a cool evening and flung it high at fresh stars. Up until recently, I had never even been to New Mexico. Instead, I've been a patient, hopeful player of life's lottery. And while it's been a pretty good run up until now, maybe, this part of me whispers, it could have been better.

When I was younger, I used to believe that my life was guided, that there was something so special about me that God himself was doing the choreography. It was reassuring but not at all realistic. The truth of the matter is that God gave us free will so He wouldn't have to be bothered.

Now I'm realizing that the only thing I'm destined for is death. In fact, the damn thought keeps popping up like a prairie dog in my consciousness, making me even more restless. It's not so much that I want to take control of my life, to seize it, to change it, to do something stupid. It's just that I'm curious as to where I might have been had things taken a slightly different turn.

I guess I need some reassurance. I need to know that I'm heading in the right direction, that I've made good choices and sound decisions, that I haven't been a total victim. So I decided to heed the advice of baseball great Yogi Berra, who once said, "When you come to a fork in the road, take it."

Using Bezos's regret-minimization framework, I imagined myself at 80, irascible yet contemplative. And I determined what would be my greatest laments, the opportunities I'd most regret missing, the moments where I'd wish I had another shot.

The 20 chapters in this book are the forks in the road of my life, the crossroads I've decided to revisit and then turn left at. I've backtracked to each one in order to give myself a second chance. Some are absurd, like trying out for the high school basketball team from which I was cut more than 20 years earlier. Others are disturbing, like using a psychic to contact my dead father to whom I'd never properly said thank you or goodbye. And a few are romantic, like finding out what might have happened had I the courage to follow up with a certain strawberry blonde who said I looked like James Caan.

A Man with No Regrets.

It sounds like an Ian Fleming novel, doesn't it? It seems just as exciting and adventurous as anything 007 did. It almost gives you goose bumps when you say it.

I read a piece of advice once from a guy named Joe E. Lewis. I don't know who he is or what he did, but it pretty much sums things up: "You only live once," he said, "but if you work it right, once is enough."

That's the journey of this book—to first determine if a regret-free life is possible and then, most important, to judge if it's worthwhile.

So join me as I begin tinkering with my fate. Join me as I look in the mirror every morning and instead of wondering "Why?" begin the day by saying, "What if?" Join me in considering our possibilities.

CHAPTER 1

getting cut from the high school basketball team

I feel like I have a knife in my heart," gasps the kid next to me. I nod agreement, doubled over in my own breathless agony, sweat puddling at my feet.

"Juniors and seniors to the line!" yells the coach, impatiently thumbing his stopwatch. "We'll do 10 in 55 seconds this time. Ready? Go!"

Basketball players call these full-court sprints suicides. But you'll never fully appreciate the irony of this nickname until you attempt to do almost 100 per day for 2 consecutive weeks with kids 20 years your junior.

I'm subjecting myself to this because although I am 40, I want to make my high school basketball team.

No, really. Over two decades after being cut from the team my senior year, I've convinced my alma mater's principal and head basketball coach to let me have a second chance.

If you find this hard to believe, then you probably were never cut from any team. It's the adolescent equivalent of being fired, except that when you're a teenager, you don't have a safety net of self-confidence to catch you. No matter how diplomatically it's done, the basic message is still "We don't want you."

I got the word 20 years ago in a dank locker-room office. The coach called me in after practice and told me that although he was impressed by my effort, he was going to have to let me go. "Sorry. Thanks for working so hard. Next!"

I remember emerging from that office pale, not wanting to meet any of my teammates' eyes because they weren't my teammates any longer. No one asked me how it went, no one slapped my back in consolation. At that age, failure freezes you, whether it's your own or someone else's. I just kept my head down, grabbed my gym bag, and fled.

But now I'm back. For a couple of weeks (10 days of conditioning, 3 days of tryouts), I'll practice with the Notre Dame Crusaders near Easton, Pennsylvania, after which I'll learn again whether I've made the cut or not. Although league rules prohibit me from suiting up and playing in actual games, for as long as it lasts, I'll be treated as just another kid.

No special favors, no fewer suicides. There are 14 varsity spots and 19 of us vying for them.

Beyond restoring some long-lost pride, the goal of this absurd experiment is to assess firsthand what a man loses and gains with age. For instance, I'd like to think I'm smarter than I was in high school. But even if I am, is this of any value when I'm squared off against a snake-quick senior point guard who spots the open lane?

In sports-bar recollections of our glory days, we never confess to losing a step or misplacing that magic touch. Our jumpers still catch nothing but net, our base hits are always line drives, and all our passes are perfect spirals.

My aim is to find out how badly we've been lying.

Lesson 1: You can train yourself to be fitter than a teenager but that's because most teenagers are in lousy shape.

It's the first day of conditioning, and we're choosing sides to run suicides.

Not surprisingly, I'm the last one picked. Since we do these drills in teams, with penalties for exceeding the time limit, it's poor strategy to have a balding, gray-haired, middle-age guy on your squad. That's like volunteering to puke.

Which is why a senior named Derrick, with a large, apparently self-carved scar on his right arm, looks sick when I hustle out to join his team. No one says anything to me. Even though Coach Pat Boyle explained beforehand what I was doing, few kids seem impressed. But that's okay. Let them think I'm a slow old man. At least I have a clear complexion.

What they don't know, however, is that I've been training for this moment for 2 months. I've been lifting weights, doing jumping drills, running, and playing lunchtime hoops with the desperate intent of not being embarrassed by any teenagers.

Conversely, most of these kids seem to have approached tryouts the same way they do algebra: Don't worry about it until the exam. This quickly becomes apparent as we run the drills, and I'm not last. In fact, sometimes I finish first as kids either give up, collapse, or retch into a nearby trash can. Still, my team finishes well over the time limit, meaning that more suicides await.

Nevertheless, it's an ego-booster to realize that I can outrun these kids, if only because I'm temporarily better trained. Exercise physiologists contend that endurance actually improves with age, and I'm apparently proving it. This may result from losing so many brain cells that pain isn't transmitted as swiftly or felt as sharply, but that's beside the point. The important thing is that I'm still standing and many of the kids are not.

Realizing that his gym has become a battlefield, Coach Boyle periodically gives us the opportunity to halve our penalty by making a foul shot. My team's first attempt, by a sweat-stricken senior named Dan, fails, and we all silently wish him dead. After we run more suicides, the coach calls my name. Instantly, I'm back in third-period biology with Sister Attila asking me to stand and detail the life cycle of a hellgrammite. I dry my sweaty hands, slowly walk to the front of the class, dribble, and let it fly. The shot arches through the air in silent, slow motion, hits the front of the rim, rebounds off the glass, and falls in. A cheer erupts, and my palm tingles from high fives.

Later that evening, I drive home in the passing lane, blasting Aerosmith. When I glance at myself in the rearview mirror, I think I spot a pimple.

Lesson 2: Every man needs a team.
Lesson 3: Every man needs a coach.

Each day's session ends with us huddling together in a sweaty knot. After Coach Boyle either chastises or congratulates us, we pile our hands together and say "team" in low, reverent unison. I look at the arms around me to see if anyone else has goose bumps.

Team. It must be the promise of commitment and glory that the word holds. It makes me feel privileged, that I'm a part of something that matters. I want to grit my teeth, whiten my knuckles, and run more suicides. Perhaps weddings should end this way, and family meals, and business meetings.

As we age, men belong to fewer and fewer teams. We become proud, solitary beings who think independence is the mark of maturity. We reclaim some of this bond vicariously by rooting for professional teams, but it's not the same. The experience is dilute. Being a member of a real team means setting definitive goals, making definable progress, and most importantly, having comrades with whom to share defeats and victories. It surprises me how much I've missed this, how much I need this.

There's a similar satisfaction in having a coach. Even though Coach Boyle is 12 years younger than I and more of a Newt than a Knute, it's reassuring to see him every afternoon. He comes to represent a very defined and focused part of my day. All I'm expected to do is follow orders and respond to the best of my ability. The only reward is his positive acknowledgment. But that is enough. There's something so enjoyably mechanical about it all, it becomes almost relaxing.

While there are lots of people giving us orders, there's a critical shortage of people acting as coaches. A true coach wants you to improve and succeed, as much for yourself as for the team. He's the objective taskmaster your father could never be, the field psychologist who understands what drives you. Coaches are the only men that guys aren't too proud to listen to and accept advice from. That's why it's important to have one in your life. It keeps you humble and on course.

Coach Boyle catches one of the kids in a lie. The kid gave a bogus excuse and skipped a couple of practices earlier in the week. So one afternoon, after the rest of us have finished running suicides, he's singled out to run some more. We sit along the bleachers and watch him suffer, the only sound in the gym being the squeak of his sneakers and the coach's admonitions to run faster. Ten, 20, 30 sprints. At one point, he collapses under the basket, and we listen for the curses that he must be thinking. But he silently rises and does 10, 20, 30 more. During his last set, the entire team spontaneously starts clapping and yelling his name. His pace visibly quickens, and when he staggers across the line, there's a certain amount of satisfaction and conquest in us all.

Team.

Lesson 4: Maybe it would help to have cheerleaders around the office.

We're into the second week of conditioning, and I'm early for practice today. In fact, I'm the only other person in the gym besides the varsity cheerleaders. I sit nervously alone on the bleachers, trying not to stare at anyone's pompoms. After a while, their coach ambles over and politely asks if she can help me. I feel like a shifty-eyed thief who has just been spotted by store security.

"I, uh, I'm waiting for basketball practice to start."

"Oh," she replies, "are you a parent?"

"No, I'm trying out for the team."

At this point, if there were a red emergency buzzer under the bleachers, I'm sure she would have pressed it. Realizing how crazy this must sound, I explain who I am and what I'm attempting to do. I even show her a business card from the magazine I work for, hoping that it carries the same weight as a hall pass. She seems satisfied, although still a bit skeptical, and goes back to the girls.

After a while, some of the guys arrive, but instead of the usual prepractice roughhousing, they all settle down next to me on the bleachers. There is no conversation. Everyone is transfixed, jaws slack, watching. When a line of cheerleaders bends over and wiggles, the kid alongside me gasps.

"What do you think of *that*, Mr. Kita?" asks Derrick with a sly smile.

"I still think of that," I reply, mentally checking off one more thing that 20 years has not dampened. "I still think of that. . . ."

All this accumulating testosterone apparently finds an outlet during practice, because we run our conditioning drills faster than ever. In fact, the junior/senior team I'm part of finishes just 2 seconds off the school record. Hmmm. Maybe we've finally stumbled upon the foolproof performance enhancer. Think of the possibilities if we could somehow get an audience with the Laker Girls.

As we huddle afterward, Coach Boyle announces that only two players have run every sprint and made every practice in these two weeks: a spry little sophomore and a 40-year-old alumnus. I have the feeling, though, that he's goading the rest of the team by displaying what has beaten their sorry selves. Nonetheless, the congratulations are sweet.

And if I'm not mistaken, I think one of the cheerleaders likes me.

Lesson 5: Speed is the first thing that goes.

Lesson 6: Smarts won't make up for it.

There's a certain nervous intensity in the locker room today. Part of it is that I feel self-conscious that I still don't have Tommy Hilfiger underwear sticking out of my gym trunks, but most of it stems from the collective realization that it's show time. The skill each of us exhibits during the next three days of tryouts will decide our fates.

No doubt about it, I'm psyched. I'm ready to call for the ball and kick some adolescent ass. But at the same time, I feel guilty about even wanting to try. On one hand, I'm expected to excel; I'm a grown man, for God's sake. But on the other, what will I really prove by doing so?

This dilemma is quickly resolved, however, once we start scrimmaging. In the first game, I'm guarding a 230-pound sophomore named Andy. The kid is like a refrigerator with limbs. He has almost 70 pounds on me—most of this, undoubtedly, Big Macs—and when he posts me down low, there's nothing I can do to stop him. Nothing.

Next, I'm up against a 6-foot-6 junior named Eddie. This still-growing boy is so tall that the Federal Aviation Administration is trying to get him to wear a blinking red light atop his head. He has 6 inches on me, which means I'm more of a pest than a test. When he gets the ball inside, it's an automatic two.

Finally, I move out to the guard position and square off against senior co-captain Tate. I outsize him by 2 inches and 15 pounds, but he is quicker than a 3-year-old in Macy's china department. Once he realizes how easily he can gain a step on me, I become nothing more than a matador.

And so the gains I've been gloating over in endurance are quickly offset by these glaring losses in strength, jumping ability, and speed. I would never have noticed a ½-inch less vertical leap or a split-second delay in reaction time had I not pitted myself against these young Bulls. But now that I have, the gap appears depressingly wide.

There is also a reckless passion among these boys that I don't share. They play the game with skillful abandon because they consider themselves invincible. When the ball squirts free, they pounce like cats—all instinct and adrenaline. Whereas when I see a loose ball, there's a moment's hesitation during which I gauge the twinge in my knee against my chance of actually grabbing the ball.

If anything, I've become a more thoughtful athlete in these 20 years, but that's not necessarily an advantage. In fact, in a game like basketball, some say intelligence hinders a player by further separating action from reaction.

Fortunately, as the scrimmaging continues, I do better. My stamina eventually outlasts their skill. Red-faced Andy begins to labor up and down the court, leaving me open for a few fast breaks. Fatigue becomes lead in Eddie's shoes, and I'm able to box him out for a rebound or two. And once, when Tate isn't looking, I disrupt his dribble and steal the ball.

Afterward, they all slap my hand and say, "Good game." And I think they genuinely mean it.

Just as I had been promised, I was merely one of the group today. No special treatment, no go-easy-on-the-old-guy. For the first time in this experiment, I truly felt like a high school kid, and no doubt it was because I was doing what kids do best: play. In fact, there were times when I lost all awareness of my outside appearance. It was my ageless soul—the one that thrives inside each of us—on that court, striving and smiling.

A senior Olympian once told me that despite all his wrinkles and white hair, he forever felt 12 years old inside. I understand now what he meant. Take away the mirrors in our world, not only those above our sinks but also those in society's eyes, and you instantly become younger. Indeed, if it weren't for the back-to-reality shake of a Tylenol bottle in my gym bag as I left practice, I very well might have hopped into my Dodge Grand Caravan and peeled out.

Lesson 7: Rest is the most delightful drug.

Time travel is not without cost. This morning I feel like a rusty tin man. Just when we had grown accustomed to suicides, yesterday

Coach Boyle replaced them with defensive slides. In this exercise, you crouch and quickly shuffle in whichever direction he points. Since the movement employs little-used muscles along the inner thighs, I am nearly paralyzed. But this doesn't worry me as much as the bizarre pains I have with no pinpointable cause. For instance, there's an annoying one in the heel of my right foot and another, of all places, in my left testicle. I mean, what the hell can that be other than my body's way of telling me I'm a nut?

Because of the 360-degree movement that basketball requires, it's the first sport I've played in adulthood that has made me feel old. What's sobering is that I see no other limps on the court this afternoon. In fact, even though I'm probably in the best shape of my life, I don't feel fit. I keep waiting for my body to shrug aside the soreness, but the one elixir an older athlete needs, the steroid all seniors crave—rest—isn't being dispensed.

I've even gained 5 pounds. Before I had been used to doing long, steady bicycle rides and runs. Now my exercise is coming in short, intense bursts, which evidently doesn't combust as much fat. Either that or I'm getting chubby just guarding Andy.

Lesson 8: What you lack in skill, you can make up for in heart.

"You nervous?" asks Coach Boyle with a grin, as our last practice ends.

"Nervous and beat up," I reply, trying to simultaneously rub my knee, shoulder, and head after a bruising scrimmage.

"Okay, everybody bring it in here!" he yells, calling us all to center court. After explaining that cuts will be made in private, he orders the juniors and seniors to the bleachers by the door and the rest to the stairwell outside the locker room.

And so the drumroll begins again. Coach Boyle first meets with the varsity captains in the hall, then begins calling us out one by one. We sit on the bleachers trying to be cool, one kid dribbling a basketball, another humming to some music in his head. When a marginal player disappears through the swinging doors, we listen for the gunshot that we know will finish him off.

"So you think you'll make the team?" asks Derrick jokingly.

"I heard I got your spot," I reply, deadpan.

Even though I realize this is all stage play, my palms are still sweaty and my smile slightly forced. I can feel the weighty hopes of every weekend warrior on my shoulders. If I make the team, then I've proved that age is not so tough a foe. If I don't, then there's always donkey basketball.

Frank, a dark-haired fireplug of a senior, returns through the doors and sits down next to me. Someone asks if he made it, and he shakes his head no, too choked up to even mumble the word. I suddenly get the urge to drape my arm around this kid and confess that I know what he's feeling—that I've been there and that it's manageable. But even 20 years later, I'm still frozen by failure. It's a contagion I can't bring myself to touch. So I swallow hard, along with everyone else, and we go back to dribbling, humming, and hoping.

"Joe!"

I spring for the door like I should have for every loose ball. And suddenly, I'm back in 1977, standing across from a coach who shakes my hand and tells me he's been impressed by my effort. "You have a lot of heart," says Coach Boyle. "You really gave 100 percent out there. And . . .

"And anyone who shows me they want to play as much as you did deserves to make the team. While you wouldn't be a starter, I'd use you on the press team. That's our 9th through 14th guys, who run the opponent. Congratulations."

I want to hug him. I want to find my old coach who cut me and tell him he was wrong. I want to ask one of those cheerleaders to the prom. I want to hike up my underwear. I want to retake my SATs. I want to finagle a second chance at everything I've ever failed at in life. I want to tell Frank not to give up hope. And most of all, I want to stay with this team.

"I'll be in the stands for your first game," I say, pumping Coach Boyle's hand, "just in case you need me."

When I eventually let go and head for the locker room, I feel as if I'm wearing Reebok Pumps inflated to cloud 9 level. There's still a bunch of underclassmen jamming the stairwell, and when they see me, someone asks if I made it. I flash them a double thumbs-up, and that stairwell becomes like the Boston Garden to me, reverberating with cheers.

Besides learning that the boy inside us never dies, I learned the value of heart from this experience. Although I still don't have the ability and skill of a lot of these kids, I trained, I prepared, and I won on heart. It's firsthand proof that the cliché is true: If you set your mind to something, you really can accomplish it. You can lead and succeed via your skill, which is easy when you're young. But you can also lead and succeed via your heart, which we often forget when we're old.

As I leave the gym for the last time, Derrick comes over to administer one more back pat. "I'm so happy," he says. "Finally, there's someone on the team who's old enough to buy beer."

CHAPTER 2

not being filthy rich

John Besteley, my 70-year-old, mail-order Romanian butler, has been patiently waiting at the Charcoal Drive-In in Wescosville, Pennsylvania, for 1½ hours. He is, however, unruffled. He explains that he took an early bus from New York City to ensure he wouldn't be late for his first day of work.

"Now, sir, after you," he says with a gracious sweep of his hand.

As we walk across the parking lot to my car, making small talk about the weather, I notice that Mr. Besteley is lagging behind. So I politely slow down. When he still fails to match my stride, I slow down further. What I'm not realizing is that he is purposely following me. A good butler is, at all times, his master's shadow—unnoticed but omnipresent.

For the next week, Mr. Besteley will be my shadow, my attendant Jeeves, my vigilant Lerch, my confidant Alfred, my abiding (but hopefully not overly friendly) Mr. French. My goal is simple: to experience the lifestyle of the filthy rich, those prim men and women who, for whatever fortuitous reason, lead lives that are far more sterling than our own.

You see, my good man, I do not come from money, nor is my breeding exactly pedigree. The only grounds on my estate come from discarded coffee. My existing staff consists of a wife who likes to sleep and two kids who seemingly never do. Indeed, the only time I'm lucky enough to have breakfast in bed is when I doze off eating a midnight snack. And rather than residing in the Hamptons, I live in a town called Schnecksville. Make of it what you will.

To live out this regret, I originally looked into renting a mansion but that was prohibitively expensive. I then called Avis and Hertz, but there were no Rolls-Royces on their lots. Neither Gulfstream nor Lear would let me borrow one of its jets, so hiring a professional butler was the sole upper-crust crumb I had left. The price was a relatively affordable $1,000 per week.

I have a couple of other motives for doing this, too. I'm curious to see just how much stress a competent assistant can remove from a busy man. (You think Bruce Wayne would've ever found the time to be Batman if he'd had to press his own capes?) Plus, since I know our arrangement will ultimately end, I want to wring Mr. Besteley, a butler for 37 years, of his most useful secrets. After all, a butler is in many ways the ideal man—sophisticated, impeccably groomed, resourceful, poised, an architect of quiet excellence. So if hiring one full-time is out of the question, perhaps it's still possible to learn how to run your life with similar aplomb.

Secret 1: To get what you want, be mannerly.

While in my employ, Mr. Besteley's foremost duties will be organizing and overseeing a Friday dinner party for 8 and a Sunday brunch for 12. While such a hectic social schedule would normally put a severe bunch in my cummerbund, Mr. Besteley is unconcerned. He has experience at four international embassies, has worked for such diverse clients as Mrs. Henry Ford and *Penthouse* magazine publisher Bob Guccione, and once even served Ronald and Nancy Reagan. ("She ran the show," he recalls, "and the president drank screwdrivers.")

He tells me this last story as we're heading to the rental car agency to claim a black Cadillac Seville. (I couldn't put someone of his stature behind the wheel of my 1989 Dodge Grand Caravan, even if it does have cruise control.) I ask him about the great automobiles he must have driven, imagining him white-gloved at the helm of Bentleys and Jaguars. But for the first time, Mr. Besteley appears disconcerted, sort of like he's about to confess catching the lady of the house in the beds with the gardener. I press him about his driving record, suspecting that perhaps there's been a minor traffic violation or two, but in fact, it's much worse. Since he's a big-city butler, he doesn't even have a license.

My first impulse is to dismiss him forthwith for misleading me. In my dealings with his placement service and our subsequent correspondence, this shortcoming was never mentioned. But the more I think about it, the more flattered I become. My man was willing to take a bullet for me. He was ready to buckle himself into that Caddy and chauffeur me through rush hour to La Guardia if necessary. He didn't want to let me down. He'll do anything I ask. Here, finally(!), was a way to rent adult films at the neighborhood video store without risk of embarrassment.

So it's I who chauffeur the butler to our next appointment, a meeting with our dinner-party chef, Tom Ney. Eventually, they both agree that to stage this affair properly, they absolutely must have 107 assorted pieces of china, 56 crystal glasses, 129 pieces of silverware, a couple of candelabras, 24 white linen napkins, 200 white cocktail napkins, and 3, yes, 3 banquet tablecloths. When I remind them that only eight people are attending, they add 10 more glasses and a second small pair of sugar tongs.

They don't agree on everything, though. The chef wants to serve champagne with the consommé. Mr. Besteley says this is simply never done. ("It's like wearing galoshes with a nightgown.") Tom wants the decoration plates removed after the second course. Mr. Besteley insists that they remain. Tom prefers that the soup be served to the guests. Mr. Besteley favors it cooling on the table before they're seated. Tom asks whether he'd consider preparing bananas Foster tableside for dessert. Mr. Besteley sniffs that a butler is never a cook at affairs like this, giving "cook" the same inflection as "pool boy."

What prevents them from carving each other up with fine cutlery is not so much Tom's patience as it is Mr. Besteley's Old-World civility. He prefaces each of his comments with "Sir" or "Mr. Ney," he thanks Tom for his opinion even if he disagrees, and, of course, he smiles. This makes a gentlemen's duel out of what might have otherwise deteriorated into a bullies' brawl.

The art of effective etiquette—it's the first lesson of butlerdom. When you want to have your way, simply try being mannerly. It's become so rare nowadays that it disarms people. It throws them off balance. Don't think of it as merely being nice; think of it as civil war. Indeed, Mr. Besteley leaves the meeting with concessions on all fronts.

It's almost dark when I drop Mr. Besteley outside his hotel. (The guest quarters at my estate have yet to be built.) I assist him in getting his valise out of the trunk and with checking in, then he bids me good night. It strikes me that something is not quite right here. I've yet to eat dinner. I still haven't read the morning paper. And I guess that snifter of Courvoisier will have to wait.

Secret 2: It's life's details that make life luxurious.

The house smells sweet, like baking pastry. It's 4:00 P.M., and I'm home from the office early, apprehensive about leaving Mr. Besteley in charge while my wife is at work. I needn't have worried. The table is set for dinner, the house is spotless, and my children are quietly reading. Mr. Besteley, dressed in white shirt and white pants, is diligently scrubbing the bottom of the cooking pots. He looks up, nods pleasantly, and asks when I would like to have dinner. I say five-ish, and he says, "Very good," adding that the week's grocery shopping has been done, all the party supplies rented, and most of my trousers pressed.

If I had a study, I would now retire to it and slip on the velvet smoking jacket I don't own. This is exactly how I've imagined it in my dreams. Stepping from a world where nothing runs smoothly into one where everything does is more soothing and pleasurable than any after-work cocktail. A butler's job is to make this transition routine, to keep your home a haven in a neighborhood of satellite offices. The only thing that would have made me smile more was a team of French maids vigorously feather-dusting the floor molding. (But perhaps that's another regret. . . .)

Mr. Besteley serves the evening meal with a paper towel draped over his wrist. (My life to this point has, inexplicably, been linen-less.) After filling our glasses with ice water, he unlids a bubbling cauliflower au gratin casserole from which my children and I spoon portions as it's offered. As we eat, he stands in the background until more water, bread, or casserole is needed. When there's a spill, it's he who springs to mop it up. When my daughter balks at cleaning her plate, it's he who threatens withholding dessert. I finish the main course without once having to stand, scold, or scream. And Mr. Besteley tops it off with his homemade custard crème.

Afterward, he scrubs all the dishes by hand, thoughtfully sets aside some leftovers, tidies up the kitchen, and as a final touch, arranges a bunch of red grapes in a bowl on the counter. "Yes, it's all done," he says, satisfied.

Reverence for the details. Most people either ignore or abhor them, but this is where contentment and true luxury lie. Few of us can be perfect in the grand scheme, but everyone can be peerless when it comes to the particulars. Whether arranging a place setting, pressing a shirt, or even scouring scalded Farberware, there's a satisfaction that springs from attending to little things and controlling what you can. It's not just relaxing; it also builds pride. A butler's confidence grows from his mastery of the mundane into a conviction that he can handle anything.

It's the details that also make a sawbuck like me feel like a million. A crisp, line-dried bedsheet at the end of a hard day. Beer chilled to 38°F and served in a pilsner glass. The diamond ankle bracelet you gave her, sparkling above a stiletto heel. Most people are too busy to bother. Most people don't have the time to linger.

But that is precisely the point. For those who do, that instant of satisfaction, that second of pleasure, is the moment of wealth.

Secret 3: If you want respect, develop presence.

Mr. Besteley and I are shopping for something for me to wear this weekend. He points out that darker shades work with my hair color best. "Navy blues, blacks, and maroons make you look more mysterious." (You don't say, old chap.)

When I find a sport coat I like, Mr. Besteley hails a clerk to fit me and hustles off in search of a matching shirt and tie. After a few minutes, he returns with a nice plum button-down that, remarkably, is on sale for $6.99. The neckwear he has chosen, however, seems a bit dull. When I hold out a flashier alternative, he beckons me aside and whispers, "It is, how we say in Romania, crap. No, this is the one you want—some color, some class. It goes with many different things." Furthermore, he points out that at $12, his choice is "significantly more affordable." (A good butler never uses the word "cheap.")

Convinced, I leave the store feeling satisfied and, because Mr. Besteley is still tailing me, even a bit mysterious.

Though having a devoted assistant at your flank is helpful, there are things that even a butler can't do—or won't do. For example, Mr. Besteley politely refuses to tee up my golf balls at the driving range, serve as my batboy during a softball game, replace the starter in my van, or refinish the basement. (Hey, you get a chance like this, you have to ask.) A butler may be a servant, but he is never a slave.

The difference has to do with presence, that quiet, dignified air he exudes. A butler is asked to do many menial things, yet when he's actually doing them, they never appear menial. Pouring wine becomes a science; deboning a fish, specialized surgery. Indeed, Mr. Besteley presses trousers with such passion that, after watching him, it infects me. I begin to delight in creating a sharp crease, and to this day, I feel strangely challenged by pleats.

The secret to developing such presence is twofold. First, whatever the deed, it must be done with quiet expertise. Never boastful, a butler always does his absolute best, and in a half-assed world, that's guaranteed to impress. A person in charge, no matter of what, is always a head taller than everyone else. Second, and perhaps most important, is the small but often overlooked matter of appearance. Spotless lapels, perfect hair, shined shoes—if it's obvious that you respect yourself, others will be more likely to respect you.

At dinner this evening, Mr. Besteley unveils his noodle soufflé. It stands 13 inches tall and quivers with cholesterol. As he sets it on the table, dressed in his royal-blue slippers and immaculate work whites, he proudly says, "I invented this."

I swear, there's esteem rising from it.

Secret 4: Treat everything you do as if it were a performance.

It's 5:30 P.M. on Friday, the guests are expected at 6, and our kitchen is filled with smoke. There has been some sort of crudité crisis as well, and Chef Ney and Mr. Besteley seem ready to serve each other's heads on the rented silver platters. But my wife and I are pleasantly sipping champagne in the sunroom, remarking at how good a year the asters have had. We are properly insulated from the hubbub.

Mr. Besteley has set an elegant table. He has even rearranged our furniture so the party can flow and grow as the evening progresses, almost as if the event were a living organism to be nurtured along with the guests. And he has given me a final dusting, fixing my tie and fluffing my pocket square until I, too, am pronounced finished.

With everything perfectly poised, Mr. Besteley becomes a sentry. Dressed in his black tuxedo, shoes gleaming, trouser crease so sharp small children have to be warned, he waits in the front hall for the press of fingertip to doorbell that will signal the start of his performance. When it is given and guests begin to arrive, Mr. Besteley is indeed on stage—serving hors d'oeuvres, cocktails, and with each extension of his silver salver, a small taste of class.

My wife and I feel like guests at our own party, as if we were finally able to secure reservations at Chez Kita. For the first time, we can sit back and enjoy the company without worrying about who needs another Old Milwaukee or whether everyone is getting enough ring bologna.

At 7:15, Mr. Besteley makes the dramatic announcement all have been waiting for: "Dinner is served." Then he ushers everyone into the dining room for a near-crippling progression of chicken consommé with lemongrass, wok-smoked salmon, chateaubriand, mixed baby greens, peach melba, and chocolate truffles. Everyone's attention is initially on the butler, but by the third course, he has been almost forgotten—a ghost who is first here, next there, then gone. And this is how it should be. Truly great butlers are invisible. Only their results are evident.

Afterward, we adjourn to the deck to sip shade-grown Song Bird coffee. (The sun-raised stuff irritates my lumbago.) It's a perfect, star-strewn night, and we're lulled by the sound of lawn sprinklers and the gentle pat-pat-pat of Rottweilers patrolling the grounds. Raoul, my burly Filipino security guard, checks to see that everything is in order, then hustles off to tend the gates for our guests' departure.

Or so it seems in this dream.

Meanwhile, Mr. Besteley has finished clearing the table, wrapping the leftovers, polishing the kitchen, and roughing out my tax return. Before he leaves, he arranges yet another fresh bunch of red grapes in a bowl on the counter.

"Thank you, John," I say while driving him to his hotel. "You did a great job."

"Yes, of course," he replies.

Unlike with the babysitter, I feel no guilty pangs of lust—just the seeds of trust.

Secret 5: The poorest men are those who pretend.

Sunday's brunch goes just as smoothly as Friday's dinner party. Even a 6-foot rubber snake planted in the hall as a practical joke cannot upset Mr. Besteley.

It is becoming obvious, however, that he is tiring of playing butler to the *"neveur" riche.* I suppose it's like asking a highly skilled surgeon to do nothing but butcher meat. To be a worthy master, not only must you use a butler to his full abilities but you must also possess a bit of aristocracy yourself. Ivor Spencer, who runs a school for butlers in London, says that although English lottery winners are a good source of jobs for his students, the relationships often don't work out. "Ordinary people aren't used to this kind of life," he explains. "They just don't feel comfortable with a butler."

I can see why. After the initial thrill of having a servant has faded and all the guests have gone, I'm left with the reality of sharing my home with a 70-year-old Romanian. And though his job is to ease my stress, I can only relax so far. It's like an extended visit from my wife's Aunt Bertha, only without the personal insults and with slightly less facial hair. To tolerate a butler, you need an entire estate, or at least a secluded wing.

Also, once you have a butler, you quickly realize that you really need an entire staff. Although Mr. Besteley agreed to pinch-hit when required, he couldn't realistically be expected to cook every meal, care for all my clothes, clean the house, wax the car, disinfect the hot tub, cut the grass, and calm my high-strung mother. For these duties, I would need, respectively, a personal chef, valet, maid, chauffeur, pool boy, groundskeeper, and pharmacist.

And though I've had a good time at our parties, I think I would have enjoyed myself more if I had been the one popping the corks and sweeping the broken glass off the floor. For me, the fun has always been in the fever. A truly memorable party requires at least a touch of the *im*proper.

I dismiss Mr. Besteley a day early, giving him the agreed-upon fee and a hearty handshake. (You never tip a butler.) That evening, I arrive home a half-hour late. The table isn't set, the house is a mess, and my children are practicing professional wrestling moves in the living room. My wife, dressed in a sweatshirt and jeans, is on the phone ordering a couple of pizzas. She looks up, nods sweetly, and asks whether I can pick them up, adding that she didn't get a chance to go grocery shopping and that the damn garage door is stuck again. I smile, give her a big hug, and breathe a sigh of relief.

I am master of my own house once more. AS

CHAPTER 3

never having the courage to ask her out

Her name was Susan Prescott. She had blonde hair and rimless glasses tinged with strawberry around the edges. That's all I remember about her appearance—two details from 23 years ago. But they're as clear as they'd be if she were standing in front of me now.

We were both freshmen in college. We were studying journalism and shared a few classes. I had noticed her and thought she was pretty. Her name—Susan Prescott—suggested a well-to-do, intelligent girl, who folds her sweaters, calls her father "Daddy," and never answers to Sue.

One afternoon in the office of our school newspaper, *The Brown and White*, she came up to me and said, "Hi." I think I smiled back. I don't know. Pretty girls make me uncomfortable, then and now. But she said something next that I'll never forget: "You look just like James Caan. And I *adore* James Caan."

I was overwhelmed. I was being compared to a handsome actor. I might have stuttered a thank you. I don't know. It was one of those moments when you're speechless and then 5 minutes later think of a hundred responses. She smiled and said, "Bye," leaving me standing there embarrassed and frustrated. I should have said she reminded me of the actress Susan Dey, in some small way. Or I should have mentioned one of Caan's films, maybe *Brian's Song*. Or I should have gone after her, started a conversation, and asked for a date.

But instead I stood there. And more than 2 decades later, I'm still standing there—in my mind's eye. I never mustered the courage to ask Susan Prescott out, not then and not in our ensuing 4 years together at school. We continued to share classes and smiles, but I was shy, and she probably thought I was either uninterested or weird. Or maybe she didn't think anything at all. Maybe I'm being hopelessly egotistical. Maybe that wasn't a come-on. Maybe it was just an innocent compliment, plucked, delivered, and then forgotten from a bouquet of others held by a genuinely nice girl.

When it comes to experiences with the opposite sex, my memory is vivid. That's because I haven't had too many of them. I'm no Wilt Chamberlain. I can remember every girl I've ever dated and even those I wanted to but never did. It sounds ridiculous, I know, but my love life is a never-ending ribbon of what-ifs. I suspect every person's is.

But I'm tired of it. In this instance, at least, I'm going to find out, once and for all, if Susan Prescott still thinks I look like James Caan.

After 23 years, I'm finally going to ask her out.

Finding her is easier than I expect. I call the university's alumni office, identify myself, and tell the young lady there whom I'm looking for.

"Let's see," she says. "Class of '81. Susan Prescott-Stone, husband Benjamin, lives in Haverford, works for Allied Health Care. Would you like her business or home contact?"

I write down both, simultaneously amazed that I'm getting all this personal information and that Susan Prescott-Stone lives so close to me. Haverford is just 45 minutes away by car. I'd been ready, if necessary, to fly to Alaska.

The fact that she's married doesn't dissuade me. After all, so am I. The affair I'm planning isn't about romance; it's about erasing a pesky regret. If it ever started to lead somewhere, I'd squelch it.

Or at least I think I would.

Also surprising is that my wife doesn't seem to mind that I'm chasing another woman in my spare time. I'd like to believe she trusts me, but I suspect it's more that she considers my quest both hopeless and pathetic.

"She said I looked like James Caan."

"Isn't he dead?"

"Back then he was a stud. I reminded her of him."

"Dear, that was when you were a freshman in college and had hair."

"Yeah, but maybe there's still a resemblance. Do you think so?"

"No."

"Not even a little? From the side maybe?"

"This woman is going to think you're crazy. You'd better hope she doesn't call the cops."

Hmmm. I hadn't thought of that. Considering that she said 12 words to me 23 years ago, maybe that does make me a lunatic for replying now. This is going to be more delicate than I anticipated. If I phone her, I'll never be able to explain myself well enough. I mean, what could I possibly say?

"Hello, Susan? You probably don't remember me, but you said I looked like a famous actor when we were in college, and I thought maybe we could meet somewhere so you could tell me if I still do."

Click.

"Hello, Susan? I'm writing a book about my biggest regrets, and you're one of them. Remember that time back in 1977 when you came on to me, and I never responded?"

Click.

"Hello, Susan? This is James Caan, the actor, calling from Hollywood. I understand that you're a big fan of mine. I'm going to be making an appearance in your area on the 9th, and I thought we could meet."

No. I'd never be able to pull off that last one. Maybe it's better to write a letter. Make it personal but professional. If it triggers a fond memory, then great. If not, then she can simply ignore it.

Dear Susan,

You probably don't remember me, but I graduated with you in 1981. I majored in journalism and was in some of your classes. I got your address from the alumni office.

I have a bit of a strange request. In fact, it's even a little embarrassing, but here goes. I'm writing a book called Another Shot. *It's about a 40-year-old guy who starts wondering about life, about how things might have turned out differently. So he makes a list of his biggest regrets and sets out to revisit each one. It's an experiment with two purposes: to see if a regret-free life is possible and to see if it's even worthwhile.*

Well, that guy is me. I've been working on the book for 9 months now (3 more to go), and I've done some pretty bizarre things. For instance, I tried out for the high school basketball team I was cut from more than 20 years ago. I hired a butler for a week to experience what it feels like to be filthy rich. I visited a psychic with the hope of contacting my dead father. And I even learned how to surf. Then there's the regret that involves you. . . .

You probably don't remember this either, but one afternoon in The Brown and White *office, you came up to me and said, "You look just like James Caan. And I adore James Caan."*

Now don't deny this. It was definitely on the record. But you so surprised me and you were so pretty that all I could say was, "Thanks"—both then and for our remaining four years at school.

So it has become one of my regrets—that I was too timid to respond and start up a friendship. Ridiculous, no? It's funny how these things stick with us.

Please rest assured that this is not a come-on. I'm happily married

*(16 years this September) and have two children (Paul, 15, and Claire, 11).
I am not looking to start anything but rather to finish something. To finally,
after more than 20 years, acknowledge your compliment and find out once
and for all if I still look like James Caan. And then, of course, to write
about it.*

*If you're willing, I'd like to meet for lunch one day. An hour or two—
I'll buy, whenever is convenient. In return, I'll send you a copy of the book
when it comes out, along with my appreciation.*

*Please let me know one way or the other, Susan, if you're open to
doing this. If you think I'm some kind of a nut, then I can certainly understand why. I won't bother you again. Nevertheless, I appreciate your
consideration.*

I write the letter on March 15, but I can't bring myself to mail
it until May 2. I read it 100 times, fussing with the words and punc-
tuation. It feels like I'm 16 again, picking up the phone, putting it
down, picking it up again, dialing, hanging up, rehearsing what I'm
going to say to the girl I'm calling. Indeed, when I finally have the
envelopes stamped and addressed (one to her business and one to
her home, for extra insurance), I hesitate before dropping them into
the mail slot.

It's not that I feel guilty about pursuing another woman.
Rather, it's that I'm throwing a part of myself to a lioness who
could either adopt or devour it. I've made a confession. I'm vulnerable to ridicule and rejection.

"If I got a letter like this," says my wife, "I'd have to read it two
or three times to make sure I understood it. Then I'd show it to my
husband, who'd probably tell me not to respond. But I'd do it
anyway. It seems harmless enough. I guess I'd be curious."

So off goes my heart, and I wait and wonder what life might
have been like with Susan Prescott. A simple acknowledgment of
one compliment could have altered our destinies forever (or, at
least, resulted in some memorable sex). When you consider all of
life's tiny choices and their potentially huge effects, it becomes
amazing how we ever end up where we are. It makes you wonder
if your existence is just a collection of happenstances, or if, in fact,

there is some hand upon the wheel other than your own. I suspect that a part of my drive to right every regret is a need to know that. Does my life have some predetermined direction and meaning, or am I just wandering? Am I supposed to be with Maria, my wife? Or could I have been just as happy with Susan Prescott? Or, even more troubling, does it matter?

Looking back is dangerous. It triggers fear, inspires worry, causes accidents. Hence my hesitation and, now, my anticipation. Every morning when my e-mail opens, I scan the inbox for a message. But nothing from her is ever there.

I ask myself, "What's another couple of weeks after 23 years?" But each day that passes without a reply from her makes me realize what foolishness this really is.

For a while, I try being rational. Perhaps she has moved and her mail hasn't caught up with her yet. Or perhaps she's on an extended business trip—Paris, Milan, Frankfurt.

After a while, I get paranoid. Maybe she has a large, jealous husband. Maybe he intercepted the letters and threw them away before she could read them. Maybe he's heading my way with a sawed-off shotgun.

After a while longer, I even get vindictive. She's probably grown fat and troll-like—too embarrassed to meet me because I'll be judging her just as she'll be judging me. Maybe she's waiting until after the liposuction.

I agonize over what to do next. Should I call her at home? Leave a message on her answering machine at work? Should I drive to Haverford, find her house, and boldly introduce myself? Should I hire a private detective to stake out her place and get some compromising photographs? Should I arrange some outrageous stunt she can't ignore, like a plane towing a banner with my name and phone number? Or should I continue to play it cool and send another letter, slightly more imploring, this time via certified mail?

Desperate for advice, I ask a friend at work what he would do. He thinks for a while, then turns wistful.

"There was this drop-dead beautiful girl who sat next to me in high school. Whenever we spoke, my heart would beat so loudly I was afraid she'd hear it. I couldn't work up the courage to ask her out, and I never saw her again after graduation. But 11 years later, my parents were on a plane, and she, by some incredible coincidence, was seated next to them. She told my mom and dad she'd had a huge crush on me back then, that she thought I was really cute, that she wished I had asked her out. But she was married now, and so was I. We had gone our separate ways, built separate lives. We had missed our chance.

"Sorry," he shrugs, "but I guess I can't tell you what to do. In those situations, I never knew."

The response is similar from everyone I ask. Instead of telling me what course to take, they tell me their stories of just-missed love instead. It must be the most common regret in the world. And not one of them, to this day, is sure of what to do. They all want to go back, but they never will. I suspect they know, like I'm learning now, that it's sweeter to just remember and romanticize it.

In a different age, I probably would have phoned Susan Prescott, rang her doorbell, hired a private investigator, rented a plane, sent even more letters. I would have been persistent. But nowadays that's called stalking, and you either get thrown in jail or go on *Jerry Springer*. And besides, I don't want to scare her. I don't want to appear obsessed. In the big scheme of things, it's just not that important. No, I am a man of my word.

And after a while longer, I become resigned. Susan Prescott doesn't care anymore whether I look the least bit like James Caan. She has moved on. And I probably should, too. But at least I have a better answer now. She's not interested; maybe she never was. As promised, I won't bother her again. We've had our chance.

"Don't be bummed," says my wife. "If you didn't charm her with that letter, then it proves that she was never the one for you."

And I hug her, like a repentant adulterer, realizing that I made the right choice after all.

CHAPTER 4

getting rid of my first car

I am on a stakeout in the parking lot of a supermarket in Bethlehem, Pennsylvania. It's approaching 7:00 A.M. on a Sunday in February—one more steel-gray dawn in a crumbling steel town. I could use a piss and another cup of joe, but I can't leave my car. Not now. Something might happen.

I've spent the past hour cruising the streets of the nearby Village. That's what we call the projects around here—the low-rent brick bunkers where the immigrant-poor cluster. From the outside, these housing projects look like prison blocks, only without the barbed wire and guard towers. No wonder the crime rate is so high here.

But the Village was peaceful this morning. No sign of life, except for its filthy refuse lying in the gutters. Still, I kept glancing in my rearview mirror. I always do these days. You never know. At the same time, I scanned the parking lots and alleys, looking for a silver 1979 Chevrolet Camaro Berlinetta, plate number unknown, possibly with a dent in the front quarter panel.

The previous owner—a thin, nervous guy named Deet (that's right, just like the insect repellent; I had him spell it)—said he sold it to a couple of "pork chops" in the Village about five years ago. I pressed him, but that's all he remembered—that and the night he had it up to 130 miles per hour on the highway coming home from the mall. Blew away a cocky Trans Am that came up in the passing lane and roared a challenge at him. Not bad for a small eight-cylinder. When he told me about it, I couldn't help grunting in appreciation.

Deet said he'd seen the car recently in the supermarket parking lot. It's still on the road, that much he knew, which is amazing after more than 20 years. But that's all he could give me. It's a shot in the dark, I know, but I've aimed at fuzzier things. After a while, you develop a sixth sense. It tells you when you're wasting your time and when you have a chance. So far, this one feels right.

But there was no sign of the car in the Village. Nothing even close. After a while, I headed here, to this lot. The store opens at 7:00 A.M. I figure that the owner of the car might work inside, that maybe I'll get lucky. Do me a favor and keep your eyes open, and while we're waiting I'll tell you a story. It's about this car, and why I'm here.

I'm not a cop. I'm just an ordinary citizen trying to beat the system. I tried doing this legally, but I got either stymied or laughed at by bureaucrats. It's tough for people to understand how a middle-age guy can start feeling about his first car—how the older you get, the more it symbolizes everything you've lost and all you want back.

This Camaro I'm searching for was my first car—automatic transmission, black cloth interior, a premium eight-track stereo system. I vividly remember the day I purchased it. I was 19, a college sophomore, stuck behind the wheel of my parents' sputtering Vega station wagon (gold, with a roof rack and wood panels, no less). I had finally convinced my father that I needed a real car, that my image was suffering. And besides, I had the money—$7,000 in cash amassed through an entire adolescence of neighborhood lawn-cutting.

So he took me to Jack Dankel Chevrolet in Allentown. It's where he'd bought his first car, a red and white 1957 Impala with outrageously flared tail fins. He seemed genuinely disappointed when nobody at the dealership recognized him.

Our salesman was named Steve, and he knew immediately what to show me. He led us through the showroom, across a back alley, then slowly raised a chattering aluminum garage door and flipped on the light. In retrospect, it was pretty dramatic.

And there was the most beautiful car I had ever seen. Its silver finish was so highly polished that it looked liquid. I half expected my fingertip to make ripples when I touched it. It had a T-panel sunroof, which was very unusual in those days, tinted black to match the interior and side piping. I swear I could feel the breeze. Its rear end was elevated just enough to make it appear impatient, like it was leashed rather than parked, like it was ready to go—with me.

I circled it reverently. Steve opened the door and let me slide inside, encouraged me to take the wheel, to look up, to imagine the sky. The scent of it was better than that of any girl or even mom's home cooking. And when he unlatched the hood, my jaw dropped.

"It's a beauty, isn't it?" he said. "The Berlinetta is our top-of-the-line Camaro. It has a more luxurious interior trim, a quieter ride, but still plenty of power. That's a 305 V-8 in there. Zero to 60 in less than 6 seconds."

"How much?" asked my father, breaking the trance.

"About $7,300, plus tax and tags," said Steve. "But unfortunately, this one is sold. Gets picked up tomorrow."

Suddenly, all my breath left me. I felt exactly like I had when my first girlfriend told me we were breaking up. I stood there feeling belly-punched. Desperate.

"It's sold?" I groaned. "Aw, that can't be . . ."

"I'm afraid so. But we can order one just like it. Eight- to 12-week delivery."

My father motioned me aside. "I know you're disappointed," he said, putting his hands on my shoulders, "but let's see what kind of deal we can work with this guy. We might be able to save you some money since we have to wait."

So my dad told Steve we were interested, which seemed like a ridiculous understatement, and we walked back to his office to begin negotiating. I was ready to surrender all my money and borrow the rest, but my dad was out to impress. He kept stressing that since he was a repeat customer, he was entitled to an extra-special deal. Eventually, even Jack Dankel himself got involved. Back and forth it went for close to an hour, until my father finally stood up and announced, "That's our final offer. Call us if you change your mind."

I couldn't believe it. We were actually walking out, turning our backs on this gleaming dream. As we drove away, I fought back anger and tears.

"Why did you do that?" I asked.

"Don't worry, they'll call back. That's the way it's done. That's negotiation, son."

"But this is crazy. You got 'em down to $6,900. That's fair. I can afford that. It's the nicest car I've ever seen. Suppose they don't call back? We're here. Why don't we just get it?"

It went on like this—my father trying to teach me an important life lesson, me sounding more and more like a spoiled adolescent. Finally, without saying anything, he swung the car around and drove back to the lot. It must have killed him to see the smug grins on the faces of Steve and Jack, but he never mentioned it again. He helped me sign the papers and congratulated me afterward—shook hands all around the table. I think part of him had realized he didn't have many fatherly opportunities like this left. I was almost grown. I didn't need his help or approval. Happiness was something I could find and purchase for myself. This was the last toy he could buy for his boy.

I don't remember much about the ensuing weeks, whether there were 8 or 12. I know that there was a strike at the factory where they made the sunroofs, so I had to cancel that option or wait indefinitely. It's strange, but I don't even recall taking delivery of the car, signing the check, or being given the keys. I guess it was a classic case of love at first sight. The relationship is forever over-shadowed by the moment you meet.

Every Sunday morning thereafter, I washed and waxed that Camaro. On my knees in the driveway, I used a toothbrush to scrub the hubcaps. For 10 years, I kept it perfect. And gradually, that car became me. In fact, when I look back at that part of my life, I see my fondest memories reflected in the car's finish.

- *Fogged windows when it wasn't even that cold outside, but our passion was hot and thick. Half naked, she'd giggle and scribble our initials with a fingertip, then look back at me and lick her lips.*

- *Empty bottles of Genesee Cream Ale rolling around on the floor, clinking with every sharp corner. Old high school buddies laughing and guzzling. Chests puffed with almost-conquests, manhood so close we could taste it, our entire lives ahead of us.*

- *Curly brown hairs stuck to the black roof above the driver's seat, escapees from the wild Afro I wore. I had to mash it down so it would fit inside. Unfortunately, I don't have that problem any more.*

- *My stereo, books, typewriter wedged into the back seat, a mattress tied to the roof, moving out. My mother crying, even though I'm almost 21, realizing that I won't be coming home. "Drive carefully," my father says. I know he's speaking of a much broader road map.*

- *White carnations tied to the door handles and antennas. Horn blaring, champagne popping, rice pinking off the metal. My new wife and I so happy we'd barely remember it all.*

- *A truck carrying panes of glass swerving into my lane. Nothing I could do. A squeal of tires, a rending of metal that I felt in my guts. An accident, my first. I'll forever feel vulnerable.*

- *Parking spots on Market Street, Aronimink, Ancinetta. The different places I've lived, the various homes I've owned, and my car waiting patiently, forever loyal, outside each one.*

- *A baby seat buckled in back. A bottle of formula in the cup holder. Driving late at night, circling the same block. It was the only thing that settled him down. Even baby boys appreciate an engine sound.*

- *Driving to the notary office with Deet, who'd spotted my car for sale on the street. Three thousand dollars cash in my pocket. No longer my car, but his. Time for something safer and more practical. Time to finally grow up and become responsible.*

That's how it came, and that's how it went. I sold it without regret. In fact, I went 10 years without even thinking about that Camaro, driving Dodges and Mazdas and Volvos—all sensible cars that get good gas mileage. Then I turned 40, and something inexplicable happened. I started noticing cars again and lusting after them. I'd pick up *Hemmings Motor News* and devour the classifieds. I'd stop at used-car lots and kick the tires on bad-ass pickup trucks. I'd do double takes at BMW convertibles.

What was wrong with me? Was this the way all midlife crises began? First an obsession with automobiles and then with the women in them?

It all came to a head when my wife totaled our 1989 Dodge Grand Caravan. This was the vehicle I'd bought to replace my Camaro, a sobering transition if ever there was one. It was a bad time to be shopping for a replacement. We were in the midst of a major home renovation, and this was an additional headache. So I took the easy way out and bought a 1996 Grand Caravan from the mechanic at my local garage. It was used but in excellent condition, with fewer than 30,000 miles.

"It'll last you another 10 years at least," he told me as I was signing the papers.

And that's when it hit me. That's when I looked at the car I had just bought—another family van, in black cherry, no less—and started questioning my self-respect. I recalled a line I'd just read in some magazine about how "a man driving a minivan is half a man." I became aware of my total lack of excitement for buying this car, for driving away in it. Sure, I'd gotten a good deal. Sure, this was a recommended model in the *Consumer Reports* magazine annual car-buying issue. But where was my pride?

That's when I remembered my Camaro.

That's when I first regretted selling it.

And that's when I started wondering if I could get it back.

6:55 A.M.

It's time. If the owner is going to show, it'll have to be soon. If I spot the car, I'll stay cool. I'll get a plate number, let it sit for a while, then I'll peek inside and check the vehicle identification number (VIN) tag on the dashboard. I don't want to confront the guy. He probably won't understand why some stranger wants to buy his car at this hour. Patience; a little while longer.

You know what's really ironic? I used to work in the liquor store across the street. Part time for 7 years. I'd park the Camaro under that light post, the farthest-away and safest spot in the lot. On slow nights, I'd stand at the register and stare at the car. The soft glow of the vapor lighting made it look showroom-new. In fact, I can still remember how great it felt to walk toward it, keys in hand on a summer night after the store had closed. I was free, and the night was sweet with possibility.

Wouldn't it be something if whoever owned it now came along and parked in that same spot? Now *that* would be destiny.

If I ever get this car back, I'm going to make it look just the way I remember it. I don't know much about restoration, but I'll learn. My son is 15, and he says he'll help. I've told him about my Camaro, about how beautiful it was, about how nicely it handled. It could be his car someday. I could bring things full circle.

I never expected my search to become this clandestine, though. When I first started looking months ago, I thought the Department of Transportation would have a record of every vehicle I'd ever owned. But it didn't. To do a trace, I'd need a complete 13-digit VIN. And even then, I'd only learn if it was still registered in Pennsylvania. Confidentiality laws prohibit the state from disclosing information about subsequent owners.

Unfortunately, I didn't have any records, and Jack Dankel Chevrolet was no longer in business. Luckily, my insurance agent was able to unearth the last 5 digits (8-5-8-0-8) from an old policy.

He explained that the numbers preceding these usually referred to the vehicle's make, year, model, engine size, and plant of origin; therefore, it might be possible to piece together what's missing. When I called Chevrolet headquarters in Detroit, however, a "customer service specialist" said that 1979 was ancient history. Not only did he not have sales records dating back that far, but he also couldn't think of anyone who'd be able to complete my VIN.

Faced with this dead end, I did what any determined American would do: I hired a private detective—a guy by the name of Tim Hoover with an outfit called Confidential Investigations. His gravelly telephone voice reminded me of a callused ex-cop, someone with a 2-day growth of beard who'd probably been shot. He sounded like a guy who could get the job done. And he did, at least partially. In a week, he turned up Deet. And from him, I learned the history of the car since I sold it, that it was still on the road, and most important, where it had last been spotted.

7:20 A.M.

I feel like a fool. How stupid to think that it would be this simple, that I could simply park somewhere and have my old car drive up to meet me. Perhaps this is the nature of the optimism that infects men at middle age, the blind faith that convinces us that we can still run a 5-minute mile, land the plum job, and pick up beautiful women. We believe it until we pull up lame, get passed over, or see her leave with someone younger.

I should have known better.

1 week later

My cousin, Stephanie, works for the city. Her job takes her all over Bethlehem, so I've given her a description of the car, hoping that she'll spot it. I even dangled a reward to make sure she stays vigilant. And sure enough, she calls with a possible hit.

"Pennsylvania plate CBK-9977," she tells me over the phone. "It fits the description. Good luck."

I stare at the scrap of paper I'd scribbled the number on as if it were a map to the lost continent of Atlantis. This could be it—my car, after all these years.

I call Hoover immediately, struggling to contain my excitement. He's not the type who responds well to emotion.

"That's C as in Charlie, B as in Bob, K as in King, 9-9-7-7," he repeats. "Okay, I'll run a check and get back to you."

Two hours later, the phone rings again. I pick up instantly.

"Hoover here. Looks like the car belongs to a Randy Foster. Lives at 7316 West 3rd Street in Bethlehem. The VIN is 1G1FP2156HN109734. It's a 1987 Chevy Camaro."

Silence.

"Thanks anyway," I finally say.

The line goes dead, along with my spirits.

1 month later

I cruise the Village whenever I'm in Bethlehem, and even my 67-year-old mother has been checking the supermarket parking lot every Wednesday when she goes shopping. I've recruited some friends who live in the area to scout for me as well, but so far, the trail has been cold. I'm beginning to think the car is no longer on the road or has been resold.

Meanwhile, my new Grand Caravan has developed an annoying problem. Occasionally, when I start the engine, the security system makes all the interior lights flash for 60 seconds. Since it's an intermittent problem, it's been impossible to pinpoint. In fact, whenever I take it to the garage, it no longer happens. During the day it's not so bad because it isn't that noticeable. But at night when I'm in a hurry and can't wait for it to abate, I feel absurd sitting there with everything blinking.

I decide to call Chevrolet headquarters once more, this time not as a customer but as a journalist for *Men's Health* magazine who's writing a story about finding his first car. There must be somebody in the Motor City who can help me puzzle out the rest of the VIN, and I figure the promise of media exposure will get his attention.

"Joe? Scott Settlemire with General Motors here. Got your message. First, I have to tell you I love your magazine, read it every month. Plus, I'm a Pennsylvania boy. Now what can I do for you?"

Bingo.

I tell Scott the entire story, building up the car, appealing to his sensibility as a middle-age guy. When I get to the part about hiring a private detective, he is suitably impressed. Then I ask him about the VIN.

"Well, we've built roughly 150 million Chevrolets over the years," he explains, "so there's no way to go back and pull the information on your car. It's too long ago. But hold on just a second. I have an idea. Let me go and get something."

Please, God. If you help me get my Camaro back, I promise I'll drive it to church every Sunday.

"Joe? You still there? We may be in luck. I might be able to reconstruct that VIN for you. In 1980 we went to a 17-digit VIN. The government made us put in random 'check' numbers, which would have made it impossible to reconstruct. But in 1979, the VINs were still 13 digits, and they were pretty straightforward."

He asks me a bunch of questions: Did I buy the car new? Was it automatic or manual? What size was the engine? Where did I take delivery? What body style was it?

"Okay, you got a pencil? I'm going to tell you what the first eight digits most likely are."

Thank you, God.

"One, because that's how they all started out; S, since it was a coupe; 87, for the body style; G, because you said it had a 305 V-8; 9, for 1979; then either N if it was built in Norwood, Ohio, which I suspect, or L if it was built in Van Nuys, California; next either 1 or 2 or 5, try all three; then the five numbers you have. Do a VIN search with all the possibilities and see what you get."

If this guy had been in the same room, I would have hugged him. Finally, a combination!

"Let me ask you one more question, Joe. How long has it been since you've driven a Camaro?"

"Must be at least 12 years," I reply. "It would have been the day I sold mine. The last time I drove it was to the notary."

"Well, we're going to have to get you behind the wheel of a new one then," says Scott. "I'll call our regional rep and have him deliver a press car for you to drive for a week, a brand new 2000. You're going to be impressed."

I am speechless. There was never a better day to be a journalist.

72 hours later

The phone rings at 10:00 A.M.

"Hoover here. I ran those VINs you gave me. We got a hit."

My hand shakes as I try to write down what he's saying.

"VIN 1S87G9N585808 is registered to an Ada Quinella, 1468 East Fourth Street, Second Floor, Bethlehem. Plate number B as in boy, D as in dog, C as in Charlie, 2-4-7-3. It's a Chevy Coupe Camaro Berlinetta. Looks like it could be the one."

Suddenly, I understand why Hoover does what he does for a living. The moment you find what you've been searching for—the instant when the key slides into the lock and turns—is like no other. The thrill, the vindication, the joy at solving a mystery, is a drug, an orgasm. I can no longer speak; I gush.

"Thanks . . . Thanks . . . This is it. . . . This is really it. . . ."

"Yeah, but you don't know what kind of condition it's in," says Hoover, deadpan. "You found it, but it may not be like you remember. That's a rough part of town. Be careful. Let me know how it turns out, okay?"

I hang up and try to decide what to do next. How do I approach this person? Is it a man or a woman? Could they ever begin to understand my obsession? And most important, would they part with the car? Or, like Hoover suggests, will I still want it?

I look up Ada Quinella in the phone book, but there's no listing. I dial information, but there's nothing. My only alternative is to drive there.

It takes 25 minutes. To do it, I have to cross the lower campus of Lehigh University, where I went to school, where I drove my

Camaro. It all seems so fitting, so right, that the car is still here, close to its old stomping ground. I drive more slowly as West Fourth turns into East Fourth and the appearance of the houses gradually starts to deteriorate. By the time I reach the 1200 block, I'm creeping along, looking for either 1468 or the car itself.

This part of town, the south side of Bethlehem, is built on the side of a mountain. It overlooks the now-abandoned Bethlehem Steel plant and the Lehigh River. This is where the steelworkers lived, my ancestors from Poland and Czechoslovakia. Now it's mostly Puerto Ricans and African-Americans. A man in an Adidas Windbreaker and a pullover hat glares at me from the sidewalk. Two guys reshingling a roof stop what they're doing to watch my progress.

The street is narrow and full of potholes. Cars are parked on both sides. I don't think there's anything newer than a 1985. Finally, I spot the number 1468 on a stuffed mailbox hanging off the front of a brick two-story. It's obvious no one is home, perhaps hasn't been for a while. And there's no sign of the Camaro. I turn the corner and drive down the back alley, where there are a few garages. But none looks like it belongs to this house. If the car were here, I would have spotted it.

I come around again and park in front, my tires crunching broken glass in the gutter. I scrawl a note on a blank sheet of paper, using large block letters: "I want to buy your car. No joke. Please call." Then I climb the steps of the rickety wooden porch and shove the message into the mailbox, taking note of Ada's name on the rest of the correspondence. I also spot an invoice from *Playboy* magazine. Good. Means he's probably a man, so perhaps he'll understand.

And then the waiting begins again.

3 days later

No word, no phone message, nothing. Maybe he read the note and threw it away. Maybe he's out of town for a few days. Maybe he doesn't live there anymore. Maybe . . . Maybe . . .

It can't end here. Not after all this work. But my previous relief and excitement at finding the car are being eroded by the realization that Ada Quinella could simply ignore me. And there's nothing I can do about it. Perhaps he's just as attached to this Camaro as I think I am. Perhaps it's all he can afford, and selling is not an option. My challenge now is to somehow get him to respond.

Dear Ada,

I understand that you own a 1979 Chevrolet Camaro Berlinetta. This is a very special car, at least to me. I have reason to believe it was the first car I ever owned. Bought it new from a dealer in Allentown when I was 19. Blew my entire life savings on it.

Many of my fondest memories involve this car. I had it when I was dating my future wife, we decorated it with lace carnations for our wedding, and I used it to bring my first son home from the hospital. I sold it about 12 years ago because I needed a bigger, more practical family vehicle. But I now regret doing that. In fact, for the last 6 months, I've been trying to track it down. And it hasn't been easy.

I was hoping you might consider selling me this car. My son is turning 16 soon, and it would really be something if I could give it to him and we could restore it together. I am willing to pay a very fair price.

Please respond.

It takes me almost an hour to write this letter. I choose the words carefully, trying to set the perfect tone. I agonize over how much information to divulge but eventually decide on complete honesty. Ada will be more likely to respond to a story than some emotionless bid. And if that doesn't work, the mention of price should certainly clinch it. Even if he considers everything else bull, greed will no doubt prompt him to find out exactly what my "very fair price" is.

With another prayer, I drop it in the mailbox.

10 days later

Nothing still. I send more letters, drive by at different times of day, even have Hoover ring a few doorbells. But neither the car nor Ada is ever around. It's very strange. Deet tells me he remembers the guy being older and not speaking English too well. Could be he just doesn't understand or, worse yet, doesn't want to be bothered.

In the meantime, Settlemire calls to tell me my brand-new Camaro Z28 is on its way. And when it arrives, it is indeed a beauty. It's the same color as my old one—silver metallic with a black interior. And although Chevrolet has modernized this model in every way, it has also done an impressive job of preserving the car's personality. I can still see my Berlinetta in its sleek lines, and from behind the wheel, the feeling is a perfect blend of 2000 and 1979. The most notable difference is the 5.7-liter, 305-horsepower V-8 engine. It's more powerful than anything I've ever driven. Working its six-speed manual transmission is like taking a puma for a walk. It's always pulling, tugging, wanting to go faster. That's not an idle you hear; it's a growl.

At almost $27,000, this car is also nearly four times as expensive as mine was. It's out of the range of most kids and their grass-cutting savings. But that's not necessarily a bad thing. This is the type of muscle car teenage boys die in—the kind you see with a No Fear sticker above a shattered windshield. The speedometer goes to 150 miles per hour, the tachometer to 7,000 rpm, and insurance rates into equally lofty territory. Actually, Chevy's target audience for this car is now a 40-year-old guy—someone just like me with money and memories.

And it sure does feel good. Arm out the window, sunglasses on, stereo cranked to nearly full volume. My wife, riding shotgun and laughing, somehow looks a decade younger—innocent and wild and beautiful. I glance at the backseat and wonder if it's still possible.

Without thinking, I find myself doing all those things older people despise in young drivers. I peel out from intersections (without even trying). I disrupt quiet neighborhoods (since the engine sounds so threatening). I scare my backseat passengers whenever I accelerate (their wide eyes noticing only two doors). But perhaps most disturbing is that after a week of driving this car, I begin to scare myself.

It's not that I'm driving faster or more recklessly. It's just that I'm realizing how many miles I've covered in these intervening 12 years. This is an aggressive car, and I don't feel aggressive any more. My testosterone gauge is no longer redlining. I've proven my manhood by procreating. And although there's no lack of desire between my bride and me, there is an embarrassing lack of flexibility when we try climbing into the backseat.

When I was young, I used to laugh at old guys driving Camaros. Now I am one. My bald spot is brushing the ceiling instead of my Afro. This car is remarkable, but it's also a reminder—a gnawing comparison between what I am now and what I was then. And that's a nudge in the ribs I can do without.

But the experience isn't as disheartening as it may sound. In fact, after a week with the Camaro, a strangely uplifting thing begins to happen. I start missing my Caravan and begin appreciating all it represents. For instance, I can really stretch out in the driver's seat, and you have to love the dual armrests and lumbar support. And since I don't have to continually work the clutch, I can relax in traffic. When I go to the home improvement store, I can fold down the bench seats and slide in entire sheets of plywood. If one of the kids drips ice cream or spills soda, it's no big deal. I get about 20 miles per gallon in the city and more on the highway. And should my wife and I ever feel the least bit amorous, we don't have to worry about wrenching our backs.

From such small realizations grows a higher appraisal of the stage of life I'm in. Twelve years from now, I'll probably be as wistful about my Caravan as I am about my Berlinetta—remembering the baby seats, the road trips, the home projects, the discarded juice boxes. Maybe I'll get the urge to hire Hoover to track it down or call up somebody in the media department at Dodge to see about road-testing a 2012.

Perhaps it's best that Ada hasn't responded. Although I'm not quite ready to abandon the search, I'm not as obsessed with reclaiming my old Camaro as I originally was. I'll probably send him one more letter saying that if he ever decides to sell the car, he should call my number. And I'll leave it at that, because I know now that I was trying to do more than repossess a car—I was trying to repossess myself. And that's fruitless.

So now I'm looking forward to the Lincoln or Caddy or Buick that I'm sure is in my future—the boat with the "Retired" license plate, curb feelers, and speedometer that goes to 30 miles per hour. I'll have it stuffed with golf clubs, wraparound sunglasses, blood pressure medicine, and gifts for the grandkids. I'll drive with my turn signal on and let anybody who wants to get in front of me. You won't catch me looking in the rearview mirror, either. I'll have realized a long time ago that it's only where you are and where you're heading that matters. ⓐⓢ

CHAPTER 5

losing my hair

My hair has been a continual source of despair.

When I was growing up during the hair-rich 1960s, my father would drag me to Benny's Barber Shop every June for a "mooney." Benny was a first-generation Portuguese immigrant with an impressive auburn bouffant. He'd buzz my scalp with his big electric razor, leaving behind only stubble that my smelly old aunts liked to rub. My parents claimed it would keep me cool during summer, but I knew it was just the opposite. "Wish I had a cantaloupe!" my friends taunted.

Fortunately, my hair would return by the time school reopened, but that only prompted my mother to start fussing with it. For some reason, she perceived it as an incredibly bad reflection on her if I was seen in public with messed-up hair. So every morning, she would slather my head with hair tonic and then sculpt the front portion into a flip curl. When the whole thing dried, it was as shimmering and immovable as an ice sculpture. "There," she'd say proudly before ushering me out the door. "You look very nice."

Being 10 and a budding ruffian, that's the last appearance I wanted to convey. So as soon as I was out of sight on my way to the bus stop, I would crush that flip curl with my palm until it was flat, and I was hopefully inconspicuous.

Then one summer, my ex-Marine father got the idea that I would look good in a crew cut. Sort of the mini-sergeant look. So he hustled me down to Benny's and ordered him to shave me tight around the ears with just a little left on top. He also bought an incredibly stiff bristle brush (I swear the label said it was good for scrubbing rust), and my mother went to work.

"We have to train it," she'd say every morning as she scoured my skull and applied more hair tonic. Eventually, I was left with a rooftop lawn, all the little hair blades cut to perfect length, well-fertilized and standing erect. I was Vanilla Ice, 20 years too soon.

You would think that puberty might have rescued me but that wasn't to be my destiny. In fact, with some testosterone to fuel it, my hair went completely berserk. It began to thicken, dry out, and curl. It was as if my body had somehow mixed up my head and my genitals. I was growing pubic hair upstairs.

I tried to comb it, but without success. It was so dense it refused passage. My hair was so bad that Benny would shake his head and curse in Portuguese whenever I walked into his shop. "I never see anything like this," he'd wail. "I can do nothing with it!"

Desperately self-conscious, I swallowed my pride and visited my mother's hairdresser. Imagine a teenage boy in a place called the Beauty Corner. The lady there suggested I stop trying to tame this lion's mane and let it grow out naturally. Instead of a comb, she suggested a hair pick. After a little trimming and fluffing, I emerged with my first Afro. My mother, impressed by the transformation, said I looked just like Bobby Vinton.

Actually, when I got home and examined myself in the mirror, I didn't look that ridiculous. In fact, I felt proud, not only that my hair problem was solved but also that I was finally in style. It was the 1970s, and all the disco kings had perms. But mine was natural.

So I let it grow. I showcased my 'fro. I swaggered to class with my pick sticking out of the back pocket of my plaid bell-bottoms. When the light was right and my head cast a shadow on the wall, I'd wave the class to silence and do my Stevie Wonder impersonation. My hair kept growing, approaching Mod Squad circumference. Friends and relatives marveled at it. It was so thick that I could dive into a swimming pool and emerge without the roots getting wet. When I bought my first car, a 1979 Camaro, my hair, like Marge Simpson's, would brush the top of the interior. In the summer, with a dark tan, I could pass for a black man.

Such a bush did attract some unwelcome attention, though. One kid, Jeffrey Gantzel, who sat behind me in English class, would shoot spitballs into my hair. He'd strive to see how many he could bury within the allotted 50 minutes. Since my hair was so thick, I never knew he was doing it until the bell rang and I stood up amid a shower of tiny white pellets. How I yearned to turn around and slug him. I must have been the only kid in the world tortured by the fear of what was stuck in his hair.

As I headed into my twenties and started a succession of jobs, I kept my 'fro trimmed and respectable. Less self-centered and more preoccupied with work and a budding romantic relationship, I allowed my hair to fall down my list of priorities. In an increasingly busy life, getting it cut and picking it out even became a bit of a nuisance. In retrospect, I should have been more appreciative of what I had.

When I turned 25, I stumbled into the most stressful year of my life. I changed jobs, got married, moved into a new house, and had my first baby. One morning in the shower, I noticed that the water wasn't going down. When I checked the drain, it was clogged with hair—my hair. "That's strange," I remember thinking. "I mustn't have cleaned this out in a while." But when it clogged again a few days later, I realized it wasn't my housekeeping: I was losing my hair. Upon closer inspection, I noticed something even more baffling: Not only was it thinning across the top, but it was also starting to straighten.

The next day, I visited my mother's hairdresser—the same

woman who had helped birth my Afro. She confirmed that I was indeed thinning, but as for losing my curl, she was also baffled. She explained that it happened to some women after crash dieting or becoming pregnant, but she'd never seen it in a guy. My hair, evidently, was not yet ceasing to surprise. (Many years later I learned that a period of intense stress like I had unwittingly encountered can trigger a condition known as shedding. This is a sudden and premature thinning, usually seen in men who are genetically predisposed to balding, which I was. Along with this, the hair can occasionally lose some of its original texture and shape. Unfortunately, once it begins, nothing can stop it.)

But I refused to surrender. After all, I was a veteran of numerous hair wars. My first strategy was camouflage. My stylist sold me some mousse and told me to comb my hair straight back. Although this successfully hid the developing bald spot on my crown, it made me feel like Vinnie the used-car salesman. As the thinning progressed, she suggested another approach: that I part my hair conventionally but leave it cut longer on one side. Yes, I'm ashamed to admit, for a short time I had a comb-over.

Compounding all this was the fact that my hair was also prematurely turning gray. Even though I had just crested 30, the once-brown strands on the sides of my head were bordering on white. Suddenly, I had another big source of stress in my life—my appearance. I had to get up earlier in the morning to work on my hair, and whenever I went to the bathroom during the day, I'd end up fussing with it.

It was time to make a bold move. It was time to throw away all this mousse and regain my devil-may-care manhood. Since it was the golden age of Michael Jordan, I started considering what I would look like if I shaved it off—not completely, but an all-season permanent mooney.

I contemplated this for months before I was able to muster enough courage to broach the subject with my new barber, Mr. Bair. This kindly old gentleman had been clipping hair for 50 years, but he wasn't much help. Being from the old school, he gave haircuts, not hairstyles. But he did show me the different settings on his electric razor. "This is a number 3," he explained. "It'll leave you with about a quarter-inch all around."

I agonized for another 2 months before finally giving Mr. Bair the go-ahead. Sitting in his chair, watching what was left of my pitiful hair falling to the floor, I felt nervous but also strangely free up there. I suddenly had one less worry. I could roll out of bed and be ready for the road. Simple soap and water could replace my bottles of shampoo. The wind was once again my friend.

What's more, I eventually found that women loved it. My wife couldn't keep her hands off my head, and young ladies I hardly knew would ask to touch it. I had suddenly become phallic. Once when I was away from home, I got buzzed at a big-city salon. The plump female stylist there finished me off by holding my head against her ample chest and vigorously rubbing it. I actually felt violated.

The biggest compliment, though, came from the guys at work. Most were at similar stages of life—their thin, unkempt hair a constant, woeful reminder of their strife. Quite a few of them stopped me in the hall, made a few casual remarks, then asked how I liked it.

"Like what?" I asked, puzzled at first.

"The haircut," they said, a little embarrassed. "I've been thinking about doing that."

Then a few weeks later, I'd see them again, aglow at their new freedom. We'd exchange thumbs-ups as we'd pass, two new members of a secret, liberating society. One day, my boss even cut his. I felt a rush of quiet pride. Imagine—me, a trendsetter.

Increasingly emboldened, the next time I visited Mr. Bair I asked for the number 2 setting on his electric razor, then the number 1, and eventually I even went to a beauty supply store and bought my own. Now my wife buzzes my head in the privacy of our own basement. I save 7 bucks, and she smiles a lot.

Although people tell me I look good like this, which has helped me regain some personal pride, the truth of the matter is that I still miss having hair. What I've done is a compromise. I've made the best of a meager poker hand and mounted a respectable bluff. A buddy of mine, similarly cursed, says he hates being bald. But he hates it proudly. That's why he shaves it all off.

I loathe having to rub sun block on my head at the beach, to put on stupid-looking hats when it's cold, and most of all, just looking so old. Every time I look in the mirror, I am reminded of what I used to be. I've made the best of what I have left, but this is only the first noticeable crumbling of my facade. Soon there will be other cracks. Next will come wrinkles and age spots.

I know that's a shallow view of life, but no matter how hard I try to convince myself otherwise, I still care. Hair is a symbol of virility, youthfulness, and strength. And the older I get, the more desperately I cling to each. So at 40, I decide to confront this regret one last time and try two bold experiments.

First, I decide to visit the Hair Club for Men to see if it's possible for me to get an entirely new top. And if that doesn't work, then I'll make an appointment at one of those swanky New York City salons and have my hair professionally dyed.

Call me pathetic. Call me insecure. But it's better to know, once and for all, than to live with a desire, a wonder, that you're too embarrassed to ever pursue.

I'm 20 minutes late for my "private consultation" at the Hair Club for Men—hopelessly lost in an industrial park of identical gray buildings. I'm not about to stop and ask for directions. That would be like inquiring whether the impotency clinic is Exit 13 or 14. Finally, after a mistaken but ironic foray into the headquarters of Allentown Valve and Fitting Company, I find it—a single wood door, in a hallway of offices with transparent glass, marked HCM.

I feel like a hairless pilgrim about to enter Jerusalem.

All those late-night television commercials featuring president/client Sy Sperling. All those amazing before-and-after photos of men transformed. All the mystery surrounding the process itself and what really goes on behind that door. Was I about to step into a roomful of guys wearing outrageous hairdos and shooting pool? Would I be greeted by a menacing bouncer who'd ask for a show of scalp in lieu of a picture ID? Until now, I could only speculate.

"Hi, I'm Diane," says a tall, attractive blonde woman with a British accent. "You must be Joe."

"I'm sorry I'm so late, but I couldn't find the place."

"Oh, we like to keep things inconspicuous," she replies. "Follow me."

I'm escorted into a teal-painted room containing a cavernous black leather sofa and, on the walls, framed pictures of whales. Subliminal messages of future virility, perhaps? You know, sperm, humpback, Moby Dick?

I had been asked to bring a photo of myself with hair. So I hand Diane a snapshot taken in college when I had my remarkable Afro.

"Oh, my," says Diane, with a flutter of surprise.

"Do you think you can make me look like that again?" I press.

"Perhaps you should watch our video first," she counters. "It'll explain the whole process. I'll be back in 13½ minutes."

Wet men flash across the screen—wakeboarding, waterskiing, hair being tossed in a storm of activity. Three clients talk about how they hate going bald. A doctor somberly points out how Propecia, a popular hair-growing drug, can cause sexual dysfunction. A beautiful stylist caresses a guy's full head of hair. She wants him; you can tell. Ageless Sy Sperling gives me his word. . . . Rewinding.

Something unevolved in me suddenly wants what these men have. It seems so easy, and it looks so real.

Diane returns with a reassuring smile and a questionnaire that probes my feelings about hair loss. Then she explains the "patented process." Natural hair that precisely matches my own in texture and color is woven onto a "matrix," a plastic web resembling a featherweight yarmulke. The top of my head is shaved and the perimeter of the matrix is "polyfused" or glued to it, allowing my scalp to perspire and breathe naturally. The new hair is then trimmed and styled to complement the old.

"Normally, you'd pay $1,600 to $2,700 for this procedure, but we're running a special promotion," says Diane, crossing out those numbers on her clipboard. "It's $1,495 for the hairpiece and an initial styling, with a 90-day guarantee."

But wait, there's a catch. The total amount must be prepaid and only 50 percent is refundable if I'm dissatisfied. "This covers our cost for creating the matrix," explains Diane. Also, the hairpiece must be styled regularly and replaced periodically (new ones cost $1,200). Thus, most Hair Club clients opt for an extended service plan. "For $199 per month, you're entitled to a new one every 3 months and a styling every 4 to 8 weeks," she adds.

After the initial investment, that's a pretty steep annual commitment of $2,400, not counting mousse. It also sounds like a lot of fuss. Sure I'd like to have hair again, but I can't afford that much. Plus, even though Diane never mentioned the word, I'm having trouble accepting the fact that I would be wearing a toupee. Despite how well it's camouflaged, that carries too much pathetic baggage.

Diane can't say how long this special promotion will last, but she is understanding when I tell her I need to think it over. She refuses to negotiate price but does offer client references if I'd like.

As she escorts me out, I pass an older man sitting sheepishly in the waiting room. His gray hair, evidently installed moments ago, looks luxurious. Diane gives me a brochure and a handshake, but before the door closes behind me, I hear her exclaim, "Oh, look at *you!*"

I blush with the guy but part of me is envious, too.

Beth Minardi surveys my scalp, her first canvas of the day, and announces that she'll take out 43 percent of my gray. Since most of my close-cropped hair has already died (and I won't be buying a new hide), I figure why not go ahead and dye some more? "Let's go for 45 percent," I say boldly, intoxicated with my approaching youth.

At that, an assistant named Michael tightens his white apron, snaps on a pair of rubber gloves, grabs some bottles from a gleaming metal shelf, and begins mixing the treatment. "You always want to go one shade lighter than your natural hair color when covering gray," explains Beth, co-owner of Minardi Salon in New York City and a color consultant for Redken. "Your hair is medium brown, so I'm using sandy brown with a hint of dark blond."

Hmmm, dark blond . . .

She then brushes the cool, thick mixture onto the sides of my head like some Dali of the dome, varying the application to "minimize" my gray, yet create a natural effect. "You don't want to take it all out," she says. "Just enough to look great for your age, like Sean Connery or Clint Eastwood."

Hmmm, Sean, Clint . . .

I sit for 15 minutes, letting the mixture work its magic, then tip my head back into a bidetlike basin to let Michael scrub it out. He then foams on the second part of the treatment, covers my head with a plastic bag, and wheels me under a radiant-heat dryer nicknamed the Ring of Saturn. I bask for 10 more minutes, reading my horoscope and gossiping, then undergo a series of washings and conditionings designed to lock in the color. "We call this a demi-permanent," explains Beth, whose clients include Tom Hanks, Brad Pitt, and Matt Dillon. "It's good for 30 to 40 washings."

What I see in the mirror afterward is demi-startling. "It's like you, only better," says Beth, with a ta-da flourish. "It's the man I married," says my wife, after being escorted in from the waiting room. "Your skin color even changed," notes Michael. "It's warmer."

I don't know what to think, except that it feels alive up there, as if each hair follicle is a bulb on Broadway. The entire transformation took only 45 minutes (and $100), and I'm still in postoperative shock. "Try to wait 3 days before passing final judgment," cautions Beth. "You need to see yourself in everyday situations, like in the mirror behind a bar or at the gym. Come back in a few months, and I'll take even more gray out."

Disappointingly, on the bus ride home, no strangers ask to run their fingers through my flaxen mane. At dinner, neither my mother nor my children notice anything different about me. And the following morning, my boss greets me as usual—with more work. Even the guys I exercise with at lunchtime (my cruelest critics) don't detect it.

I supposed this is the desired effect. As Beth explained, you don't want anyone to make a fuss. People should look at you and see a youthful subtlety, but nothing they can pinpoint. If the world's attention is immediately drawn to your head, then your venture has failed.

I understand all this and am grateful for the lack of laughter, but somehow I expected more. After 3 weeks, I'd have to say I'm discouraged that it hasn't made one thin hair's worth of difference in my life. I'm not suddenly getting laid more or paid more, and younger guys aren't asking me what brand of gel I'd recommend.

I suppose it has to do with where a man is in life. I'm 40, married, mortgaged, with two kids and a job. I'm not trying to prove anything other than that I can survive the stress. Under these conditions, graying hair is expected and even esteemed. However, if I were 40, single, and vying with some youthful guy named Todd for district manager (or, more important, for a *date* with the district manager), then any slivers of silver I saw in the morning mirror would undoubtedly eat away at me like rust on a Corvette's underbody.

I suspect that the drive to color your hair is inversely proportional to your level of self-confidence. If this is right and you consider the fact that sales of men's hair-coloring products have tripled in the last decade, it's a sobering comment on modern male evolution.

Some of the best life advice I've ever received was from a buddy who, in the face of thinning hair, shrugged and said simply, "I am what I am."

After this hint of dark blond grows out, that's what I'll return to being. 🅰🆂

CHAPTER 6

not getting along with mom

My 66-year-old mother drives a 1996 Chrysler with 2,626 miles on it. Last Thursday, on her way home from the hairdresser, she was almost hit by someone she says was driving "erotically." For Christmas, she gave me a Great American Steakhouse Onion Machine she bought from QVC. It makes whole, deep-fried onions in the shape of chrysanthemums. When it snowed a few months ago, she called to warn me not to let the kids go sledding without helmets "because of what happened to Sonny and Cher." And by the way, did I know that Aunt Chubby's hemorrhoids are bothering her again, iceberg lettuce is up to $1.29 a head, and I'm going to regret never calling her once she's dead?

From what I can gather, this woman is not unique. Colleagues have confessed that their mothers twist them up in similar ways. One was told to "be careful leaving the dog out back because it might eat the tires off the car." Another was warned repeatedly to "get that cracked windshield fixed in case it hails." A third is under orders to visit every Sunday; otherwise "I just sit here alone in the dark." And then there's the fellow whose mom gave him two neckties for his birthday, one red and one blue. When she saw him in the red tie, she asked, "What's the matter, don't you like the blue?"

Is this some kind of organized plot? Did the mothers of America gather at a bingo hall in the Poconos and take lessons on how to confound, belittle, and confuse their kids, even once they're adults? It appears so.

I often wonder how I survived my childhood to become a relatively normal, sane individual. (Never mind the twitching—it comes and goes.) As the only child of a full-time housewife, I was constantly in my mother's crosshairs. If I'd wander off into some neighboring field with my best buddy, Mark Kovaleski, a piercing cry would soon split the suburban tranquillity, actually scattering birds.

"JO-O-O-E-EYYY!"

Her constant worry made me jumpy. I grew up convinced that I was toeing the precipice of some horrible physical disaster. Here are just a few examples of the dire warnings she delivered. (I now know that they're not true because I finally asked a doctor for his professional opinion.)

Warning: "You're gonna fall and crack your head open!"

Truth: Your skull can split like an egg, but it would require a severe impact, such as falling into the corner of a coffee table, says Larry L. Alexander, M.D., an emergency room physician. "You're much more likely to fracture your skull."

Warning: "Wear clean underwear in case you're in an accident!"

Truth: When emergency room personnel cut the clothes off trauma patients, Dr. Alexander says it's done so quickly that they never pay attention to whether the underwear is stained, dirty, or full of holes.

Warning: "Keep touching yourself and it'll fall off!"

Truth: There's no evidence that "pocket pool" or masturbation will cause any damage. Such exploration is "a normal part of growing up," says Dr. Alexander.

Warning: "Someday your face will freeze like that!"

Truth: No matter how far you stretch the corners of your mouth, how much you cross your eyes, or how deeply into your nostril you plunge your tongue, facial muscles will never become paralyzed as a result.

Warning: "Don't go outside without a coat, or you'll get sick!"

Truth: Colds and flu are not caused by catching a chill or getting your feet wet. This myth persists only because most people get sick during winter, when it's naturally colder and more damp. Dr. Alexander adds, however, that such a warning can become self-fulfilling. "If you dread damp feet, your brain may depress your immune system when it happens."

Warning: "You'll poke someone's eye out with that!"

Truth: It's impossible to "poke out" an eyeball with a sharp instrument. What you'll probably do is pierce or rupture it. To actually pop an eyeball out, Dr. Alexander says you "have to get in there with your fingers and pull it out."

Warning: "If you break a leg, don't come running to me!"

Truth: It's unlikely that you'd be able to run with a broken leg, but you could still walk. Dr. Alexander has seen people with broken legs walk into the emergency room. "It hurts like crazy," he says, "but the muscles spasm and produce enough support to bear weight."

Feeling smug, feeling vindicated, I had my mother read all this.

"Oh, what does *he* know?" she said. "You grew up healthy, didn't you?"

Well, come to think of it, *no.*

The subtle anxiety I lived with manifested itself in persistent childhood bellyaches. Specialists did all kinds of tests but couldn't immediately pinpoint the cause. Eventually, they attributed it to my vitamins, but I think that was bull. They just had no way to gauge the stomach-knotting effects of my mother's oppressiveness.

What's more, by the time I got to college, I weighed 200

pounds, a natural by-product of my mother's favorite foodstuff: Crisco. She used to feed me black coffee and a tray of pecan twirls for breakfast, then wonder why my grade school teachers said I had a discipline problem and might be hyperactive. When I was a baby, she accidentally dropped me on my head. And once, when I'd really pissed her off (I think I dented the aluminum siding with a ball), she took a wild swing with a plastic bat and hit me in the nuts.

I swear, the woman is a lunatic.

My father, bless his soul, can no longer act as a buffer. He's dead. Make of this what you will.

Lately, our relationship has become so maddening that I've practically given up. It's extremely stressful to drive my mother anywhere because she tenses visibly and starts muttering "Oh my, oh my" whenever we're being passed by a truck. Dinner at her house is equally challenging because she makes a stultifying amount of food, including her signature pork-kraut roll. When I try to explain that I don't eat like this anymore (I weigh 165 pounds now), she insists I'm too skinny and packs a sack of leftovers that usually includes canned goods she's had in the basement since the war. The last time I spent an afternoon at her place, she chastised me for drinking four Corona beers with one of the neighbors. "Do you know how long it took me to get the limes out of those bottles so I'd be able to put them out for recycling?" she ranted. "And what is the garbage man ever going to think? That I'm an alcoholic!"

Even talking to her on the phone is difficult. Here's a typical conversation which, to be accurately reproduced, should be read as loudly as possible and without any pauses. You be the judge.

"*Joey!* Joey, my refrigerator's acting screwy. What should I do? Who should I call? How come you never help me? I have to do everything myself. You don't even call. I could be dead for all you know. How I suffered for you! All that time in the delivery room while your father was out on the golf course jumping in mud holes. Don't think I'm too old to put you over my knee, either. You'll get yours someday. You'll see how it feels when you get to be my age. This arthritis! It takes me 10 minutes to get up the stairs. But don't you *ever* put me in a home. Mildred's kids are trying to do that to her, and it's awful. Just awful. I want to die right here. Then you'll know. Then you'll appreciate me. Did I tell you I just bought a Hummel from QVC? My sister is sick about it. She wasn't home, and she missed it. But I don't trust those operators. I don't like giving out my credit card number. I've heard what they do. There was just something on *Oprah*. Marion wants me to go on a bus trip to Atlantic City, but I told her I can't do that. I have too much work around here. Especially now with this refrigerator. What am I going to do if all my food goes bad? I just bought a pound of fresh mince bologna at Shop-Rite. You want to come over and eat it? Did you hear about Eleanor? Oh, she's not doing good. She has to wear those Depends now, those big diapers? And Rita is going in for her operation on Thursday. I don't know how I'm going to get to the hospital to see her. That's my hairdresser day. . . ."

See?

Spending more than 10 minutes with my mother, in whatever medium, completely twists me up. But I have not gone totally cold. The situation still bothers me. I know that someday when she's gone, I'll regret never having been closer to her. After all, she is my mother, and deep down under all the calluses, I guess I do love her.

A part of me really does want to make things right, to have the sort of kinship that Jimmy Carter had with Miss Lillian—the reassuring, womblike bond of mother and son. But you know what's really pathetic? You know what most embarrasses me? It's the fact that I can't bring myself to call my mother anything—not Mom, not Ma, not even Grammy (like my kids do). It's as if I'm resisting closeness at the most basic level, as if I'm remembering all the battles we've ever fought and refusing to put her name next to mine on even a small truce.

But I know I have to change, or at least try, because if I don't, it'll haunt me.

So last winter, I swallowed my pride and asked my mother to join me for a night at the Metropolitan Opera in New York City.

She loves Pavarotti and occasionally watches opera on PBS, so I thought she'd enjoy something like this. It would be a date, an adventure, but most important, 12 uninterrupted hours together. Actually, I'd asked her once before, about a year earlier, when two tickets to a performance by José Carreras unexpectedly became available. But it was too spur-of-the-moment for her, and besides, "Why would I ever want to do *that*?" she said. "I have his tapes. I can listen to him in my kitchen."

Nevertheless, when the opportunity arose again—this time to see *The Tales of Hoffman*—I decided to risk another invitation. I asked her 2 months in advance, making sure it wasn't her "hairdresser day" and then checking that she didn't own any tapes of that opera. As I had hoped, she was cornered and feeling guilty about refusing me before. Indeed, she later confided to my wife that she'd had to accept because "Joey never asks me to do anything twice."

Seven weeks before the performance, she called to find out what time I'd be picking her up, what everyone else would be wearing ("I'm thinking about a nice pantsuit"), and since the trip was in February, what would happen if it snowed. Fortunately, Debbie the hairdresser had been to the Met, said it was fantastic, and had gotten my mother somewhat excited.

Six weeks before the performance, she called to ask all these same questions again, and the interrogation intensified the closer we got to departure. ("It's that blue pantsuit. You know, the one I wore to Dick's funeral. Uh-oh, in the long-range forecast, they're calling for light snow!") Since the bus was supposed to arrive in New York by 6 o'clock and the opera didn't start until 8, I made dinner reservations for two at a trendy Chinese restaurant called Shun Lee, a few blocks from the Met. The *Zagat* guide describes it like this: "For exquisite, high-end Chinese fare in a bizarre, glamorous movie-set atmosphere, this Lincoln Center legend is in a class by itself; the out-of-this-world food is as good as Chinese gets."

I read my mother this, hoping she'd be impressed. "Well," she said, "it sounds good. But do you think they'll have number 11, chicken chow mein? You know that's what I always order when we get Chinese."

As the big night approached, I started getting nervous. It was that old childhood queasiness inside me again, but this time, it couldn't be attributed to vitamins. It was cold, raw apprehension.

To appreciate my dread, you need to understand that I haven't spent more than 30 minutes alone with my mother in the last 30 years. To minimize my stress and frustration, I learned to surround myself with insulation—my wife, the kids, our dog, neighbors, relatives, headphones. I used them all to deflect and muffle her craziness. This evening, however, would be an intensive, one-on-one experience. Although the trip had been arranged by my employer, few people I knew had bought tickets, and I purposely hadn't registered for the group dinner. This was about her and me, meeting for perhaps the first time. Intimate strangers.

"Where do you want me to sit?" she asks loudly, clutching her purse as if the bus she's entering is filled with furloughed convicts. "Don't put me by the emergency exit or the bathroom. Lots of times it stinks back there."

I direct her to a nondescript spot about halfway back, but it's not long before she starts moaning about her seat. "How do I get the back of this chair to come up? Where's the lever? How do they expect anyone to reach *that*? My arthritis. Here, reach across and yank it for me."

So before we've even left the parking lot, I'm already humbled—my head buried in my mother's lap as I reach over and tug at the handle. Worse yet, she's wearing so much cheap perfume, I'm going to smell like a dandy for the rest of the evening.

When the driver is delinquent in pulling out, she starts nervously checking her watch. Even though she generally has nothing to do and no place to go, she likes being punctual. And it worries her when she's not. "Are we going to be late? You know how I hate to rush."

Fortunately, the delay isn't long and the drive to New York is uneventful. There's an entertaining movie, and no one befouls the bathroom or has to use the emergency exit. But my mother is uncharacteristically quiet. She sits clutching her purse, hair perfect, watching New Jersey traffic. When I ask if something is wrong, she says she's making an effort not to be negative, because she knows that upsets me. She's purposely not going to talk about her sick friends, how much her knees hurt, what a no-good son I am, the refrigerator. . . . She wants us to have a nice, pleasant evening.

I am momentarily stunned. Maybe there's hope for us yet.

We arrive in New York on schedule. It's an ugly night—sidewalks mounded with melting gray snow, streets mined with puddled potholes, air heavy and damp. "You should have worn your rubbers," she says, clutching my arm as we walk down Columbus Avenue. "You know you always get sick when your feet get wet."

But I don't hear this. Instead I'm noticing how strange it feels to have my mother holding my arm, to actually be touching her. We haven't hugged or kissed in decades. It's not the Kita way. We are stoic, private people. Resolute Poles. Affection is just one more thing that makes us nervous. In all my 40 years, I have never said "I love you" to my mother, either. In fact, affection is so foreign to our relationship that I can vividly recall the only time I offered it. I was 8 or 9 and had picked a handful of buttercups from our backyard. I gave them to her in the kitchen. She smiled, checked them for bugs, then put them in a glass on the windowsill. But afterward I felt ashamed, as if I were somehow less of a little man for having done this. I don't know why, but it was never repeated.

We stroll past Lincoln Center, heading toward West 65th Street and the restaurant. My mother gets out of breath quickly and keeps ordering me to walk more slowly. When we're halfway across an intersection and the "Don't Walk" sign flashes, she is gripped by genuine panic.

She is depending on me, like she once did my father. In fact, I feel as if I am him, like he's come back to dwell inside my overcoat. This is what he and my mother used to do. Walk arm-in-arm on special occasions. The subtle infusion of him makes me feel strong

and proud. Those taxicabs are no threat. I am finally grown up
enough to steady and protect.

The restaurant is packed. It's Chinese New Year, something I
hadn't anticipated, and people are bickering with the maître d' to
get in. Fortunately, with an Asian-sounding name like Kita, I am
usually given more attention when making telephone reservations
at places like this. So unlike these other unlucky couples, our name
is in the book, and I smugly escort my mother past the line and to
our table.

The dining room is decorated predominantly black, but since
this is the Year of the Dragon, it has been accessorized to match.
Coiled around the entire perimeter, just beneath the ceiling, is a
giant, gold, papier-mâché dragon. The head of the serpent, with
green eyes, gaping jaw, and fiery tongue, is directly above us. My
mother looks up, obviously intimidated, purse still on her lap, hair
perfect, and says, "My, this is different."

I order a glass of cabernet and encourage her to do the same,
but she declines, insisting it'll make her fall asleep at the opera. The
menu is vast and pricey. I can tell it's swimming before her eyes.
She's searching for her favorite number 11, not realizing that in a
place like this it's probably been elegantly renamed.

I eventually settle on a selection called the Fisherman's Net, "a
harvest of seafood served in a delicate potato basket," and steer her
toward the jumbo prawns, "lightly breaded in a Grand Marnier
sauce."

And so . . . now that dinner is ordered . . . and we're here . . .
with plenty of time to spare . . . well . . . uh . . . what do you want
to talk about? This is all unspoken, of course. I sit sipping my wine,
looking around, squirming. We're at one of those famously narrow
New York tables, people at either elbow. I wonder what they think
of us. Is it obvious we're mother and son, or do they fancy us a
May-December romance, or worse, that I'm her gigolo?

"I have to go to the bathroom," my mother announces loudly.

"Sure, it's right over there. Not even any stairs," I reply, pointing.

"I'm not going to go."

"Why not? It's right over there."

"I'm going to hold it until we're done. That way I won't have to go at the opera. You know I don't like sitting on all those strange toilets."

I detect a few stares.

My mother does not take well to new experiences. She is a creature of habit, avoiding change as if it were the freeway's passing lane, preferring to cruise along at a familiar 45 and take no exits. She has lived her entire life within a 10-mile radius of where she was born, never worked, and rarely traveled. She is a taut pool that resists being rippled by any pebble.

For my son's 14th birthday, we invited her along to his favorite sushi restaurant. After building her confidence with cucumber and crab rolls, he talked her into sampling a small piece of raw fish. "Oh my," she yelled in the crowded restaurant. "I can't swallow this! I'm gonna gag! *Joey!* Hand me your napkin!"

Thankfully, she remains composed when our waiter delivers her entrée—an elaborate arrangement of shrimp and broccoli, glazed in an ethereal, shimmering sauce.

"I'm never going to be able to eat all this," is the first thing she says.

"Just try it, maybe it's really good," I coax.

"What time is it now?"

"Six-thirty. We have a whole hour."

"I'm almost too nervous to eat. You know I don't like to be late."

Fortunately, her dinner *is* good, absolutely nothing to complain about. But what I'm finding is that, without negatives, there isn't anything left to discuss. My mother believes that her life ended the day my father died. Nothing, not even the salve of time, has been able to convince her otherwise. They had been married for 34 years, and although the relationship was more tolerance than happiness, in retrospect, it was so much better than the alternative.

My mother was so sheltered in her marriage that she had never even written a check. I had to show her how to do it, her hand trembling as she scripted the name of the funeral home and endorsed it. She had never dealt with finances, business people, the outside world, life in general. My father handled all that. She was responsible for cooking, cleaning, shopping, and overseeing me. Perhaps that's the problem right there: a mother with good intentions but no perception of reality.

In the 8 years since my father's death, I've refused to replace him. I will not do everything for her. Friends and relatives consider me heartless, but I know she has the capability and the toughness. Nothing gripes me more than her dismissal of a new challenge, her insisting, "Oh, I could never do that." And so we bicker and spar and drift further apart. And in the meantime, we've grown so accustomed to arguing that we no longer know how to relate when we're not.

And so we just sit here, each of us silently eating. It is so sadly disconcerting.

Finally, she says she can't eat another bite and pushes her plate in my direction, urging me to finish it. I acquiesce not because I'm still hungry, but because it gives me something to do.

"I'm going to the bathroom," she says. "Keep an eye on my jacket."

"Do you really think someone's going to swipe it?"

"Just watch it."

But I watch her instead, walking away almost as if she is a kid, all nervous and naïve in such a strange environment. Even at 66, the woman is still attractive. Blonde hair, unwrinkled complexion, a little overweight, but after such a soft life, that's to be expected. She could easily remarry if she wanted. In fact, one of the most unsettling moments of my life came when I witnessed an older gentleman hitting on her at a dead relative's viewing. That's even worse than catching your parents having sex.

Eventually, she returns wearing fresh lipstick and even more perfume, complaining just briefly about "the attendant in there who I had to tip; I hate when they do that." When the bill arrives, she furtively opens her purse and tries to push cash into my hand, but I tell her she's embarrassing me and I pay with a credit card.

Compared to dinner, the opera is anticlimactic. There's a show to preoccupy us, to keep us separate. It lasts for 3 hours and 45 minutes. I fall asleep during the second act, and I think she's bored, too, even though she won't admit it. During the intermissions, I walk alone through the crowded halls, frustrated by the expectations I had for this evening and my failure to meet them.

We ride home together on the bus, and I feign sleep so we can both relax. She stares out the window, still clutching her purse. I can't imagine what she's thinking, what she's feeling, or how she reconciles us. The woman is a mystery, even though we share the same life, the same blood.

I have a buddy who is a psychologist. He mentioned to me once that conversation is like WD-40. It keeps our connections lubricated and operating smoothly. It's easy for me to see now that our relationship has seized up because we've never been able to talk. What few words we do exchange almost creak with effort. It's partly her fault because she never laid a foundation of respect and trust. Instead, she used ridicule so I would grow up tentatively and remain her little boy as long as possible. It's not that she was selfish or cruel, it's just that being a mother was all she knew. My blame is that I've refused to forgive her for this, even though I know how lonely and desperate she is. My behavior remains childish. I've never given her the chance to treat me any differently.

I'd like to say that our evening ended with an exchange of heartfelt thanks, but it didn't. I'd like to say that we squeezed each other's hands when I pulled up in front of her house, but we didn't. I'd like to say that we mumbled something simple like "Hey, that was fun, let's do it again," but even that didn't happen. It was late, I was tired, so was she. I waved in the dark as she unlocked the door, and pulled away.

My mother later told my wife that she had a wonderful time and that I was a perfect gentleman. For a while, she stopped pestering me with phone calls and all her petty troubles. It was as if I had pumped some much-needed attention into a near-empty hold, and it was enough to sustain her for a while. For that, at least, I was thankful.

But in the days that followed, I became cynical about our lack of progress and tried to forget about the evening entirely, to let it fade like the last note of that opera. I convinced myself that this was one regret I'd probably carry forever. It was simply too complicated to ever remedy.

At dinner a few weeks later with friends, after I'd told the whole story with much hyperbole, one woman stopped me: "Maybe that was the first step," she said. "Maybe that's all you can really expect."

It was such a simple analysis that I couldn't believe I had over-looked it. Amid all the other regrets I was swiftly trying to resolve in my life, here was one I was ready to abandon merely because it lacked a clear-cut resolution.

There had been progress in those 12 hours we spent together. I'd made an effort, and so had my mother. It was a big first step for both of us. And although we'll never discuss that night in such a sentimental context, I know she'll always cherish it.

What makes me so sure of this is something that happened 3 months later. It was during my obligatory Mother's Day visit. I was sitting on her sofa, nearly comatose after a lunch of mashed pota-toes, lasagna, breaded chicken, "crap patties," and cheesecake. ("You're such a picky eater, I never know what to make.") She was rambling on in her usual way, and I was barely listening.

"Don't forget to take a look at my bank statement before you leave. I can't make heads or tails out of it. And I think there's some-thing stuck in my chimney. See if you can look up there and find anything. I hear it every night. And you know how scared I get, all alone in this house. My blood pressure! My arthritis! Someday when you're my age, you'll appreciate all I go through. Mildred's kids chipped in and sent her a big bouquet for Mother's Day. You never do that. The only time you ever gave me flowers was when you picked those buttercups from the backyard. That was 30 years ago! Mildred hates the home, though. She moans about it every day."

"What did you say?"

"I said Mildred hates that nursing home, and you better never put me in one. I want to die right here."

"No, about the buttercups."

"Don't remember that, do you?" she said, tapping her head to indicate its Vise-Grip qualities. "You picked a bunch from the lawn and gave them to your mommy. A mother doesn't forget *anything*. Just remember that. Now take a look at this bank statement before I forget."

And as I do, I can't help smiling to myself. I *had* broken through.

"Hey, you want to go out for Chinese next Thursday?" As

CHAPTER 7

never being able
to find God

I am sitting with my family in a back corner of the Calvary Temple Baptist Church—a remote spot from which we thought we could anonymously observe the ceremony and then sneak out. But a television camera has found us. Like a bloodhound, it has gotten a whiff of fresh soul. While panning across the vast, theaterlike interior, it hesitates and then zooms in. We try to act natural, inspired—our voices and visions raised toward heaven.

What I'm visualizing, though, is some frail old widow in an Arkansas trailer park sitting in front of her Zenith watching us. We're supposed to be a peephole of light for shut-ins like her, an example of how Jesus can buoy you, a compelling reason to call the toll-free number on the bottom of the screen right now and make a modest donation. No wonder we're feeling uncomfortable.

In between verses of "Amazing Grace," the preacher calls the afflicted forward, inviting them to kneel at the long marble altar and ask Almighty God for forgiveness. A steady stream of people shuffles toward him, heads bowed, hands clasped, seemingly so tortured by physical and mental devils that they may not make it. It's compelling footage.

Yet the camera remains focused on us.

A few pews over, a brittle Black woman with white hair, who looks about 90, starts clapping her hands and swaying to the music as nimbly as if it were 1929. Someone should tell her to be careful. Her navy blue bonnet is already askew.

But still the camera doesn't move.

In the choir at the front of the church, a blind woman dressed in an ivory gown and standing beside a seeing-eye dog suddenly throws back her head and begins speaking in tongues. Her eyes are wide open and white. It sounds and looks like she's possessed.

But the camera couldn't care less.

The preacher's son, a broad-shouldered young man in a perfectly tailored suit and gleaming shoes, pounds on the piano. Despite the effort, his clothes never rumple and his hair never moves. Another miracle.

Suddenly, I know what that camera lens represents and why it's staring at us. It's the eye of the Almighty Himself, letting us know that nothing escapes Him, that He's aware of our indiscretions, of our skepticism. And it's far more interesting than any of this.

A fat woman five rows over throws up her dimpled arms and screams something unintelligible.

God knows what we're up to, that we don't belong here, that we're lifelong Catholics playing a game we're not supposed to.

The singing and dancing grow louder and drums join the piano. The whole scene is increasingly manic. At any moment, I expect leg braces to come off and crutches to fly through the air. In fact, I'm tempted to take off my thick glasses and feel my scalp for a miraculous regrowth of hair.

What on Earth are we doing here?

Afterward—exhausted, relieved, disturbed—we drive home

feeling like we've been touched by Jimmy Swaggart and need hot showers.

"That wasn't church," says my son. "That was a TV show."

"Yeah," adds my daughter, visibly relieved. "We were lucky to get out of there."

Church isn't what we normally do on Sunday mornings. Usually, I'm off riding my bike across the quilted farmland of southeastern Pennsylvania. I tell my family that this is my church. This is when I contemplate the glory of the world and renew myself for the week ahead. This is my Sunday worship.

The problem is that my kids have heard me say this so often over the years that now they've adopted the same argument. My wife used to be able to take them to Mass while I was out cycling, but now that they're older, they've ceased being so cooperative.

"How about if I take the dog for a walk?" asks my 15-year-old son. "It's a beautiful day. That can be my church."

"I'm going to meditate while I sleep late," suggests my 12-year-old daughter.

As a result, Sunday mornings are not the quality family-bonding time that they should be. Instead, they're filled with grousing and finger-pointing.

The easy solution, of course, would be for me to just go to church. Put on a suit and tie, order the kids into the Volvo, and drive off with a blank smile like all the other neighborhood dads. But I can't do that. I spent 12 years in Catholic school, and it wrung the faith right out of me. Instead of becoming spiritual, I became skeptical.

It all stems from my junior year, when our high-school principal (a priest) ran off with a woman he was counseling. Nuns were crying in the halls, and at the subsequent assembly, we were told that "Father has been called from us."

Yeah, right. The only call he answered was a siren's song.

The lesson I learned that day was that even those with religious authority are human. And those nuns weren't honest about what happened, because they didn't want us to know that. They didn't want us to see that even those who purport to represent God are as weak, confused, and vulnerable as the rest of us. They didn't want to risk losing our fear, our awe—which is how they controlled us.

Since then I've realized that the entire Catholic Church operates this way. It says it understands heaven and hell, that it has accurately interpreted all the rules, that this is the one true faith. But the truth is that no one really knows. The church and the people who run it are human. They believe, and they want you to believe, that they're slightly above us. But they're really not. And what I object to most, what keeps me from sitting pleasantly numb at Sunday Mass, is somebody telling me what God is all about and what I have to do to win His approval. I believe that spirituality is an intensely personal thing. It's between you and the Big Guy (or Gal, if that's how you choose to interpret it). There doesn't have to be an intermediary.

So I stopped going to church as soon as I was old enough to disobey my parents and get away with it. Part of it was laziness, sure. But part of it, too, was that I was taking my first moral stand. I got increasingly pissed off hearing priests use their sermons for fundraising rather than soul-lifting. I became steadily more angered by the blank faces of the congregation and their obvious lack of motivation. I remained Catholic only so my children could receive the basic sacraments and so my deeply religious mother-in-law wouldn't excommunicate me from the family.

The parish we belong to serves 2,500 families. On holidays such as Christmas and Easter (the only times I visit), people don't arrive early to celebrate the season's special blessing; they do so to get a good parking spot. If you don't arrive on time, you end up in the Parish Center for a sort of makeshift, overflow Mass. None of the priests knows our names, and every three months we get a computer printout of our contributions, just like a bank statement. It's the business of God they're in—an assembly line of souls operating at maximum capacity.

I've tried, but I just can't derive anything beneficial from experiences like this. To me, church can't be an obligatory transaction where you show up, get grace, and then leave. It has to be something I want to do, something I draw nourishment from; otherwise it's a waste of my time, and probably God's as well.

What I never planned on, though, was my children's adopting my skepticism. It seemed like such a bold and worthwhile crusade until my own soldiers got wounded. Even my wife, who's religious at the bone, has been influenced. She's less devoted than when I first met her, less sure of her spiritual self, and I feel bad about taking that from her. Sometimes I feel downright evil, like I've corrupted my family's spiritual health. Sometimes I wonder if it wouldn't have been better to just swallow my doubt until the kids were older and be a good religious robot.

Although I don't agree with the church's methods, I do value the qualities it teaches: love, truth, humanity, charity, respect. These are the cornerstones of every good person, the qualities that every father should be nurturing in his children. But lately on my Sunday rides, I've been feeling like I'm failing mine. At its core, religion is simply the line between good and evil. And every child needs to be aware of where that is. In fact, the more reminders you can deliver, the better. Although Catholic school ultimately made me suspicious about religion, it also made me conscious of that line and the traits that separate the people on each side of it. I absorbed this knowledge without realizing it. The soul must be porous.

But when are my kids exposed to this? Certainly not while walking the dog or sleeping late, no matter how deeply or meditatively. Although my wife and I try to set good examples, we make up an ever-dwindling slice of their world. When they're away from home, what values do they have to depend upon? When they're alone in a difficult situation, whom can they turn to for consolation? Realistically, not us. They need something else.

So one Sunday morning, alone in my church, I get an idea. Suppose I postpone these bike rides for a while and take my family to a different service every Sunday? There must be dozens of denominations in our area. Suppose we visit some of the quaint churches I've been pedaling past for years? It would make my wife happy, because we'd be worshipping as a family. It would renew my interest, because each service would be unique. And it would get my children's attention, simply because it'd be fun and different. It would be a spiritual adventure, a religious education for us all.

It makes perfect sense. If we're having trouble finding God, then why not go looking for Him? He has to be out there somewhere.

Obviously, someone is still paying to light this world.

St. John's United Church of Christ belongs on a postcard. It sits atop a knoll along Rising Sun Road in the village of Laurys Station, Pennsylvania—a tiny white chapel set against a backdrop of hazy blue mountains and yawning valleys. While scanning the church listings in the Yellow Pages, I spotted an advertisement for it. This seemed a novel way to attract "customers" and, considering its idyllic location, I thought it a good place to start.

We arrive 15 minutes before the scheduled Sunday service, just like perfect, punctual Catholics. But the parking lot is already full, and the sound of a congregation in song greets us at the door. Did I read the ad wrong? "No, no," says a pleasant, round usher. "Everyone just enjoys getting here early."

We are temporarily dumbstruck.

He escorts us to the very front of the church, the first pew. We *never* sit this close. This is the mosh pit of souls—the place where the priest can actually see you, make you feel guilty, and prevent you from sneaking out early. But although there are probably only about 150 people inside, the church is so small that these are the only seats left. My wife and I are among the youngest attendants and one of the few couples with children. We feel immediately uncomfortable, like we've been put on a pedestal.

What's worse, everyone is smiling at us.

"Fresh meat," whispers my wife.

I nervously look at the bulletin the usher handed us and am pleased to see that the title of this week's sermon is "Don't Go to Sleep!" At least the pastor is direct. It puts me slightly more at ease.

Despite how beautiful and quaint the church looks from the outside, its interior is suffering. Like most of the parishioners, it's old and crumbling. There are water stains on the ceiling, runaway cracks squiggling up the walls, and a large piece of fabric draped over the deteriorating entrance to the steeple tower. But this isn't as disappointing as it sounds. In fact, I kind of like it. It hints of poverty and struggle. When you don't have much to work with, you know what's important.

The service turns out to be just as no-nonsense. Some singing, a Scripture reading, the sermon, some more singing, and that's it. The whole thing takes maybe 20 minutes. To a guy who once had to carry his sobbing children from a 2-hour Holy Saturday Mass, it is a refreshing experience. When worship is this brief, you're automatically focused. There isn't any time for daydreaming.

But as we gather our things and prepare to leave, we notice that no one else is stirring. The woman behind us whispers that there's a congregational meeting the last Sunday of every month. So we dutifully sit back down and watch as the church becomes a boardroom. The pastor relinquishes control to a secretary, roll is taken, minutes are reviewed, new officers are nominated, votes are counted, and budgets are debated. Eventually, a skinny man in a powder-blue suit flips on an overhead projector and plucks the top layer off a thick sheaf of slides. These turn out to be detailed plans for the church's Phase I expansion, architectural renderings of a piece of heaven brought to their earth. Everyone sits transfixed as he painstakingly projects one image after another onto the cracked wall. After about 20 minutes, my wife and kids start giving me the hairy eyeball.

The meeting plods onward, and the stack of overlays refuses to dwindle. The skinny man drones on. Finally, I nod a signal, and we get up as quietly as possible. We duck under the projection of the new west facade and head for the rear exit, embarrassed yet determined. But before we can escape, the pastor himself hustles after us. In the vestibule, he shakes our hands, insists we sign the guest book (a thank-you note arrives 2 days later), and apologizes profusely for the length of the meeting. He's sincere, almost begging, when he says he hopes we come back.

My family is wrung out by the experience.

"Do we have to do this *every* Sunday?" my daughter moans, throwing herself across the backseat of the car as if she's been shot.

"This is your father's idea, not mine," says my loving, supportive wife.

My son is already listening to his Discman.

I try to salvage what I can by mentioning what I found interesting; namely, how this little church isn't just a place of worship, but rather a meetinghouse—how it's intended for people and their business as much as it is for God and His. It was nice to see the two intermingled. But despite such a strong sense of community, I still felt out of place. This wasn't my faith. This wasn't my spiritual home. That wasn't my dream projected on the wall. It was almost like I was cheating on someone.

"Yeah, it didn't feel like our church," says my son, temporarily lifting off one earphone.

"Yeah," agrees my daughter. "It didn't feel like we belonged."

Well, how about that. Deep down, they do feel connected. They know a place where they're welcome, even if it's so vast their names aren't known.

Maybe their faith isn't so shallow after all.

One of the things I've never understood about religion is why everyone has to wear a costume. If you're supposed to be focusing on what's in your heart, why does it matter what's covering your skin? Why all the special vestments, whether worn by the person conducting the ceremony or by those in attendance?

Catholics are particularly obsessed with this. During my 12-year sentence in parochial school, I was forced to wear dress slacks and shoes, a collared shirt and tie, and occasionally even a blazer to class every day. The girls, of course, had to wear uniforms. It was as if the nuns, who had some pretty nifty costumes of their own, had us forever poised to attend Mass—an infantry fully outfitted for the Second Coming. For a while, I actually believed that wearing sneakers to church was a mortal sin.

So I was instantly intrigued when I heard about the Baha'i faith, which must be the world's most casual religion. There is no dress code, pastor, church, or organized service. It's simply a group of like-minded people coming together wherever is convenient. Founded in the mid-19th century by a Persian nobleman who surrendered his princely existence for a life of deprivation, it is the second largest and fastest growing of the world's many denominations.

But you'd never guess that from the looks of it. When we accompany some Baha'i friends to a Sunday morning gathering at a local university, there's even a dog in attendance. The congregation (if you can call it that) is an eclectic mix of 2 dozen people with diverse nationalities and occupations. There's an Indian doctor and his family, a college professor, a couple of students, and a young actor with white hair who's playing the role of Scrooge in a local Christmas pageant. For refreshment, there are cartons of orange juice and bagels, plus casual conversation with these friendly people. The sole guy in a suit is apologetic, explaining that he has an appointment immediately afterward.

After about a half-hour of socializing, everyone sits down in a circle, sings along to some music from a tape player, shares a few inspirational thoughts from the week, then reads a paragraph or two from a book of reflections written by the faith's founder. This isn't worship of some deity but rather a quiet striving toward spirituality. This is a little search party trying to find the key to a slightly more satisfying life. They are not here out of habit or fear or ego. They're here simply because they find it enriching, and they want to be here.

Although there are no religious icons in this scuffed classroom and the windows are clear instead of stained glass, I can still detect

something holy here. It's goodness. It's happiness. It's peace. It's acceptance. It's all the things that religions attribute to God but then
obscure with ceremony and regulation.

After the readings, we break into groups. The children go off
for a makeshift Sunday school while the parents adjourn to an upstairs classroom for what would normally be an hour-long discussion. But today is different. The woman who owns the dog will be
giving us a lesson in Chinese meditation—teaching us how to redirect the energy or *chi* inside our bodies. She starts by giving very
specific instructions for how to sit. She wants us on the front
quarter of our folding chairs, backs straight, hands palms up in our
laps. This, she claims, will activate the all-important acupuncture
point between our genitals and anuses. (I wag my eyebrows sug-
gestively at my wife.) Furthermore, she tells us to periodically touch
the tips of our tongues to different spots inside our mouths. Any
saliva that accumulates should be gargled and swallowed since it's
beneficial to health. Oh, and one more thing. She warns us not to
be alarmed if any parts of our bodies start to move spontaneously.
(I'm slightly alarmed, praying that it's not the bowels of the large
gentleman next to me.)

And with that, she hits the button on her tape player to start the
guided meditation. The first 10 minutes are agonizing. I can't understand one word the guy on the tape is saying, and my all-important acupuncture point is cramping. I'm feeling generally
ridiculous as, I think, are most of the people in the room. But I
close my eyes, smile softly, and try to appear serene, not wanting to
offend the woman (or her dog, which could turn mean). Eventually, I catch on to what the Chinese master is saying and begin
"opening and closing my lungs like a lotus flower." Breathing in
such a way must induce a mildly hypnotic state, because once I get
the hang of it, the remaining 50 minutes go by swiftly. I emerge
feeling strangely refreshed (and checking to see if anything of mine
moved spontaneously).

Afterward, a succession of people take me aside and explain that this isn't typical of the Baha'is. It's as if they don't want me to get the wrong impression, to expect that next I'll be forced to drink the Kool-Aid. But I haven't taken it that way. Rather than New Age zealots, I see only a group of ordinary people who are open-minded enough to allow something like this. That's encouraging. Most religions are too close-minded, too paranoid of new inter-pretations. They don't see that fresh experiences help you grow, while rote ones keep you where you are. Or maybe they do, but that's part of their plans.

I don't know if it's the meditation or the experience of this laid-back faith, but a strange sort of lethargic peace lingers in me for the rest of the day. In fact, I see it in my entire family. My kids admit that they had fun (largely because there were lots of other kids around). They picked up on the genuineness, too, and for a while at least were content just being there and being themselves.

I think part of the problem we're having is that our Sundays have become routine. There's nothing special about them anymore, nothing to set them apart from the other days of the week. That's how it is for a lot of people these days. Stores are open early. Ac-tivities are plentiful. The bustle is usual. But I'm realizing that it's important for one day to retain some small measure of specialness. If nothing else, religion provides this. Beyond the community of the church (which you may or may not feel), there's the commu-nity of your family. And this is vital to cultivate. This is the glue that keeps you together—whether as a group or as an individual. This is what we felt today, and this, perhaps, is what we most need to re-claim.

If Baha'i is religion at its most relaxed, then Ukrainian Or-thodox is the faith that's most choreographed. The friend who introduced us to it explained that it's headquartered in Constan-tinople (Istanbul), where services can last up to 13 hours. I try to keep this in mind as we're blessing ourselves for the umpteenth time at the Assumption of the Virgin Mary Ukrainian Orthodox Church in Northampton, Pennsylvania. We're 4 of maybe 100 people, each one a relic. The majority of the 90-minute service is in a language we don't understand, resolutely sung by a priest in ornate vestment and high hat with a severe black beard reminiscent of Rasputin's.

This is the church of goose bumps, the first one we've visited that feels like God is in here with us. The deep chimes that began the ceremony seemed triggered by His fingertip upon the doorbell, and we all respectfully rose to greet Him. From the gold dome atop the building, to the thick doors that protect the sanctuary, to the scent of incense that pervades everything, to the secret prayers and holy books, to the fact that this liturgy has remained unchanged for almost 1,300 years—there's a sense of permanence and awe, a feeling of certainty and eternity here. This is underscored by the ending to every prayer: " . . . and unto ages of ages." It's the way things always have been and the way they forever will be, just like God Himself.

I feel suitably small and meaningless, dwarfed by the immensity of time and my insignificant role in it. But this isn't such a bad feeling. To bow your head and acquiesce, to finally surrender after a week of petty struggles, imparts an unexpected sense of relief. I don't have to think at all here. All I have to do is follow along in the program. In a world with fewer and fewer clear-cut rules, it's surprisingly nice to be told so precisely what to do. Although the Catholic Mass is similarly rote, this service is so intensely ritualistic that it makes the Catholics look like wild Baptists. In fact, there is something almost hypnotic about it. Repeating a meaningful word or phrase in monotone has been scientifically shown to slow heart rate, lower blood pressure, reduce respiration, and ultimately induce a pleasing, meditative state. (Plus, who knows what's in that incense?) This is called the relaxation effect, and it has significant health benefits. Whether or not you believe in salvation or any of religion's other metaphysical effects, this might be its most tangible gift—a single hour of calming meditation.

But while overwhelmed adults can appreciate this, impatient children certainly cannot. While at first the seriousness of this faith has my kids intimidated, eventually they wither under its ponder-ance. By the end of the service, they're both bent over the pew with heads in hands.

Perhaps the older you get, the more attractive a religion like this becomes. Maybe when you're 75 and sick of change, a service like this is bliss. For these people, too, this religion is more than a way to stay connected with God; it's a link to their Ukrainian heritage. It seems the strongest religions have this—Judaism, for instance.

Although it feels nice to be wrapped in the thick, wooly com-fort of a faith this ancient, it's obvious we don't fit in. This religion is as foreign to us as the language it's celebrated in. What's be-coming increasingly worrisome, though, is that there may not be a denomination we instantly understand. When I first set out to right this regret, I believed we'd eventually walk into a church or hear some preacher and it would suddenly feel like we were home. But the more places we visit, the more I suspect that that isn't going to happen. Perhaps instead of searching outside ourselves, we should be looking within. Maybe all these churches are nothing more than distractions.

And that's what eventually brought us to the Quakers. What intrigued me about this religion, when I heard a friend describe it, is that it isn't a faith of pomp, but rather of person. Quakers be-lieve that there's a piece of God inside everyone, and the way to find Him is by looking there. As a result, Quaker "churches" aren't any more sacred than any other place. In fact, they refer to churches not as places of worship, but rather as "meetinghouses." Everything in them is simple, straightforward, and without airs—no preachers, kneelers, altars, artifacts, or even sacred scripture. Everyone already has all that's needed to access God. You just have to believe in yourself.

On the Sunday morning we visit, a hundred or so people grad-ually filter into the lobby of the meetinghouse. Sweaters and jeans are the order of dress, since there's no need to impress. As we chat and shake hands, we feel no hopeful pressure to join the faith, as we immediately did at some other churches. Perhaps it's because these people already know we belong. Rather than being subtly recruited, we are genuinely welcomed.

After a while, everyone meanders into a large upstairs room—the heart of the meetinghouse—and takes a seat on wooden benches arranged circularly beneath a skylight/atrium. And then the service begins: 1 hour of complete silence.

I can't remember the last time I sat still this long with nothing to do. Most people avoid being conscious of themselves without distraction for any sizable length of time. I suspect they're afraid of meeting that intimate stranger within or, worse yet, being terribly bored by what they find. It certainly makes me uncomfortable. I sneak peeks at the people around me, searching for a clue as to what to do. Most have their eyes closed, some are staring blankly up through the skylight, but everyone appears to be having a peacefully good time. There are children in the room, too, and all are sitting just as quietly, making a minimum of fuss. (They stay for the first half-hour, then go off to Sunday school.)

The friend who had originally explained this religion to me said she discovered it when she was in her late thirties. At first, she was an unwitting member. She had twin baby girls at the time and simply started cherishing this oasis, this single hour of calm. She didn't necessarily find God, but she found herself, and as she eventually realized, that can be just as enlightening.

Although the Quakers encourage thoughtful silence, they also welcome meaningful interruption. If in the course of your meditation you are inspired to say something to the group, then so be it. A few people take advantage of this today. One young man confesses his addiction to violent video games; a Vietnam veteran states his struggle with the Quaker view of pacifism. No one rebuts or expounds upon any of these comments. They are taken as mere statements—paper-airplane thoughts that have been carefully folded and tossed into the air.

As I sit here, I think of nothing and everything simultaneously. I try to clear a room in my mind so I can just *be*, but random thoughts keep slipping under the door. I chase each one out, but eventually there are just too many scurrying about. So I sit amid their swirl, finally realizing that just to be conscious of the thought process is a worthy separation of self. If I can step back and observe my brain functioning like this, then there must be something beyond it doing the observing. I am not my mind. I do not exist only in its neuron sparks and synapses. I am something else. Could it be that this is the small part of me that is God?

These are big thoughts—too big, perhaps. But it's invigorating to think on such a scale. Normally, I am preoccupied with "little-think"—the myriad to-do lists of our days. This has been an opportunity to go beyond that. I can see how it can be classified as worship.

The hour ends with just as little fanfare as it began. Visitors stand up to introduce themselves, announcements are made, but no collection is taken. At other services, the entire worship seems built around donation. At one in particular, the pastor even raised the basket up to God—as if He cared.

My family likes the uniqueness and informality of the Quakers. Although my kids are too young to grasp the deep worth of meditation, just having the discipline to sit quietly for 30 minutes has to be valuable to them. Thinking is a skill not all children realize they have.

Three days later, my son gets an e-mail from a girl named Chloe, whom he met at the meetinghouse. She wants to know when he'll be coming back.

"You know, I've been thinking," he says to me. "I kind of liked the Quakers best."

Over the next few months, we visited lots of other churches and temples and houses of worship. For most of this experiment, my family remained cooperative. We were buoyed by praise from co-workers and friends, who genuinely admired what we were doing. It seems a lot of people want to start their own search, but are either too lazy or too overcome with religious rigor mortis to begin.

But no matter how noble the cause, my kids eventually began grousing about these forays just as they had about going to our old church. Our quest for God hadn't turned out to be the Easter-egg hunt they originally envisioned. It wasn't that straightforward, or even that thrilling. When you set out to find something, it's with the assumption that it's hiding and that it can, in fact, be found. But I've learned that that's not necessarily true when it comes to God.

God isn't hiding. He's pretty much everywhere. What's happened is that we've disguised Him with all these religious interpretations. It's like we've been playing one long game of "whisper down the alley" for generations, and the message is now so far from the original that it no longer makes sense to an increasing number of us.

When you look objectively at religion as we did during that time, Sunday morning becomes a fascinating phenomenon. When we stepped out of our routine, we noticed all these polished people scurrying about in different directions to their chosen denominations. It's a vibrant, colorful underworld. It's like looking through the glass at an ant farm where everything is so organized and busy. But you can't help wondering what they are trying to accomplish. I would bet many of the "ants" aren't even sure.

It's convinced me, though, that there is a God instinct. It's no different from our need for food or warmth or love. It's an embedded part of us, something that's required if we're to thrive. But it's a subtle drive, especially at first. Only with age does it gather momentum, become noticeable, and ultimately, send us off searching.

There was a time, for instance, when I didn't care about any of this—when I believed myself invincible, when the hereafter was pallid compared to the here and now. I had no need for God, no use for anything beyond myself. The world was full of enough wonder. But religion is all about need. At first, it's someone else's—

the poor who need your help, the souls who need your prayers, the church that needs your money. It's easy to shrug off such requests. But slowly and inevitably, the need becomes your own. It's not necessarily that you need help or prayer or money. It's something far less tangible than that. It's something that can't be thrown into a collection basket.

At 40, I'm starting to feel that need. And it's difficult to explain, even though I explain things for a living. The best description I have is a hole—freshly dug in the pit of my stomach. And the older I grow, the more it grows, widening and deepening until some days I feel like I am the hole, and there is nothing else to me. There is no associated pain; it doesn't ache or burn or throb. It's just there, waiting for something to fill it. And I suppose that something is God.

My children don't have this need yet, and that's why our search left them largely unaffected. They have no regrets about their relationship with God because it is naturally intimate, even though they don't realize or acknowledge it. They already know goodness and wonder and truth. They don't need some church or preacher to explain it. They live this way every day. It's only with "education" and "maturity" that it drifts away and they develop a young adult's attitude.

But just as we all lose our physical attributes, we also eventually lose these proud attitudes. We begin as children and end childlike, both physically and emotionally. And somewhere during this progression, perhaps around age 40, comes the turning point.

I know now that all this has been *my* regret, *my* quest—not my children's. They have lots of obvious meaning in their lives; I have increasingly smaller amounts. But I don't feel I was wrong in making them come along. Although it had a meager effect on them now, I think one day the benefit will compound. One day, when they reach their turning points, they'll remember that even though their old man didn't find God in a miraculous way for his family, at least he had the sense to look.

And now each Sunday morning when I'm pedaling my bike through the Pennsylvania countryside and my children are home grousing to my wife about going to church, I am no longer plagued by guilt. I know that even though we may be "without religion," we are not without God. I am praying, I am meditating, I am touching my soul in the best way I know how. And they are, too, in the many mindful activities they pursue. And although we may not worship together conventionally, that doesn't make us any less of a family. There are other ways to appreciate and love and inspire one another that are just as valuable.

I'm not absolutely sure yet, but I think that's pretty damn close to where God must be.

CHAPTER 8

missing my sexual peak

The lion mates for 36 continuous hours, copulating and ejaculating hundreds of times. It's one of the chief reasons he's called the king of beasts.

Deep in the neural circuitry of man are remnant memories of this. Hundreds of thousands of years ago, as hunters and gatherers in the Rift Valley of East Africa, our male ancestors witnessed this grand performance. The lion with his pride—confident and potent and tireless. Because men are impressionable beasts, they dreamed of possessing just as mighty a drive and becoming sexual lions themselves.

This is just a theory of mine, but I don't think it's that much of an anthropological exaggeration. I believe it to be true, because I've seen this performance firsthand and felt what it can do to you.

When I was in Kenya in 1989, I witnessed the lion's mating ritual on the plains of the Masi Mara. It was one of the most captivating things I'd ever seen—primal yet tender, powerful yet peaceful. Watching this huge animal growl and nip and quiver and eventually fall back languid in the dust, only to rise shortly thereafter and do it again, was the most impressive of encores. It is the definition of raw maleness. It is the essence to which all men can be distilled. It is sex without psychological interference or morality. It is pure. It is selfless. It is unending. It is inspiring.

Science tells us that men reach their sexual peak around age 18. This is when their sex drives are highest, their sperm counts greatest, and even their penises the longest. In other words, this is when they are closest to being lions, when the male juice called testosterone fills their veins like spring rains swell a farm stream. This is when they are most obsessed and ready. This is when 36 hours of continuous sex is possible.

But the irony is that our society discourages men from having sex that early. They are still too immature, irresponsible, and self-centered. So most are left to satisfy an imaginary pride of lionesses culled from Victoria's Secret catalogs and the Internet. Instead of being proud of their manhood, they're embarrassed at what it drives them to do late at night when they're alone in bed or when they're in the shower with a bottle of shampoo.

No wonder so many adult men find it difficult to express emotion and love. They've grown up suppressing their urges, controlling their sexuality, until it no longer feels natural.

I regret missing my sexual peak. When I was 18, the furthest I'd gotten with a girl was a clumsy exchange of hand jobs in the back seat of a Camaro. Now that I'm 40 and significantly less horny, I can't help feeling sorry that I missed my only opportunity to be that lion.

When it comes to sex, the male brain is a pest. It never stops questioning its owner's reproductive prowess. No matter how virile the body remains, no matter how physically satisfying the current relationship, it always wants to know "Was it good for you?" and "How do I compare?" These are two of the most stupid, egocentric questions a guy can ask a lover, especially one he's been married to for 15 years. But nonetheless, this is still the first urge I get immediately afterward. I, like most men, am incapable of feeling completely satisfied unless I hear, however distant, a smattering of applause.

It's this insistent need-to-know mentality that drives middle-age men to cheat on their wives. When they look in the mirror and it's no longer evident that they're young and desirable, they go searching for assurance elsewhere. Even though they rarely find the lies they want, or some woman to tell them for more than a night, they doggedly continue the hunt. It's the curse of our lost lion-hood.

But is it really lost? Without resorting to a nubile 25-year-old mistress, is it possible for me to arrest my slow slide into monoga-mous limpness and reclaim my sexual peak? Sex has to be the most intimately studied topic in the world, both at the psychological and physiological levels. Suppose I enlisted some professional and chemical help that would allow my 37-year-old wife, who is just now approaching her sexual peak, and I to meet? Would I be ca-pable of one final mighty roar?

a weekend at sex camp

"The diaphragm!" Maria screams. "I forgot the diaphragm!"

My wife and I are speeding toward the airport to catch a flight to Atlanta, where we're supposed to attend a weekend retreat called the Sexuality Playshop.

"Are you kidding?" I shout back, vainly searching her face for some hint of humor. "We'll have to turn around! Damn it! How could you be so dumb?"

"Hey, I wasn't the one who kept hitting the snooze button," she yells. "I wouldn't have been so rushed if you'd gotten me up on time, *stupid*!"

And so begins our romantic, restorative escape to the idyllic mountains of north Georgia where, as the Playshop brochure promised, we'd "discover a new level of communication and sexu-ality." At the rate this was unfolding, though, I'd be lucky to find my wife in the same bed.

The Sexuality Playshop is a racier version of the traditional

Marriage Encounter weekend offered by pastors, psychologists, and counselors nationwide. The Playshop preaches similar principles of love, integrity, and honesty, but it is much more sexually explicit. (Ever attend a dinner buffet where the entertainment was X-rated videos?)

The two-day $595 course (renamed Retreat for Couples since our stay) is held four times annually by Jeanne Shaw, Ph.D., a certified sex therapist and licensed psychologist. She's also a grandmother, but all maternal comparisons end here, as she's not afraid to say "penis" in public and admits to having had an orgasm while reading erotica in a bookstore.

Unlike the classic marriage retreat, though, the Playshop is not designed solely for troubled couples. Rather, it and a growing number of similar workshops nationwide advertise themselves as a way to build and revitalize sexual energy. Indeed, when you consider all the other experiential, skill-building camps available—from flying a combat jet to learning to barefoot water-ski—it's no wonder some entrepreneur didn't think of this sooner.

My wife was attracted by the Playshop's sentimental trappings: the flowery pastel stationery, the opportunity to "move away from an emphasis on body parts to a greater emphasis on heart and mind," and the promise of becoming more "intimate." I, on the other hand, was enticed by the "explicit audiovisuals," the opportunity to move away from an emphasis on heart and mind to a greater emphasis on body parts (did I read that wrong?), and the promise of wild, hoot 'n' holler sex in a King Villa rented at my publisher's expense.

Despite that spat in the car, our 15-year, two-child, dual-career marriage was not in any precarious position. We were merely out to learn, have fun, and hopefully, end up in a few precarious positions.

Check-in at Villagio di Montagna, a resort in Cleveland, Georgia (just down the road from the Cabbage Patch Kids factory and the "I Got Mine" Gold Mine), is a bit awkward.

"Ah, yes, the Kitas. You must be another Playshop couple," says the gentleman at the front desk.

"Uh, that's right," I reply, casting a baffled glance chestward to see if I'd forgotten to latch the top five buttons on my shirt.

"Just to let you know," he says, winking, "your King Villa has a Jacuzzi, a fireplace, and a large, multijet shower. Enjoy."

Since this is our first sex camp, I immediately check the room for hidden cameras, giving special attention to the lower shower jet. And later that evening, at our group's first meeting, I can't help imagining what the other 15 or so middle-age couples might look like naked. A large woman, snacking on honey-wheat pretzels and possibly thinking the same thing, smiles at me from across the room.

As I suspect, some men look as if they've been dragged here by their wives. They slouch in their chairs, name tags askew, polite scowls on their faces lest anyone suspect *they* need sexual instruction. Meanwhile, the women are all doe-eyed and hopeful, hanging on Dr. Shaw's every utterance as if it will magically transform their relationships into romance novels. Their elbows are poised to prod.

"We are taught reproduction in school but not sex," says Dr. Shaw, in a move to assuage our egos. "Procreation is easy and spontaneous but being sexual is not. Let's brainstorm a list of things that good sex is dependent upon."

Our group's answers include foreplay, fatigue level, time, where the kids are, how long it's been since the last time, desire, atmosphere, chemistry, smell, size, good health, skill, toys, degree of danger/intrigue, and so on. Soon we've listed 35 prerequisites for good sex.

"It's a miracle we ever have it!" says Dr. Shaw. "And isn't it amazing that no one mentioned love? I once gave this exercise to 100 psychotherapists, and they forgot it, too. Can you remember when the only requirement was that your partner be there? The more years you spend together, the more requirements there are."

Since the majority of the couples who enroll in the Playshop have been together more than 15 years, this observation is met with lots of head-nodding. "Sexuality is good energy," she continues. "It shouldn't be stifled or rigidly controlled."

I half expect some people, especially one particularly friendly guy with a perm, to begin stripping after this declaration but none do. In all her literature, Dr. Shaw stresses that this 16-hour program is the most fun you can have with your clothes *on*. There are no pants-optional sessions nor is there pressure to disclose details of your sex life.

"Normal sex in our society is boring," adds Virginia Erhardt, Ph.D., a psychotherapist in Atlanta who is assisting Dr. Shaw. "It's functional sex. The erotic component of sexual arousal has been socialized out of us so we can feel virtuous. Arousal brings our genitals to life, but eroticism brings our hearts and souls to life. Our goal is to help you be more erotic and realize your sexual potential."

Unfortunately, by the time our first session concludes at 10:00 P.M., Maria and I are feeling about as erotic as a Ron Howard film. Once back at the villa, she dons her flannel pajamas, and I don't even bother to brush my teeth. Better leave the police whistle and leather chaps in the suitcase tonight, honey. I'm beat.

"Your assignment," says Dr. Shaw, as she walks through the room distributing pink and blue index cards, "is to write what you would most like to do sexually with your partner or what would most turn you on. Don't worry, no one will know what you wrote."

Ten minutes of mad scribbling ensues. I finish way too early and can't resist peeking over the shoulder of a good-looking woman in front of me. Her card reads: "Being persuaded by a wildly attractive stranger." I fight the urge to tousle what little hair I have left and look swarthy.

Dr. Shaw then seats all the women in a tight circle and randomly distributes their pink cards. We men are invited to sit in another circle, outside of theirs, and listen as they read these fantasies aloud. No doubt about it, this is like peeking through a hole into the sorority shower. Whoa! Lisa wants to roll naked on a putting green. Dainty, demure Cindy Lou yearns to be lashed to a piece of driftwood on the beach. The descriptions are vivid and, at times, raw. And to hear these supposedly normal women vocalize them is akin to dialing 1-900-TALK-HUSKY. Most of the men in the group are dumbfounded. In fact, when it's our time to step into the inner circle and read from our cards, it's evident how woeful our imaginations are by comparison.

The point here, though, is not who can spin the most provocative yarn, but rather that it's commonplace for everyone to harbor these erotic scenarios. Couples encounter problems when they keep these fantasies to themselves or, worse, disappear within them. "Our culture teaches us that fantasy and friction mean good sex," explains Dr. Shaw. "But if you're totally focused on the physical sensation, you're not focusing on connecting with your partner mentally, emotionally, or soulfully. Yes, the physical part is important, but if you're having fantasies instead of relating to your partner, you're making orgasm the focus instead of the connection. Try sharing these fantasies or simply looking in your partner's eyes."

Since my fantasy happens to involve a multijet shower and lots of Camay, I suggest to Maria that we "freshen up" on our break. So we dodge the couple from L.A. who want to talk about their time in therapy and hustle back to the villa, only to find the maid slowly scrubbing our bathroom.

Throughout the presentation, Dr. Shaw distributes handouts that reinforce her messages. Some are instantly intriguing, such as *Toning Your Orgasm Muscles* or *External Prostate Massage*, but others are lame surveys and conversational prompts that she encourages us to take outside and complete together.

One of the weekend's most interesting discussions, however, involves the relationship between eroticism and anxiety—those twin engines that always seem to be revving against each other. "Most people are nervous coming to a workshop such as this," says Dr. Shaw. "But if you pay attention to this anxiety, you'll grow.

"What is eroticism, anyway?" she asks. "How would you define it?"

"Passion," volunteers some guy with a ponytail. "Reckless abandon," offers the woman with the "stranger" fetish.

"Teasing . . . forbidden . . . wild . . . oily . . . daring . . . hot . . . kinky . . . sensual . . . nasty . . . creamy . . . mysterious . . ." Once we get rolling, it's difficult to stop, which brings us to the puzzling realization that if eroticism is so easy to define, then why is it so difficult to practice?

"Erotic sex is a balancing act between arousal and anxiety," explains Dr. Shaw. You'll only be as erotic as you think your partner will let you be. "As you can see, we all have hidden knowledge about how to have a steamy affair with our mates. We just have to risk being real and using that knowledge."

Dr. Shaw suggests using anxiety as "fertilizer for growth," explaining that its presence in a relationship is not so much a sign that something is irreversibly wrong as it is a signal that the relationship is ready to mature further. It's your challenge to help it grow. Ultimately, it's the issues that are the most difficult and embarrassing to broach with your partner that produce the most gain.

To underscore her point, Dr. Shaw choreographs some unusual dinner entertainment for Saturday night. I'm dribbling ranch dressing on my salad when I happen to glance across the table into the living room of the lodge where our group is dining. Playing on the television is an X-rated massage video in which a very tan, fit couple is slowly working the lactic acid out of each other's love muscles.

Unaware of what's unfolding behind them, the couple across from Maria and me continue jabbering about their European vacation and all the beautiful lace they bought in Brugge. We nod politely, push away our salads, and crane our necks so as not to miss anything. Meanwhile, this other couple thinks we're extremely interested in what they're saying.

"Unbelievable," I mutter.

"Yes, we were shocked at how cheap the lace was, too," replies this woman, "especially given its quality."

"Really well-hung," murmurs Maria.

"Well, my husband is pretty handy around the house. But it wasn't difficult. Just a few simple brass curtain rods is all."

It's not until someone turns up the volume that they glance over their shoulders to see what's going on. Then a cloud of uncomfortable sociability descends upon the room. Conversations continue, but they're distracted. Jokes are made, but they seem forced. We're a bunch of sexually mature adults, but no one knows how to react.

"One part of our culture says sex is bad and dirty. We don't talk about it, and we keep it behind closed doors," explains Dr. Shaw. "Another part exploits the lasciviousness of it. In either case, the message is that sex is not okay. My rationale in showing this video during dinner is to desensitize you to your anxieties about being sexual—to show you that it's perfectly fine to eat and watch sex videos at the same time." (Warning: Don't attempt this while eating hot soup or steamed clams.)

Saturday evening ends with a dance. Lights are dimmed in the banquet room, and a disco ball is illuminated by a strobe. Dr. Shaw and her assistants distribute silk scarves and balloons, encouraging us to use them creatively as we dance. I immediately bolt for the door before anyone asks me to do the horizontal polka, but Maria catches my arm and tells me to be polite. Fortunately, this is nothing but a forced attempt at sophomoric gaiety, and we escape unscathed—albeit after 2 hours.

It's late when we stumble back to our room. I'm about to suggest a "massage" when my wife starts complaining about all those mashed yams she ate for dinner and heads for the bathroom. I slip into a pair of silk boxers and try to wait up but fall asleep before the first flush. At this rate, we may be the only couple who goes to sex camp and never has sex.

The course ends on Sunday morning with a somber exercise. Dr. Shaw has us write our partners' epitaphs, pointing out that "you don't get to keep the love you find—without fail, one of you will bury the other." I try to write one for Maria and find that the anticipated loss instantly makes me appreciate her more. But this is not Dr. Shaw's sole intention. She wants to impress upon us the importance of maintaining independence in a relationship, becoming mature enough to survive such a setback by balancing love for our mates with a love for ourselves.

"In order to be part of a couple, you have to be an independent person first," Dr. Shaw explains. It's easy to leech off a partner, seeking comfort and security. But if this is done for any length of time, you'll lose your personality and integrity. And should your partner die, you'll die, too.

"Personal integrity is the greatest aphrodisiac," continues Dr. Shaw. "Couples spend their whole lives trying to change one another, when in fact they should be accepting their differences. Anytime you compromise your integrity, your independence, you grow resentful of your partner. If more men and women would take responsibility for their own experiences in a relationship, I'd be out of business."

It's little lessons such as these that have stayed with my wife and me. Playshop didn't transform us into insatiable sexual animals. We left no holes in our villa walls, nor did either of us come close to drowning in that multijet shower when we finally did consummate the camp. But neither of us had had this kind of training before, and it reminded us how much heartache could be saved if we educated our children in a similar way. As one ex-Army guy in our group concluded, "This was the first time I was ever with people who talked so freely and honestly about sex. It's made me a lot more comfortable."

There were other benefits. The open atmosphere of the course seemed to make everyone feel younger and more playful, as evidenced by the entwined hands and loving glances exchanged on the final day. I guess any experience that wrenches sex from the darkened bedroom and positions it center stage for adult discussion is beneficial. Besides, when was the last time one of your conferences ended with directions to a great place along the interstate to make love?

hiring a love coach

Marriage partners are like beer. Those first sips are full of luscious flavor, but as your taste buds gradually adjust, each successive mouthful becomes more ordinary. Eventually, the head fades, things go flat, and the can dimples.

Now I'm not saying that my bride has become a quart of Pabst. No, she's still Blue Ribbon to me. But we're often just too busy to be as intoxicated with each other as we once were. We both realize it. We both bemoan it. But we never really talk about it. And that's why the next step in my quest is a 2-month experiment with Ed Shea, a new breed of relationship coach who prefers to do his counseling over the telephone instead of across a polished maple desk. Sex camp brought us closer, but it didn't set us on fire. Perhaps some private, one-on-one coaching will rekindle the passion.

What attracts me to Shea's style of therapy is that it's relatively anonymous. After all, as a man, I have my pride. The only guy I've ever felt comfortable confessing to was old Father Gallo, and that's because he had narcolepsy. With this arrangement, I can still hide, although more physically than emotionally. By being a long-distance referee, sort of the soft-spoken voice of a wise conscience, Shea says he's better able to get couples to open up (men especially) and really listen to each other.

"My job as a coach is to help you strengthen your communication muscles," he explains. "The exercises I prescribe will feel awkward at first. But you'll become more coordinated."

Our customized 8-week training program entails 15 three-way telephone conversations with Shea, kind of a *ménage à AT&T*. Our 10-hour bill (not including phone charges) totaled $1,000. But before you balk, let me dangle one tantalizing outcome before you. During this time, my wife and I had the best sex of our married lives—and with each other, no less!

Do not be surprised if that grand suddenly seems like a paltry sum.

What Shea had us do was remarkably simple in retrospect, but it is the very overlooked basis of marriage (and sex) itself. As promised, he taught us how to be more effective communicators. Here's what we learned.

Voice your appreciation. Every one of our sessions began with a 5-minute warmup in which I would tell Maria what I appreciated about her. Then she would do the same for me. Such back-pats ranged from the profound to the incidental, but their effect was always the same: It made us feel good, confident, and loved. Plus, it put us in a positive mood for the discussion that followed. In these hectic times, the words *I appreciate you* have become even more special than the often trite and expected *I love you.*

Feel for soft spots. One of the ways Shea uncovers weak spots in a marriage is by having his clients complete a questionnaire that probes 10 common areas of disharmony in a relationship. These are money, work, sex, communication, religion, children, in-laws, problem solving, mutual appreciation, and shared leisure activities. The most troublesome among them then becomes fodder for future discussion and a focal point for growth. We learned to take the temperature of all of these things periodically.

Repeat what the other person says. "When most people are in a discussion or are having an argument, they aren't listening, they're reloading," says Shea. "They shoot and reload; shoot and reload."

To break this bad habit and keep battles from escalating, Shea teaches a technique called mirroring. It involves repeating or "reflecting" everything your partner has said. The trick, though, is to be a "flat mirror"—never interrupting and always using the exact words instead of summarizing in your own words. You have to listen closely in order to do this—hence the value. Ultimately, this process will make the other person feel heard and understood. Regardless of how the argument turns out, that's significant progress right there.

Negotiate a solution. You can't demand change from your partner. That just results in stalemate, war, and most hurtful of all, no nookie. What's required to overcome a bothersome behavior or situation is tactful negotiation. Here's the bargaining language Shea recommends. We simply picked a soft spot, then filled in the blanks.

"When this happens, I feel _____."

"I react _____."

"I'm afraid of _____."

"I hurt so much when _____."

"It reminds me of _____ from my childhood."

"If _____ could happen, this wound would be healed."

Although this exercise also felt awkward at first, it did help us to address and even correct problems that would have otherwise been ignored, perhaps to the future detriment of our marriage. For instance, to give me fair warning of any impending PMS, Maria agreed to write on our refrigerator calendar those days when I should be most cautious. The result has been a longer fuse on my part—because I now understand what's driving her behavior—and remarkably fewer arguments.

"What you're striving for," says Shea, "is a conscious marriage in which you think before you react."

But enough about that. What you're really interested in, no doubt, is what caused the sudden spike in our sex life. I wish there were a more revolutionary explanation other than that for the first time in a long time, we stopped talking about our workdays, the news, and the kids, and started discussing each other. I guess we were excited by meeting a new person, just like when we were dating, only this new person was the one we had been sleeping with for 15 years. This connection, this newfound intimacy, naturally enhanced our love life.

"It's a simple process that can have profound effects," concludes Shea. "It's a way to take your relationship from the functional to the exceptional, from the ordinary to the extraordinary."

I agree so much, I just might buy another round.

So what did I learn from these experiments?

The most important sex organ is the brain. Despite how magical sex may seem, it is a well-defined physiological process. Blood flows into the genitals and stimulates the nerve endings there—nothing more. In order for this to happen, the brain must initially release certain hormones and redirect the circulatory system. It all starts up there. When a man is young and close to his sexual peak, this connection is imperceptible. But with age, he becomes increasingly aware that for his body to fully cooperate, his mind must first be engaged. That's why sex is absent from boring, predictable relationships. And that's why fantasies, whether real or imagined, are so effective and exciting. Age is just a physical condition. Inside, I still feel like a 12-year-old boy. And now I realize that in my mind, I am forever 18. I just have to give myself permission to regress.

The next most important sex organ is the tongue. But not used in the way you might assume. Communication is the ultimate aphrodisiac. A relationship does not begin with physical contact but with conversation. Words, however hesitant, are what eventually seduce us. Before two bodies can truly connect, their minds have to. And this is done in the simplest of ways—by talking and sharing. Is it so surprising then that when I was at my sexual peak, I was also my most outgoing—my most willing to hold a lover's hand and earnestly confess the secrets of my soul? Great sex requires nakedness not only of body but also of heart. The two involved must be able to see *everything*.

And so I realize now that anyone can be that lion, regardless of age. Even though my supposed sexual peak may have passed, I can still reclaim it to a degree. But ironically, that is no longer the most alluring challenge. Having felt an occasional deep connection of heart and mind with my wife during these experiences, I now realize that there's another peak out there, one that we've just begun to approach. It's the culmination of our life together, the zenith of our love. Although we'll probably never reach it, I suspect that won't be a regret.

Each step higher is enough of a reward.

CHAPTER 9

having dad die without saying goodbye

What questions do you have at this point?" asks the psychic.

I don't immediately reply. What do you say to a dead man, especially when that dead man is your father to whom you never properly said goodbye?

"You can see him?" I ask after a while.

"Yes. He's sitting right behind you," she says. "You walked in here with him. You must have been talking to him, because he's ready. What would you like to know?"

I'd like to know what killed him. Why he simply, suddenly, didn't wake up one morning when he was only 61. Was it entirely natural, or did he encourage it somehow? I'd like to know what he thought at the end, if he was aware of what was happening, if death came as an adversary or as a friend.

I'd like to know how he managed to die so heavily in debt, why he thought he could become rich on credit. What was it like living with that secret, seeing everything eaten away by the cancer of compound interest? I'd like to know if that's what caused his alcoholism. Or was it being forced into early retirement from a job he'd worked at for nearly four decades? I'd like to know if he was bitter.

I'd like to know why he went to church every day and prayed the rosary. Was it out of fear or real faith? I'd like to know whether he still loved my mother after 30 difficult years, and whether he ever regretted marrying her. I'd like to know if he was disappointed in me, if I could have somehow helped. I'd like to know where he is now, *if* he is now, and whether what we do in life makes any measurable difference.

But I can't vocalize any of this. I just sit there on the couch, uncomfortably silent. Evidently, my relationship with my spirit father is the same as it was with the real one. I still don't know what to say to him, how to begin difficult conversations, how to express emotion. So I hesitate. I stumble. And, not surprisingly, so does he.

I'm here because I regret not saying goodbye to my dad, missing the clichéd deathbed scene where I could finally have connected with him and thanked him. I'm here because I regret never having a meaningful relationship with him, never talking as friends, never sharing our thoughts and perceptions. In the years since he died, I've romanticized what a father-son relationship should be. I've researched it, written books about it, even given TV and radio interviews on it. I've become smug in my belief that if I had another shot, my father and I would be the best of friends. So I sought out an opportunity to do so. I contacted a medium, a woman near Philadelphia with an impressive reputation as a conduit to the dead.

Except when she opened the door to her small apartment on a July evening thick with the threat of thunderstorms, it all looked so disappointingly ordinary. Instead of stepping into the next world, I simply crossed the threshold into the home of a fiftysomething schoolteacher with bare feet and a billowy skirt. The local news was on TV, her mail was scattered across a table, a few nondescript paintings hung on the walls, stacks of books teetered in the corners.

There were no signs of witchcraft—no burning candles, incense, or crystal balls. In fact, to begin, she merely opened the blinds to a large window. And then she sat on the sofa and for the next 60 minutes stared into the light that was filtering in—eyes glassy and faraway and occasionally glistening with tears. Never was it a dark experience.

"Your father was/is an interesting guy," she says, apparently studying his spirit as she would a photograph. "Here's a man who lived his life in a very orderly fashion and who tried to learn everything about every new situation. He wants you to know that he's just getting used to the place he's in. He says, 'I was thorough in life, and I'm thorough in spirit.' And he looks at you and says, 'Hi.'"

A chill passes through me because that's exactly how my father was. His handwriting was so exact, it looked painful. No long drive was undertaken without a TripTik. But I caution myself to remain quiet and objective. I've told this woman nothing about myself, not even how to spell my last name for fear she might do a quick Internet search. She knows only that I wish to contact my father. She is ignorant of me and of the circumstances of his death.

"He says that he can swallow now and that his chest feels a lot better," she continues. "And he's showing me how he can move his legs and his knees and his feet, and how pleased he is to be able to do that. I don't believe he was particularly old when he died, and I think he was surprised by his death. He was a strong force in life, and he remains strong as a spirit."

I have never been to a psychic, although I've read quite a bit about paranormal experiences. I think charlatans abound in the field, but I also believe there are a select few who've found actual lines of communication. I've felt these channels myself at times—inexplicable intuitions of things about to happen or shivers of recognition at an unseen presence. But at the same time, the logical, educated part of me insists that it can't be, that such phenomena are nothing more than imagination and coincidence.

Unfortunately, when you're trying to contact someone who's dead, there are few alternatives. I stopped visiting my father's grave because it's obvious he isn't there. And no matter how fervently I've prayed to him, there's never been an answer. So despite my skepticism, a clairvoyant was my only remaining option. But as I sit on the couch and listen to her, I'm having a hard time identifying any theatrics. There is something she sees, and she's just too close to the facts.

"He was so tired in the end," she says in a tender monotone, "tired from his illness and tired from becoming more and more dependent. He was too proud to accept that. So I think he died partly from natural causes and partly from despair of the situation he was in. But don't get me wrong. Your dad wasn't sad when he died. He says he made peace a long time ago with everything. He was more bewildered than sad. He just didn't expect it. And he apologizes for the legal mess he left. But he says not to worry. He's in a good place now and, once again, he's showing me how well he can walk and keep his balance. Any idea why he keeps doing that?"

The coroner surmised a heart attack, but since he hadn't been hospitalized and my mother wouldn't allow an autopsy, the cause of death was never pinpointed. He had been weakened by the flu a week before, so it could have been pneumonia, heart failure, or as his actions seemed to suggest, a stroke. It was a possibility I'd never considered up until now.

"And there's someone named Paul," the psychic continues.

Another chill sweeps through me. Paul is my only son, the first grandchild. My father died 4 months after Paul's 7th birthday and 2 weeks before he was to take him to Disney World. Paul was a miniature replica of me, and my father loved the reincarnation. On Sundays, he'd take him to the Democratic Club to play shuffleboard and drink birch beer. Paul would come home with the sticky sweet scent of a barroom and a pocketful of crumpled dollars from the old drunks there. On Saturdays during the fall, my father would take Paul to college football games, buy him anything he wanted, and sit as high in the stands as possible.

Paul is 15 now, on the fuzzy edge of remembering these things.

"Your father is reaching out to Paul and telling me Paul's going to take part in some type of activity this summer, or he likes sports, or there's something very competitive about him. Your dad is very proud that he helped instill this competitiveness. It sounds like he hangs out with Paul a lot."

I am dumbfounded. Paul is going to lacrosse camp in a few weeks. And there's nothing, not even girls, that excites him more. How could this woman know? Is she actually speaking with my father, or is my hopeful subconscious interpreting her generalities as specifics? I can't tell. In a situation like this, your hearing becomes selective.

I cross my legs and continue listening. The psychic tells me there's someone named Ellen or Helen that my father is waving at. There's somebody named Harry who's been dead for a long time and to whom my father often speaks. She says that my father wants my mother to get a new roof on her house and visit the eye doctor. He wants to thank his doctors, because they all did a helluva job— even his teeth feel better now. She says she thinks he was in the Navy, a salesman, a leader in his community, and perhaps a Sunday school teacher. He says hi to his sister-in-law. And she says he wants to know if I have any toothpicks in the house. There's something about toothpicks. . . .

I let her ramble, skipping from name to name and subject to subject as if searching for buttons of familiarity to further depress. I try to remain stoic, unaffected, giving her as few clues as possible. None of this latest stuff makes any sense. I don't know any people with the names she mentioned. My mother already got a new roof and glasses. And one of the most frustrating things about my father was that he never trusted doctors or took medication, which is probably the reason he's dead. He was an ex-Marine who thought he could tough out anything. He was also a supervisor at AT&T, not a salesman; a one-time volunteer fireman but hardly a community leader; a committed churchgoer but never a peewee preacher. As far as I know, he barely tolerated his sister-in-law, whom he considered a troublemaker. And the only thing I ever heard him say about toothpicks was that I should never run with one in my mouth.

It's as if this psychic were tuned in to a short-wave radio transmission from a faraway place. The broadcaster is almost breathless, rushing to deliver a lot of information in a short time, and she's only able to grasp words and phrases. Sometimes the reception fades out. Sometimes her translation is accurate, but other times it's not. She interlaces just enough truths, however, to keep me believing her and tolerating her errors.

"Underneath the orderliness, underneath the tidiness, your father really did have emotion. He just didn't have time in life to include it in the equation. . . ."

"He notices you've lost weight. . . ."

"Your dad wanted to be as pure as one could be without being tainted by immoral or amoral positions. . . ."

"He sure did like to eat. . . ."

"If he had it to do over again, he says he would just go fishing. . . ."

"You have a bicycle that you ride for exercise and recreation? He says be careful about the front gear, double check it. He says sometimes it exhausts him to watch you ride so much. . . ."

"Your mother suffers from high blood pressure. . . ."

"He visited California, and he has fond memories of it. . . ."

"He wants to tell your wife (is it Mary? Marie?) how much he loved her, that she was the daughter he had always wanted. . . ."

"You used to work for a newspaper. . . ."

"Your father was emperor of his own little island, but in reality, he was emperor of empty space. . . ."

"I think you loved your father. It wasn't easy to do, but in many ways you understood him better than he understood himself. That's what he's saying now. That's quite an accolade. . . ."

I interrupt. "Ask him about the book," I whisper, surprised at how my voice is hardly there. "Ask him what he thought of it."

A few years ago I published a book called *Wisdom of Our Fa-*

thers, which was essentially about him. Plagued by his sudden death, I asked nearly 150 other older fathers all the questions I wish I had asked my old man—big questions of life, such as how do you find God, and what's the secret to happiness? I interspersed their advice with deeply personal stories about my father—true stories that made my mother cry and, she says, embarrassed him and the entire family.

"Ask him," I repeat.

"Well, he smiles when you mention it," the psychic replies slowly, as if straining to interpret. "He's smiling, but he's not jumping up and down with any great joy either. There was a book written that told a story about his life? I don't know that he was thrilled. He's proud on one hand, but I don't think he believed that family stories and journals should be out like that. But he says it's okay. He's funny, actually. He says, 'It's all about me!' But I guess his final comment is that it was honest."

I feel vindication and relief. That's exactly what I always thought my father would say. But did it actually come from him, or am I somehow hearing what I want to, yet again?

Overall, the hour goes by quickly. The psychic contends that there is no rush, that she'll stay in touch as long as I'd like, but eventually, I feel the need to leave. I'm confused and frightened and reassured and angry and empty, all at once. I don't know what happened here, and I suspect that I never will. I need to go away and try to make some sense of it.

I hand her the agreed-upon $75 fee and tell her to double check the amount, but she scoffs. If nothing else, we must have trust. In exchange, she gives me her card (a name in blue letters floating in the sky), plus a cassette tape of what went on here.

"Listen to it," she says, pressing it into my hand. "It gives many people a further understanding."

When we parted, I realize later, neither of us said goodbye.

And a few nights later, I gather my wife and children together. We sit on the floor in my son's room, pop the tape into his stereo

system, and listen. They are wide-eyed, too, at some of the revela-
tions. They feel the chills. And in the end, we all agree that
somehow this woman was right more often than she was wrong.
And my daughter, Claire, makes an interesting observation.

"Did you hear it?" she asks.

"Hear what?" I say.

"The heartbeat. It's the first thing I noticed. It's always there."

And sure enough, wherever I jump to on the tape, I hear it—a
barely discernible thump, thump, thump. . . . Not mine, I'm sure,
and no electronic trickery, I believe.

Perhaps my father does live on, if only in me.

CHAPTER 10

never learning how to surf

Maybe it's because the women spectators wear bikinis. Maybe it's because, like Jesus, you're walking on water. Maybe it's because you finally have an excuse to always be at the beach, a half-naked escapee from responsibility. Or maybe it's because you're doing something that lies at the edge of plausibility, not only for science but also for the majority of men.

Whatever the reason, I've always considered surfing to be the coolest sport ever invented. Nothing in even the X Games can match it. To call sitting in front of a computer and exploring the Internet "surfing" is like calling podiatry "professional football." To me, surfing is the ultimate.

When I was a landlocked kid in Pennsylvania, my favorite TV show was *ABC's Wide World of Sports* and my favorite segment was surfing from Hawaii's famous Banzai Pipeline. The camera would peek into the massive green tube created by the breaking wave and inside would be a bronzed madman crouched low and grinning. That's who I yearned to be.

I wanted to travel the world like those guys in *The Endless Summer*. I wanted to date a girl as hot and bouncy as Annette Funicello in *Beach Blanket Bingo*. But the closest I got was 1 week at the Jersey shore each summer with a bottle of Sun-In and my mother yelling at me from the beach not to go out too far.

Decades later, I am still enamored. Whenever I'm at the beach, I watch the surfers or, if none are out, the waves. Both are ageless, powerful, and hypnotic. For the skinny, unsure weakling that still lives inside me, they continue to represent a way to instantly be cool, admired, and free.

So before I get too old, before I hand off these dreams to my grandkids, I decide to give it a try. I'm inspired by an ad for Lou Maresca's Surf School in Vero Beach, Florida. The fee of $150 for 3 days of personal instruction sounds reasonable. But what really cinches it is when Maresca tells me over the phone that 90 percent of first-timers stand up during their initial class.

"Unless you weigh more than 250 pounds or are extremely out of shape, you're never too old to learn," he says. "If the Beach Boys can still tour, then you, my man, can still surf."

Faced with the cold-water reality of being a balding, middle-age guy in flowered surf trunks, I decide to reserve at least some dignity by learning the lingo before I go. I figure if I can talk the talk, it'll be less immediately noticeable that I can't walk the walk. So I buy a stack of surfing magazines and books at the local Barnes and Noble and immerse myself in the culture.

The first thing I learn is that I'm a Barney, a beginner. The Hawaiians, though, have a less cuddly word for it. They call rookies like me kooks, a derivative of their native *kukae*, meaning "crap."

Like all Barneys, I'll be spending a lot of time in the weak surf or slop. Even then, I'll probably get cleaned up or smashed by waves regularly. A common mistake is putting too much weight on the front of the board, which causes its nose to pearl or dip under the surface. When you're tumbling in the whitewater or soup, that's when you're most vulnerable. Ding or hit your head, and you'll sink unconscious to the bottom. Since the surfboard is attached to your ankle via a leash, it'll stick straight up or tombstone out of the water above you.

The more I read, the more I realize I'm not going to be riding or ripping any big waves with just a few days of instruction. Hanging ten toes over the end of the board, let alone even one, is probably out of the question. And as far as visiting that big green room, the hollow tube formed as a large wave crests and curls over itself, I'll just have to be content with those *Wide World of Sports* memories for now.

But I'm going to do this. Whoa, dude.

Two weeks later, I'm feeling lithe and lean in my skin-tight O'Neill wet suit, posing for any thonged blondes who might be bunning on the beach at Fort Pierce State Recreation Area on Florida's Atlantic coast. Maresca shatters the moment, however, by pointing out that I have the suit on backward.

Oh.

After I straighten myself out, he motions me away from the water and explains that before I try riding any waves, I need to practice one key move. "It's called a pop-up," he says, "and this is what you do."

Maresca lies face down on his beached surfboard and assumes the same position you'd use to begin a pushup. Then, without moving his hands, he deftly jumps one foot forward so it's midway along the board and pivots his rear foot. Next, he rises into a low crouch, with knees bent, butt low, leading hand about 6 inches above the board, eyes focused on its nose.

"That's how you stand up," he explains. "Your belly button represents your center of gravity. The trick is keeping it low."

Maresca does it a few more times, then tells me to try. But whereas his pop-ups were quick and fluid, mine are slow and hesitant. I keep practicing until I approach a fair imitation. But

Maresca still isn't ready to let me near the water. Next he delivers a 20-minute talk about its dangers. In fact, by the time he finishes warning me about lightning ("the guy was rinsing off right over there when it hit him"), man-of-war jellyfish ("their tentacles dig into your skin and make it feel like there's a blowtorch on you"), rip currents ("I almost drowned in Costa Rica"), big surfboards ("you don't want to get hit on the head with one of these"), and sharks ("that fin chased me right out of the water"), I'm not sure I want to surf (or even wade) anymore.

But just as you need good physical balance for this sport, you also need a measure of levelheadedness. Cockiness is a fool's trait when you're dealing with something as powerful and guiltless as the ocean. Respect and even fear are healthful. If your knees quiver as you stride down the beach and your skin goose-pimples when you toe the 80-degree water, then you're ready. If not, then you probably need to think some more about what you're about to do.

"But those sharks, Lou. . . . Are there really some around here?"

"Taste the water," says Maresca. "If it's salty, then there are sharks in it. Here on the East Coast, surfers are mostly bitten on the hand. That's because it's lighter in color than the rest of the body, and it's going in and out of the water like a bait fish. Watch out for schools of bait fish. You don't want to get caught in the middle of one. And when you're walking out, always shuffle your feet. This will keep you from stepping on a crab or a shark that's lying there, lethargic from the cold water."

Other surfers can be like sharks, too. Hungry for action, territorial and vicious if repeatedly crossed, they regard newcomers as mullet. There's a complex etiquette to surfing that's not readily apparent. Although it may seem as if there's an abundance of waves, in actuality, there are few worth riding and an even smaller area where you can catch the best. That's where the veterans, the real hammerheads, have their board meetings, and you should stay out of their way. The worst thing you can do is drop in ahead of someone who is surfing or paddling at the peak of a wave. It's not only bad manners, but also it's dangerous. Maresca advises that I tune my technique in the small stuff first. Then—if I feel ready to join the big boys—to hang back, be patient, and paddle hard when an opening does arise.

"When you eventually catch a good one," he says, "you'll earn their respect."

With his prefatory lecture complete, Maresca finally allows me to pick up my board and head for the ocean. We wade out a considerable distance, but the water remains only waist deep and the waves disappointingly gentle. I'm wondering how I'm ever going to surf in this when he orders me to lie belly down on my board. While standing behind me, he scans the horizon like a veteran sea captain until he spots a 2-foot swell heading toward us. Just before it arrives, he grabs the back of my board and launches me along with the wave, counting, "Three, two, one. Up!"

Suddenly, I feel as if I'm in the barrel of a 20-footer on Oahu's North Shore.

The rising power of even this tiny swell carries me along amazingly quickly. I try to recall all the things we rehearsed on shore—the importance of those last few powerful strokes to get atop the wave, the single fluid pop-up, the exact spots where you have to plant your feet, the crouch you're supposed to maintain—but I forget them all in one adrenaline-pumping instant. As I try to stand, I panic, submarine the nose of the board, and gulp a mouthful of water. I do remember, however, to cover my head as I tumble about, since my giant 9-foot board (ironically emblazoned with the word Impact) is tethered to my ankle by a 12-foot leash. When I surface, I can't speak or see. I gag, cough, and check if my wet suit is now on inside out.

Meanwhile, my adolescent son, who insisted on coming along, skims by on my left, having no trouble standing up on his first-ever ride. The 47-year-old Maresca whoops and punches the air as if it's his grandson surfing that wave and motions for me to quickly paddle back out.

"C'mon! Here comes another one!" he yells, looking out at

what seems to me a glassy sea. But sure enough, an almost imperceptible swell slowly builds into a breaking wave. As it approaches, he grabs the back of my board again, swings me around so I'm pointing toward shore, and pushes me off with another countdown. This time, I'm up for a split second, and I catch the feeling—a magical, intoxicating flash of balance—before somersaulting into the ocean.

It's the mystical sweet spot of sport—the line drive up the middle off the meat of the bat, the tingle in your fingers after a perfect baseline jumper—only more intense. This is the coca, the nicotine, that addicts surfers. It skews reality, promotes daydreaming, and slurs speech. And I've just had my first hit.

Maresca says that sometimes after he's been cleaned up by a big wave, he'll just linger underwater and laugh. It helps him regain his composure and saves energy that would otherwise be wasted trying to surface in turbulent surf. I try that now, resting just briefly beneath the wavering skylight of water. It's calm and cool and pleasant down here, and it makes me want to smile, too.

When I surface, Maresca is there grinning, waving me back out. "C'mon," he screams, "here comes another good one!"

Although Maresca is a patient and thorough teacher, his promise of getting me up on a surfboard on the first day is not unusual. Most surf camps (and there are dozens of them) make the same claim. What makes this possible are giant surfboards, most of which are 9 to 10 feet long. Called long boards, these cruiseliners of the surf world are more stable and easier to paddle, and allow novices to ride smaller, safer waves. The lighter you are, the more you're just along for the ride. My 85-pound son is but a bug on his.

The alternative to a long board is—you guessed it—a short board. These are generally 6 feet long and have the opposite characteristics of their bigger brothers. They're very responsive, more difficult to paddle, and perform best on large waves. These are the boards you'll see sticking out of sunroofs near Encinitas or being ridden by professionals in competition. Thus, it's the board that many novices mistakenly rent or buy and try to learn on.

"Too many beginners buy short boards because they look cool, fit under their arms, and are ridden by the pros," says Maresca. "But they're useless when you're starting out. An adult male needs a big board."

To prove his point, Maresca lets me try his short board later that day. I can't even begin to stand on it, and my many futile attempts send sand into places I never guessed could feel gritty. My son, however, finds it much more manageable than the long board, which underlines the importance of proper sizing. Just as with a bicycle or a pair of running shoes, the better the equipment fits, the more fun you'll have and the faster you'll progress.

The other intriguing thing about surfboards is the apparent contradiction of staying planted on a smooth, speeding surface, slickened further by rushing water. (I mean, some mornings I have trouble enough in the shower.) What makes this feat possible is the thin coating of wax that surfers rub on the top rear half of their boards for traction. This is the tread, the tire chains, the stuff that makes you stick. It's an almost religious process. Every surfer pauses to wax his board on the beach before heading out. "Mr. Zog's Original Sex Wax" is one of the more popular brands. But if you buy some, make sure you use it for its intended purpose. Leaving it on the nightstand is tacky.

I wake up at 4:32 A.M. barely able to move my arms. Reaching up for the bathroom light switch makes me wince. Unaccustomed to the windmill, paddling motion that's used to smash through the surf and reach the wave break, my shoulder muscles feel like they've rusted. Even my never-tired, rubber-muscled boy is groaning in his sleep.

Most people don't realize what a great workout surfing supplies, says Maresca, a scrappy 5-foot-10, 170-pound game fish of a man. Look at pictures of lifelong surfers and you'll see near-perfect physiques—broad shoulders, well-defined pectoral muscles, powerful arms, and abdominals that resemble dune-buggy tread. This is surprising, since the sport looks so effortless from shore. But as Maresca explains, the ride is just 10 percent of the game. The rest is a brawl for position against a giant, tireless adversary. Even if you're wily enough to find the seam and flirt with its fury, it can still blindside you at any moment with a force equal to that of a crumbling building.

Despite my soreness, so far I've been surprised at how straightforward surfing is. In fact, of all the sports I've tried, including downhill skiing, sailing, and auto racing, it is by far the easiest to learn. But when I say "easy," I'm referring to that 10 percent—the glamour pose that is really not much more difficult to strike on a moving long board than it is in an anchored basement. To paddle into position to catch a wave, to read it and gauge its demeanor—that's the unseen 90 percent that both startles and exhausts the beginner.

I've also been surprised that you don't have to be a great swimmer to take surfing lessons. In fact, at Maresca's school, most of the time I'm in water shallow enough to stand in. What's more important, at least to start, is upper body strength, since you're continually paddling and pushing yourself up on the board—not to mention carrying the thing. Plus, you need a reservoir of endurance, because the combination of effort and excitement keeps your heart rate at a chest-quaking level. Although you don't have to be superfit to learn how to surf, the better shape you're in, the more you'll enjoy the lessons, the more in control you'll feel, and the longer you'll be able to stay out.

Maresca estimates that he has taught more than 500 people to surf since beginning his part-time business in 1993. But if you want to go beyond those initial lessons and really get good at it, you need a serious level of commitment. He has noticed the salty smile on my face, the glint in my eye, and he knows what I'm dreaming: Trade the Caravan for a Woody, switch coasts, rent a beach house, and practice, practice, practice—eventually sticking a toe in the water of master's competition. As a splash of reality, he explains that the real surf gods swim laps in a pool three or four days per week, then hone leg strength, balance, and endurance by running or cycling. Plus, there are the daily pushups and crunches, hundreds of them.

This is all preparation for the good one, as Maresca refers to it—the perfect wave that can become a never-ending life quest. In his bathroom at home is a National Oceanic Atmospheric Administration weather radio that he flips on every morning for the latest marine forecast of wave height and swell interval. He watches the Weather Channel as others do soap operas and wears a tide watch instead of a Timex. He has a web of contacts across the hemisphere (including a son in Hawaii) who are quick to call with surf reports and flight schedules when conditions start to build. There are even wave fax services and Internet sites with live video feeds to keep him abreast. When a hurricane threatens, he scrambles for a board—not to shutter his home, but to surf on.

"Yeah, a hurricane does it for me," he says, starting to lose his concentration at the mere thought. "When I hear '10 feet, 15 seconds,' I'm heading to Monster Hole. It's my favorite spot around here, a little jewel. Places like that are like pornography to a surfer."

But a good one for Lou and a good one for me are very different entities, I realize as my lessons continue. When colleagues heard I was heading for surf camp in Florida, their initial reaction was that I was 3,000 miles off target to the east. "Ain't no big waves there," said one guy from Gainesville. But that's the common misconception. The last thing a fledgling surfer needs is big waves. That would be like sending a Little Leaguer to bat against Roger Clemens. As I've experienced firsthand, the best waves for learning are 2- to 3-footers. In fact, it's amazing how much pure liquid power even these relatively small breaks have and how much snot they've knocked out of me.

"You know how heavy a bucket of water is," says Maresca. "Well, imagine having an entire swimming pool unloaded on you.

Beginners don't need that kind of threat. Usually when you're learning, the surf will never be too small."

As my instruction winds down, Maresca gradually draws back. Whereas initially he had two hands on the back of my board, now there's just one or sometimes none. As we wait in the surf, he gives me pointers for reading the weather conditions and the water. This incoming tide is best, he says, because I'll benefit from the combined energy of the breaking wave and the tidal surge. And that offshore wind I feel on my face is another good sign. As it blows gently out to sea, it'll hold up the cresting waves as if they're liquid sails, giving each one a clean, rideable face.

This time, instead of depending on Maresca to holler "Three, two, one. Up!" I'm belly down on my board, craning to see what might develop. It's like merging onto the expressway at rush hour. I'm looking over my shoulder, watching the approaching traffic, searching for an opening, then quickly accelerating. Once in the flow, I feel the wave begin to lift me onto its back, and I paddle harder in a mad dash for the apex. "It's just like sledding," Maresca had told me. "When you're out in the snow, you want to put your sled at the top of the steepest part of the hill to get the best ride. It's no different with a surfboard."

I remember that, and it helps. Soon I feel the nose of my board begin to tilt down and its tail lift, which means I've reached the summit. Instantly, I pop up and angle the board toward the smooth, open face of the wave. If this were a sizable wall of water, its lip would now begin to curl over, enclosing me in the famous barrel or green room that surfers dream of visiting. Spend even 3 exquisite seconds in there, and you'll be forever preoccupied.

But there is no barrel to this wave, nothing special to separate it from all the others. Except that I ride this one out, crouching atop its back until I feel its strength ebb and collapse. As I gently hop off, Maresca is there waiting for me, looking thoughtful, arms crossed.

"Surfing is so cosmic in a way," he concludes. "You come to

the beach at a tiny moment in your life. The wave has traveled thousands of miles, and you blend with it and ride it. When you hit a good one, it feels like magic."

That was the last wave I rode, the last time I surfed. Even though I left Vero Beach with all kinds of plans, the sport has proven too impractical for a guy marooned on a partially wooded acre in Pennsylvania. The ocean is a 2½-hour drive away, which isn't exactly conducive to spontaneity. And what am I supposed to throw out of my garage if I'm to squeeze a surfboard in—the lawn tractor? the extension ladder? God forbid, the garbage cans? Although I'm ashamed to admit it, such trades are no longer realistic.

But when I do get to the beach nowadays, usually for one fleeting weekend in July, I no longer sit in the sand with regrets. I can look out to sea and say I've done that. And even though I didn't do it particularly well and may never do it again, that is reward enough.

Now where is Annette Funicello?

CHAPTER 11

working my life away

Fifty days off.

These three words always seemed like a dream to me, just a bit less improbable than dating a supermodel or hitting the lottery. Even though I received 20 days of paid leave each year, my job as the executive editor of a national magazine made it difficult to spend even a week away. I'd sneak a day here, a half-day there, but I never felt like I entirely escaped. Work was always simmering in the back of my mind, and I guess it eventually cooked me. Like so many other driven men and women, "well done" was no longer just a compliment to swell my head. It was the way I felt every night before I collapsed into bed.

For almost 20 years, I'd been working. Lawn maintenance, liquor store clerk, newspaper reporter, magazine editor. During one stretch I had a full-time job and was moonlighting part-time at two others. The money was good, and while I was young and single, I even enjoyed the bustle. But once I got married and had kids (each an additional full-time obligation), I started enjoying work progressively less.

It's a sobering moment when you catch yourself snapping at your babies not because of their behavior but because of your job frustrations. It's a frightening time when you realize that the person you married is drifting away, and you don't have the energy to reach out. And it's a dark day when you sit in a corner office with a sunny view and begin to question the meaning of the word successful.

I've been there.

And I decided to get out.

Quitting isn't a difficult thing to do. It's always easier to run away than it is to pursue. The problem is society's perception and acceptance of the two. One is viewed as shameful and the other, supposedly fun. But I had been chasing for nearly 2 decades, and I was tired and not even sure what was ahead of me anymore. I'd become uncertain about the worthiness of the reward. The adrenaline that once produced a satisfying buzz was just making me stressed and desperate.

There was no moment of insight, nothing anyone said that made me realize all this. It was just a knowing, a gnawing, a bone-deep calling that it was time to move on. I suspect that many people harbor it, but they resist, year by year growing more miserable. Job dissatisfaction is the most widespread cancer in America, eating away at the senior workforce. Ironically, there's a treatment that's 100 percent effective. It's just that nobody thinks they can afford it.

There was no major outpouring of emotion when I resigned, just handshakes, back pats, and quiet good wishes. There was no gala send-off or thank you, just greasy bags of fast food bought with petty cash and shared among the staff at a park pavilion. It was obvious that everyone was more jealous than happy. I was moving on and they were staying put. How could I expect them to be demonstrative? My leaving made them face their entrapment.

I cleaned out my desk and drove away on my final day, feeling like a schoolkid on the brink of summer vacation. Tomorrow there was no place I had to be, no schedule by which I had to abide. For the first time since I could remember, I was living my own life, and it felt instantly exciting.

Fortunately, the journalism business is such that, if you're competent enough, you can easily find work elsewhere, often in the same publishing company. I had assurances of another job when I decided to return. So my departure was eased by the knowledge that this was more of a sabbatical than a severance, that I was heading into an extended vacation rather than a serious financial challenge.

So I stepped into the dream and took a crack at one more regret, escaping work for what would become 7 weeks. Like other retirees, I could proudly say that my sidewalk was perfectly edged, my garage floor swept dinner-plate clean, and my lawn clipped to a precise crew-cut length. All the working guys in my neighborhood hated me.

But beyond landscaping, there was some serious mental yardwork that also got done. My near-retirement experience enlightened me in several ways that don't typically happen during 1- or even 2-week getaways. Here's what was born when the labor ended:

I started dreaming again. I never used to remember sleeping. I'd pass out after a hard day then awaken 6 to 8 hours later feeling crusty and kind of dazed. Occasionally, I'd dream about our latest nubile intern or (once) being swept away by an in-box tidal wave, but most of my downtime was black, blank.

Then, after a few days away, I started having these incredible dreams. It was as if Spielberg, Hitchcock, and Coppola were directing my subconscious. What's amazing is that all the activity was somehow very restful. I awoke feeling fresh and alive—sort of the same "Whoa, *now* I'm ready to go" exhilaration you get after riding a roller coaster.

Robert Van de Castle, Ph.D., author of *Our Dreaming Mind,*

says that no one ever really stops dreaming—the average is 100 minutes per night. "It's just that in your hurly-burly world you weren't giving yourself the opportunity to lie in bed and recall your dreams. They were off with the sheets because your mind was preoccupied."

Dr. Van de Castle adds that the longer you doze, the longer your dream-rich rapid eye movement periods last. With no morning deadline, I was sleeping later, dreaming more, and waking up better rested.

I lost track of time. I used to marvel when my children would ask what day it was or puzzle over the necessity for a watch. But during my hiatus, Monday morning lost its dread and Friday afternoon all its unproductive wishfulness. I had no reason to clock-watch or even look at a calendar. And guess what? Time finally slowed down. It was like being a kid in mid-July again. After years of feeling as if my life was speeding by, the brake lights came on and living became luxuriously unmeasured again.

I walked the mile to the grocery store. I stopped in to get my hair cut without an appointment. I nearly bought a hammock. And I learned to enjoy driving 55, especially during rush hour.

My memory returned. Harvard psychologists have demonstrated that the mere expectation of memory loss with age seems to encourage that fate. While there's much to be said for the power of positive thinking, I'm also convinced that men and women become increasingly forgetful because of "information saturation."

Say there's an important remembrance—your wedding day, to choose a crucial example—that you want to retain. But as more passengers board the ol' brain bus, it gets pushed further and further back, until the driver—that's you—can only make out vague bits and tuxedo colors.

Nowadays, we're bombarded with more daily intelligence than J. Edgar Hoover ever was—through newspapers, magazines, television, e-mail, and that annoying Larry King. But when the shelling subsides, even for a short time, you'll be surprised at what's still standing.

"Why, how silly of you, dear. They were gray *Pierre Cardin* tuxedos, of course."

I became thoughtful. When I was working, I never read anything; I scanned. I didn't listen; I heard. And I didn't see; I glanced.

The result was a harried, superficial existence—the information saturation thing again, dumbing me down. What I realized during my time off is that you have to chew your food if you want to digest it properly. I also discovered that it's better and more healthful for the mind to know a few things well than a great many things slightly.

I got taller. No kidding. Two different people said I actually looked like I'd grown. The worries and responsibilities of my old job must have been hunchbacking me. Quick, measure yourself.

My hair got fuller and the gray disappeared. Sorry, my mistake. That was a dream.

I stopped yelling at my kids. It's not that they were any less devilish, it's just that I hadn't been previously pushed to the brink of tolerance by the 9-to-5 office equivalent of spilled SpaghettiOs, unflushed "boom-booms," and Legos chattering through the heating ducts. I learned that I have more patience with children when I'm not dealing with their grown-up counterparts for most of the day. What a relief: I'm not an ogre after all.

All my energy went into my life. Imagine that your life is your job, your career, and that you're working exclusively toward its success. Fifty, 60 hours per week are spent solidifying the assets, balancing the books, and otherwise perfecting the product. What a life and business that would be!

When you no longer have to devote so much time and energy to someone else's bottom line, it's amazing what you can accomplish. I painted the outside of my entire house. I bicycled at least 20 miles every day. I analyzed and restructured my investments. I cleaned out my T-shirt drawer. And yes, I went to Disney World.

I noticed my wife. You hang a new painting on the wall—a true work of art, it is—and for the first few months, you admire it daily.

But as the years pass, it becomes just another part of the room—no less beautiful, just less appreciated. My wife of many years has soft sienna eyes framed by matching brown hair, and there's a dimple on her left cheek. When she's daydreaming, she'll touch the tip of her tongue to her upper lip. And she looks best in red—no, make that crimson.

I started having incredible sex. The two biggest obstacles in the sex lives of most working people are time constraints and fatigue. Since I suddenly had all the time in the world and was never really tired, my libido returned from Toledo.

I gained perspective. Funny how the closer you get to something, the less of it you see. In my previous life, I was the editor of *Bicycling* magazine. For 8 years the job and the sport consumed me. Then I quit and realized that cycling is just a game. For that matter, accounting is only playing with numbers, banking is a lot like Monopoly, and even complex urban planning is just a real-life version of SimCity.

After all the career noise had subsided, I realized that very few jobs carry any life-or-death consequences except your own. And, hey, I'll never be remembered eternally. I'll never do the twist with Uma Thurman. And isn't work really just something you do for hours a day so you can afford more toys?

I realized the value of doing nothing. To hell with all those articles and experts that tell you how to make your free time more productive. I say it's productive to sometimes be unproductive. Channel-surf until your eyes swim. Lie in the grass and stare at the sky until large, squawking vultures circle overhead. Linger in bed until your spouse gets nervous and feels for a pulse. Drool.

Don't feel guilty about occasionally doing nothing. It's calming. It's rejuvenating. This is your mind. This is your mind in neutral. Any questions?

It's only fair to point out that not all the side effects from this time away were positive and fun. Although it was a life-altering experience to have my dry-cleaning bills dwindle to nothing, there were some troublesome wrinkles that developed.

I lost a bit of my self-worth. While it's everyone's fantasy to retire young and live large, I got a taste of what can humble, and eventually even defeat, some older people. The message light on my phone stopped blinking. My circle of friends condensed. And my old job continued without me.

You don't have to be a social psychologist to know that men and women become their careers. The careers are their identities, their pocket squares, their reasons for being. Standing at the school-bus stop without mine, however temporary, left me feeling undefined. Imagine hesitating, searching, when someone asks what you do for a living. Why is it so painful if the answer is "Nothing"?

I felt a little guilty. It was as if I had found this huge box of Godiva chocolates, but I couldn't share it with anyone. In fact, people had to watch me eat them, one by luscious one. It was a sadistic treat at first, but I eventually noticed the jealousy, and believe it or not, it bothered me.

I started looking forward to going back to work. Somewhere into the 6th week, after the kids had returned to school and I had painted even the bathroom roof vents, I got this twang, this gentle mind nudge, this almost-evolutionary urge that maybe it was time to go back.

It had something to do with boredom, I'm sure, and a bit more with ego and reproving myself professionally. But a large part stemmed from simply being satisfied that I had completed one job and was ready to move on to the next. I had siphoned off the stress, gotten reacquainted with my family, read a few good books, got into respectable shape, and made the house presentably suburban again. I had proven to myself that I could control my life and be relatively happy and content.

But most important, I had realized that *I was still here.* That fun person my wife had fallen in love with; that carefree father who used to play weekday Wiffle ball with his kids; that positive, energetic journalist who gave every story his all; that guy I used to like.

The realization that I hadn't changed significantly and that I was still alive down deep inside made a huge difference in how I felt about myself. Although I'm certain the afterglow from this time off will fade and that I'll eventually forget a lot of its lessons, I know now that everything isn't inevitable. It's just a matter of how you handle it.

Oh, and one more thing.

I ran out of cash. And that was when I knew I really better go back. 🅰️🆂

CHAPTER 12

never pulling the trigger

We're sitting on a bench in Idaho's Treasure Valley watching a cat named Tip hunt field mice. Buz Fawcett, owner and instructor for the Wingshooting Workshop: An Instinctive Shooting School, has momentarily surrendered the podium to the expert.

"Watch her," he whispers.

After spotting something in the brush, Tip has frozen in mid-stride. Her chin rises slightly to point at the prey, and her eyes focus with a laser's intensity. Then, in an instant, she attacks—one smooth, sudden strike leaves the mouse struggling between her teeth.

Like most domesticated animals, Tip no longer hunts to survive. She has all the Meow Mix she needs in her bowl in the old mobile home parked on the shooting grounds. Instead, she hunts out of instinct and primal satisfaction, explains Fawcett. Then, with a gaze similar to Tip's, he looks at me and says, "You have that in you, too. It's the predator."

I have enrolled in Fawcett's school for two reasons. One is to learn how to shoot a gun, which I have never done. And the other is because I could not resist. Something compelled me to come.

Like every boy, I played with toy guns—cap pistols, air rifles, homemade grasshopper guns. But I never fired a real one. Never pulled a genuine trigger. Never saw what was between my sights stumble and fall.

My best childhood buddy, Mark Kovaleski, had a .22 and a .30-06 in his house. His dad occasionally took him target-shooting down by the river, but I was never invited. We were too dangerous together. Mark and I both knew where he kept those guns, but we afforded them our utmost respect. We never let our curiosity or our wonder tempt us. It was the first time we exhibited any maturity.

As a result, I never hunted, never developed any fascination for weaponry or war. The few opportunities I had to touch a gun made me nervous. It was as if I were seeing beyond it, feeling the death rather than the pleasure intrinsic to it. But as I grew and eventually became a father myself—a supposed role model—I often wondered whether I should have one around the house for my family's protection, whether it would be wiser to familiarize my children with this necessary evil rather than keep it forbidden. I guess you could say I regretted my ignorance.

Then one day, I happened to dial Fawcett's number. I was writing an article about summer adventure camps for men and had pulled his advertisement from some magazine's classified ads. As a journalist, I typically talk to dozens of people every day, and this guy was just another on a long list. But the instant he answered the phone, I felt something different. Confidence, knowledge, wisdom. What was supposed to be a 5-minute conversation lasted half an hour and ended with an invitation. I was drawn to this man for no apparent reason. He had an important lesson to teach.

Somehow, I convinced my editor to let me visit Fawcett, which was pretty amazing considering that I worked for a health magazine and this was an exercise in shooting things. Normally, I am not given to spontaneity, nor do I believe in predestination. But there was something out there, something powerful, and I needed to finally face my gun fear and take aim at it. For perhaps the first time in my life, I was operating on instinct rather than logic. And it felt good.

Sixty-three-year-old Fawcett has been described as a "crazed shotgun prophet" who is "part shaman, part showman." He calls his brown shooting fields on the brink of the Great Basin near Boise his sacred place, where he hears ancient voices, he says, and gathers inspiration.

"I'm surprised I don't see crop circles or some damn thing out here," he says while scratching his reddish-white beard. "It's where everything comes to me. If I were a religious man, my hair would probably stand on end."

The flyer for Fawcett's small school advertises a "master gunner program," guaranteeing to raise an experienced shooter's accuracy to between 75 and 98 percent after just 3 days of one-on-one instruction. He goes as far as to claim that most shotgun shooters in this country are lousy shots and most instructors don't know what they're doing. While his 300 graduates can attest to his unique expertise, he's even more adept at infusing them with an intriguing theory of life that goes far beyond this sport and his 30-acre shooting compound.

"It was worth taking the class even if I never pulled a trigger," said Tracey Harmon, a 39-year-old entrepreneur in nearby Moscow, Idaho, whom I met later. "What really surprised me is that we didn't instantly start banging away," he explained. "Instead, we discussed philosophy, the evolution of men, tribal aspects of a baseball team, all before shooting one round. Buz taught me more about being successful than any business school I ever attended."

Fawcett's philosophy is based on something he heard in class decades ago. A teacher once said that the average person consciously uses only 10 percent of his brain; geniuses employ maybe

15. Like a burr in his trademark breeches, this knowledge pestered him. Why would nature, so efficient everywhere else, tolerate such a wasted resource? "I couldn't believe it," he says. "There had to be a purpose."

Drawing from observations made during 30 years as an army shooting instructor and outdoor journalist, photographer, and filmmaker, Fawcett developed a theory that he calls the Predator. Inside each of us, occupying that remaining 85 to 90 percent of our brain, is a dozing creature. It is an extremely intelligent and powerful beast that harbors untold years of human experience and instinct. Awaken it and you not only benefit from this wisdom but also gain self-confidence, improve athletic performance, ease stress, and take better control of almost every part of life.

"It's like software that's already programmed into the computer," explains Fawcett, who speaks with the velvet eloquence and deep conviction of a minister. "You just have to know how to access it."

Even if Fawcett's philosophy sounds a little outlandish, most people can usually recall at least one instance when they met their inner animal. If you've ever hit a home run, for instance, it was your predator who spotted that fastball and swung the bat so perfectly. If you've ever surprised yourself with a reaction so swift and sure that it left you wondering where it came from, then it was your predator on the pounce.

"The introduction usually occurs when you're startled, say, by the sudden flush of a prey animal or bird when you're hunting," explains Fawcett. "Your body moves, seemingly of its own will, and in a moment, the quarry is down. You're astonished. What most people don't realize is that it's possible to replicate this experience over and over in many different activities."

The key, Fawcett insists, is surrendering the conscious mind. That fastball, for example, reaches the plate in 0.4 second. Considering the time it takes to swing a bat, this leaves only 0.15 second to decide what to do. Likewise, instantly calculating the speed, trajectory, and angle needed to make a shot that can bisect a bird in midflight seems impossibly complex.

"Yet we can do it in a twinkling," he says. "That's why so much of our brain is devoted to it. The predator is the reflex action that shuts down our conscious self and takes over with the pure genius of instinct."

And oh does that feel good. When the predator stirs, it takes over our entire being, focuses all of our energy, compresses time, and then, when it's finished, leaves us with a "fierce sense of satisfaction," says Fawcett—"a roaring elation."

It is, quite simply, the essence of being alive.

It used to be that the predator and the man were almost indistinguishable. When human beings first roamed the Rift Valley or, more recently, the prairies of this fledgling country, they had to depend on their wits and intuition for daily survival. But in the last hundred years or so, the predator has been progressively contained, caged behind the bars of mindfulness and socialized behavior.

"Society is trying to turn us into benign creatures," says Fawcett. Today's man is discouraged from crying, yelling, slamming doors, coming on strong to the ladies, smashing brandy snifters, and asking adversaries to step outside. Hunting is considered barbarous in many circles, red meat is bad for your health, and sports are something we watch more often than play. Our traditional release valves are being soldered up, while life inflicts more and more pressure. "But to deny the predator is to risk a buildup of aggression, hostility, and stress," he warns.

Fawcett sees the repercussions of this in the twin epidemics of stress-related illness and escalating violence. He even goes so far as to suggest that we've gotten so out of touch with our predators that we're becoming prey—exhibiting such typical "hunted" behavior as living in a near-constant state of adrenalized alert and herding together in apartment complexes and suburban developments for safety.

As an antidote, most men have taken to feeding their predators with raw, vicarious experiences such as Bruce Willis films, pro football, and violent computer games. It's the Roman Colosseum with 21st-century lions. "But simulations are not the same as actually doing it," says Fawcett. "It doesn't give you the same release, the same purring sense of satisfaction."

Fawcett isn't suggesting upending china cabinets to attain inner peace. Despite its name, the predator is not intrinsically angry or violent. It does not thrive on malevolence or murder but rather on the pure, synchronized joy of the instinctive attack, whether the prey is a 12-point buck, a fastball on the inside corner, an opponent's queen in a game of chess, or a clay target launched across the blue Idaho sky. Like the muscles in the body, the predatory instinct needs to be exercised. Its health and well-being heavily influence our own.

If Fawcett is beginning to sound less like a crazed prophet and more like a wise old guy who might be on to something, then welcome to the club. Chris Bryant, a 39-year-old student/disciple, who runs a vineyard and importing business in Summit, Mississippi, later told me that recognizing and regularly exercising his predator has helped him become more relaxed, focused, and emotionally healthy.

"The mind is an unbridled horse," he said. "It wants to run free in a daily flow of consciousness. But Buz pointed out the need to give the conscious mind a rest and let this other part of the mind take over."

Patricia Price, a licensed mental health counselor and psychotherapist who specializes in consciousness studies, generally agrees with Fawcett's theory. "I like to call the experience a cerebral orgasm," she explained to me, "a connection with something deep inside yourself. It can be addictive, it feels so good."

To find and unleash my inner predator, Fawcett gives me a crash course in instinctive shooting. Despite how I may feel about guns, hunting is still the oldest and easiest way to make the animal in me stir. Plus, the three main lessons he guides me through have a certain carryover value in the rest of my life. This isn't just about instinctive shooting; it's about instinctive living.

Practice, then forget. "Tell me something," says Fawcett, adjusting the brim on his beaver-fur hat. "Do you dance?"

"Do I *dance?*"

"Yeah. Shooting a shotgun should be like ballroom dancing. An instinctive shooter has a beautiful appearance. The movement is almost hypnotic; the firearm seems to be part of the body. The predator makes it look easy. Here, follow me."

And so I rumba with the master, mimicking his every smooth move. Our right legs step forward and our back knees slightly bend until we've assumed the proper shooting stance. It feels awkward at first because it's the opposite of the way most right-handed people hold a gun, yet he claims it results in better balance, accuracy, and protection from recoil. Using imaginary guns, we mount, point, fire; mount, point, fire. Instead of tracing a lazy arc across the sky with our barrels, we practice shooting like the rattlesnake strikes.

"Rehearse this in your mind before you go to bed tonight," says Fawcett, a 99.9 percent shooter himself. "Your inner predator is still a baby. The way to make it grow is through repetition. Teach it the rules, the basic movements, then forget them. Move out of its way and let it do what it does best."

Point, never aim. Fawcett is careful to never use the word aim in his instructions. That's because when you aim, you think—consciously trying to direct the gun toward the target. It's better not to see the gun barrel at all, he contends. In fact, he removes the sights from the tips of all his firearms so there are no distractions. You point the gun as you would a spear or, more simply, your finger.

"Stand behind a child and tell him or her to point at something that's in motion," he says. "What you'll see if you follow the child's finger is that the baby predator automatically builds in an allowance for the moving target."

This "pointing" is vital to the instinctive response. Pitchers do it with their gloves, quarterbacks with their opposite arms, archers with their bow fingers—and they all do it without thinking. It represents the moment at which all the necessary calculations are made, the pause before the attack, when that 90 percent of the brain is humming. In shooting, you point with the extended arm that grips the barrel and, in honor of Tip, with a lift of the chin.

Get a pair of snake eyes. Part of being able to point is seeing the prey *exactly*. Before she springs, the lioness is not looking at the entire wildebeest, says Fawcett, but at the tip of its nose—the leading edge of the target. Anyone can teach himself to do the same by narrowing his focus on everyday things. Don't simply watch a crow fly overhead—search for its beak. Don't just look at the person you're talking to—zero in on the pupils. Train yourself to look at the corners, the crannies, the edges of things.

Such heightened awareness will crack the gloss we put on life, sharpen our experiences of the world, and enhance performance. "When you're playing darts, don't focus on the bull's-eye; choose a spot within the bull's-eye," says Fawcett. "If you're whitewater rafting, look at the one rapid that can hurt you most. Ted Williams could see the stitches on a baseball."

Fawcett uses two tricks to help his students see like predators. One is a pair of glasses with yellow lenses that heighten contrast and shrink the pupils to pinpoints. The other is a detailed description of his favorite scene from *Little Big Man*, in which Dustin Hoffman's movie sister explains that the secret to shooting a six-gun is going "snake eyes."

"That's it! That's the look of the predator before it strikes," says Fawcett, almost trembling with vindication. "Face slackened, eyes hooded over as if in a trance, focus absolutely zeroed in."

"You hungry?" asks Fawcett, after almost 3 hours of verbal instruction inside the mobile home.

"Yeah, I could use a sandwich."

"Good," he says, making no move toward the cooler. "You shoot better when you're hungry. Otherwise, all the blood is in your stomach. Let's go."

So I follow him outside, ready—I suppose—to finally meet my predator. There are 16 shooting fields scattered across the grounds. It's like a golf course, except that the cups are small clay disks or "birds" sent spinning at various angles through the air, and the par for each is a single shot. I carry a beautifully burnished, 12-gauge, side-by-side shotgun Fawcett calls Hop-a-Long. Since I've never shot a real firearm before, I'm scared, both by this weapon and by the expectation that I'm actually supposed to hit something. But Fawcett tells me not to worry. Just relax and let the predator take over.

It's no simple matter out on the firing range. As a novice, I have so many things to remember that I can't possibly permit myself to relax. As with any other challenge, my intellect wants to dissect and control it. So target after target falls to the ground unbroken.

"This is tough," I say.

"Only if you *think* it is," he replies.

To ease my frustration and remind myself of how simple this should be, Fawcett has me set aside the gun and point at a few airborne targets with my finger. Then, with Hop-a-Long back in hand, he calls, "Bird!" I react, and the target is dust. It all feels so smooth, so natural, so fulfilling that I rejoice and immediately want to do it again.

The damnedest thing about it is that time seems to crawl. Whereas I had previously been rushing to mount, point, and shoot in the few milliseconds afforded, now it's as if the bird flies in slow motion and my reaction to it is liquid. Suddenly, instead of trying to hit any part of the target, I'm looking for the front edge—and Ted Williams doesn't seem so extraordinary after all.

"The predator has the ability to compress time and view speed differently," explains Fawcett. Ping-Pong players, for instance, don't see the ball moving as fast as spectators do. It's an illusion created by the focused mind.

"Time is an experience," Price explained to me later. "That's all it is. When you take yourself out of the measurement of time, then you can be in the world in a different way. There's a lot of paradox. To think clearly, you have to not think; to have energy, you must be still; and to perform well, you just have to *do* it."

Before long, I'm shooting more consistently, and I even nail a "following pair"—two birds launched in quick succession. I shoot 50 rounds of ammunition that afternoon and 250 more the next day. By the end of the workshop, I'm shooting better than 70 percent—marksman territory for a tenderfoot.

But my gun handling isn't the sole source of satisfaction. I know the "feeling" now, and how to evoke the beast within. I realize, with newfound clarity, why in certain situations my conscious mind gets in the way. And I can laugh along with Fawcett at the framed motto inside his trailer: *"Cogito ergo non ferio,"* or "I think, therefore I miss."

Most important, I've begun to see my predator in other aspects of life. When I emerge from a writing groove to look at the clock and see that hours have passed, I know that it was my predator crafting those sentences, and they are good. When I finish a long run or bike ride and recline in the cool renewal of contentment, I know that it was my predator's legs that brought me here, and it is healthful. And when I find myself in a tough situation where my heart races and my voice cracks, I know that I can draw guidance from this force inside me, and it will be right.

"Buz gave me a different outlook on everyday occurrences," said Harmon, who plans to return for a refresher course. "I don't care if you're playing ice hockey, swinging a baseball bat, or organizing a business: Before you can achieve what you want, you have to understand who you are. Then you can decide on your purpose, lay the groundwork, and focus on this edge."

"I set aside 15 minutes every morning and afternoon to clear my mind of all its traffic," added Bryant, a former Junior Olympic swimmer. "Call it meditation if you want, but for me, it's simply a quiet, restful state. It's tough to do because the mind doesn't like to be handcuffed. But once you train yourself, it's like a natural drug, and it helps you to focus better. That's how I stay in touch with my instinctive self."

"I hope you realize," concludes Fawcett, snapping closed the latches on his gun case, "that I haven't really taught you anything new here. I've simply led you down an ancient path that already existed within you."

Somewhere Tip purrs contentedly, and I know now why she is satisfied. I know now why I came. 🅰🆂

CHAPTER 13

not having washboard abs

f it's true that God lives inside each one of us, then God is undoubtedly an abdominal muscle, because that's what people are worshipping these days. In gyms and homes throughout America, men and women are doing endless sets of crunches or using contraptions bought on TV infomercials to flatten their stomachs and unveil their abs. After these workouts they look expectantly in the mirror and flex, searching for some small measure of definition that will finally permit them to wear a belly shirt.

I am guilty of this obsession, I confess. I want a six-pack just like those buff guys on the covers of men's magazines. I want to give my wife the option of doing laundry on my washboard abs should her Maytag ever quit. I want to dare little kids to make tiny fists, rear back, and punch me in the stomach as hard as they can. I want to bask in their awe and admiration.

It's not that I'm vain; it's just that no other visible body part symbolizes youth and fitness more than a rippled set of abs. As long as you have one, you can never be old or out of shape. It is the stamp of vitality. And perhaps that's why, at 40, I'm suddenly spending so much time doing situps in my basement.

For most of my life, I've been skinny. Muscle has never seemed to stick to me. I bought my first weight set when I was 13—an entire new body in a cardboard box. But no matter how many squats or curls I did, it never seemed to make any noticeable difference. My pecs failed to pop shirt buttons. My forearms never rivaled Popeye's. A skilled tattoo artist might have been able to squeeze MOM on my biceps, but never MOTHER.

When weightlifting didn't work, I tried eating lots of muscle foods like steak, eggs, and milk shakes. My goal was to weigh 200 pounds. When I reached it in college, I wasn't imposing—I was fat. Bicycle riding and running eventually helped me shed those extra pounds, but in the process, I returned to being chicken liver. Nowadays, when I take off my shirt in public and a lady swoons, I'm more likely to suspect a lack of Mitchum.

So before I'm too old to add any muscle tone, I decide to get serious once and for all. I hire Mike, a personal trainer with an impressive reputation, to design me a no-nonsense, ab-building workout. Judging from the size of him, "no-nonsense" shouldn't be a problem. He's 6-foot-4, 218 pounds, and rock hard. In fact, the guy looks more chiseled than the presidents on Mount Rushmore. I tell him I want the workout to be tough. I want to be cursing him as I near the end of every set. I want my money's worth. But most important, after it's done, I tell him I want to be able to look in the mirror and finally see something.

A man of few words, Mike gives me a level stare. "No problem," he says. "Let's see what you got."

I interpret this to mean he wants me to remove my shirt. But when I do, standing next to him makes me feel like I should be wearing a skirt. He looks me over and grunts, then from his gym bag he takes what resembles a pair of ice tongs. (God help me if he's going to make me turn my head and cough.) But they're calipers, used to gauge a person's fat level by pinching folds of skin at various places on the body. Mike takes four readings—from my hip, chest, back, and thigh—and scribbles down each one in a notebook. Then he takes out a tiny calculator and tries to punch in my numbers with his sausage-link fingers. Just when I think he's about to dash the thing against the wall in frustration, he succeeds in hitting the "equals" button.

"You're 11 percent," he says. "Pretty lean."

I don't know whether to be proud or embarrassed. He tells me that's well below average for men my age, bordering, in fact, on being skeletal. But while low body fat is conducive to good health, it's a challenge to look ripped with a chestful of ribs.

"Ever consider supplements?" he asks.

He's referring to the myriad products sold at nutrition stores and through muscle magazine mail-order. Most come in tubs, no doubt to underscore their promise of hugeness. The labels show massive, bronzed creatures that vaguely resemble humans. Everything on the packaging ends in an exclamation point: Mega Muscle! Bicep Blaster! Net Weight 5 lb 2 oz!

Although there are some exotic formulations, most are simple protein powders that you mix with water and drink every day. Protein is the brick that builds muscle. It's impossible to dump a big enough load into the body for really fast construction; most people just can't eat that much. But they can pinch their noses and slug down a protein shake for breakfast, lunch, and dinner.

I've always resisted doing this, though. It seems unnatural, like cheating. Plus, I don't want to be paying for and drinking such slop for the rest of my life. Who knows what other effects it has on the body? I'd rather do it the hard, natural way.

"Your choice," Mike shrugs.

Next, he orders me onto the floor and bends my limbs in various directions to test my flexibility. Evidently, he wants to be sure I'll be able to do the exercises he gives me.

"Tight hamstrings," I hear him grumble. "Okay, get up."

After a few more minutes of studying his notebook, he nods as if satisfied with himself.

"If you follow the program," he says, "in 8 weeks, your abs will pop."

As he demonstrates the five exercises I'll be doing, I begin to wonder if he means that last statement literally. Most are moves I've never heard of, and when I try a few, they instantly make my gut burn. Is it possible for an ab to rupture? Should I be wearing safety goggles?

Let me give you an example. The hanging leg raise is an exercise that's done from a chinup bar. While hanging, I'm supposed to slowly curl my thighs up to my chest. No problem. I can do one, two, even three of these. But Mike wants me to do three sets of 12. To make it slightly more manageable, he clips a pair of support straps onto the bar. These are pads that cradle each elbow, allowing me to support my body weight with my arms instead of my hands. Okay, now I can do four, six, even eight, but that's still a long way from my assignment.

"Don't worry, you'll work up to it."

A close second on the torture scale is the oblique crunch. This is similar to a conventional situp, only instead of fully raising my upper body off the ground, I'm supposed to stop halfway and then alternately pivot to each side. This works the oblique muscles that run along the sides of the torso. The crunch part evidently refers to the sound you make when collapsing to the floor afterward.

"Three sets of 12 for this one, too," Mike deadpans.

It should be pointed out that although I'll never be mistaken for the Incredible Hulk, I am in fairly good aerobic shape. In other words, I'm not a complete Don Knotts. I've taken on Jack La Lanne, tried out for my high school basketball team, and even gone surfing. But what Mike is showing me here is an unfamiliar kind of fitness, and it has me feeling like a novice.

No exercise underscores this more than the cable crunch. I do this one while kneeling in front of a cable-pulley machine—a metal tower with an enclosed weight stack at the bottom and a pulley/grip at the top. The idea is to lower about 90 pounds to my forehead and slowly curl my upper body downward. When I do it correctly, it feels like there's a knife in my gut. The problem is, the exercise looks totally benign. In fact, while other guys in the gym are buckling on kidney belts and grunting up huge slabs of iron to build their bodies, it looks like I'm merely praying for the arrival of mine.

"Three sets of 12," Mike repeats.

The good thing about all this is that I'll only have to do these exercises two times a week, and since there are just five, it shouldn't take me more than 20 minutes. I can easily fit that into my lunch hour.

"See you in 2 months," Mike says as his handshake buckles my knees. "Call if you have problems."

The very next morning, I have problems.

It feels like my intestines are in a big knot, like I'm coming down with a severe stomach virus, like I've been up all night vigorously belly dancing. I am so sore deep in my gut, the back of my navel needs an ice pack. No string of situps ever made me feel like this, and I take it as proof of the program's effectiveness. I am hurting, but I am encouraged.

So I follow Mike's orders and become a gym regular. The number of sets and reps I can do for each exercise gradually grows and the soreness diminishes. Soon I start to feel strong, and not just in various appendages like I did when I lifted weights before, but at my very core. What most people don't realize is that the ab-dominals are not just a vanity table but a functional slab of muscle that stabilizes the entire body. Strong abs give you an epicenter of balance that reverberates through everything you do—from everyday posture to sports performance.

Of course, immediately after each workout when my abs are as pumped as possible, I examine myself in the locker room mirror. If no one is around, I'll strike a quick pose. And by damn, something *is* happening! A ripple here, a trace of new definition there. It's like a child is being born, and I'm catching the first glimpse. "Congratulations, sir. You have a brand new baby ab!"

It's ridiculous, isn't it? How a man's whole persona can be changed by a little new muscle. Suddenly, I feel more handsome, more masculine, more intelligent, more *worthy*. I pat my flattening gut at least a dozen times each day. It gives me confidence. It lends reassurance. It comforts me.

And, I'm surprised to say, it also reminds me of my Uncle Henny. He used to pat his stomach, too, usually while laid out in a lawn chair with his shirt off on a summer Sunday. Only instead of rock-hard abs, he had a beer belly the size of a Thanksgiving Butterball. He had survived the depression and a world war—a hardworking Hungarian with plenty of battle scars. But the medal he wore most proudly was the one that hung just below his chest. He carried it like a trophy. To his generation, a belly like that was a status symbol—a sign of prosperity and success. It, too, gave him confidence, reassurance, and comfort.

So what happened in those intervening years to change our perceptions so dramatically? What's the difference between my gut instinct and Uncle Henny's? Well, besides light beer, there's overwhelming scientific evidence nowadays that being overweight (and sedentary) increases the risk of premature death. And the fitness craze of the last 2 decades has elevated the hardbody to almost gladiator status. But perhaps most intriguing is the theory that in an age of increasing conformity, we need something to separate us. Throughout history, men have decorated themselves—with piercings, tattoos, uniforms. Now we're doing it with muscle. Abs have become our tribal mark. Those who have them are, in some way, special.

But like most men and women, I don't often think of what

drives me when I'm working out. All I know is that when I catch a glimpse of myself in the mirror, it feels good. And when one of my wife's girlfriends catches me with my shirt off and kiddingly asks if those are abdominal muscles she sees, I become totally obsessed. Six weeks into the program and I've reached Mike's three-set, 12-rep prescription—really working up an impressive sweat. I have dreams of being a body double for Brad Pitt.

But then, at the peak of self-absorption, something totally unexpected happens. One day in the locker room after a particularly intense workout, I notice that my abs are crooked. *Crooked.* It's not that one side is more developed than the other. Rather, the ones on the right are all about an inch higher than their partners. At first, I think it must be an optical illusion—a smudge on the mirror or the angle from which I'm viewing. But as I step closer, I realize there is no mistake: Something is definitely wrong. Instead of looking defined, I look deformed.

"Huh," says Mike, when I call him to break the news. "I'll meet you at the gym in an hour, and we'll have a look."

"Huh," he says again later when I pull up my shirt like an ailing patient before a doctor.

"Well, what the hell's the matter?" I press, increasingly worried and angered by his speechlessness.

"Everyone's body isn't perfect," he finally replies. "Just as some people have legs or arms that are slightly different in length, others have muscles that aren't perfectly aligned. Maybe you broke a rib when you were a kid, or maybe it's genetics. But whatever it is, there's nothing you can do about it."

And just that quickly, my six-pack dreams are shaken and popped open, left to fizzle out in a depressing anticlimax. I'll never appear shirtless on a magazine cover. I'll never be approached in laundromats by beautiful women who are conveniently out of quarters. I'll never win "Best Middle."

This crushes me more than I expect. But eventually I come to a realization. Unlike most of the other sweaty men and women in gyms and basements throughout America, I now have an excuse, and a foolproof one at that. After the initial disappointment fades, I actually feel some relief. Abs are one less thing I have to worry about. This is one goal that's not realistic for me, and I know that now unequivocally.

But I can't escape it entirely. Wouldn't you know it? Lately, I've been looking in the mirror and thinking about my chest. If I really worked at it, maybe got Mike to draw up a new plan, I wonder how these pecs of mine might come in?

CHAPTER 14

being very afraid

T hese fears. Tell me about them," says Dr. Mario, closing his eyes and preparing to see as I do.

Slowly the room darkens, and the sky grows purple like a bruise. The air becomes still, tense, and difficult to inhale. A red bar scrolls across the bottom of the TV screen with a warning to take cover. So I close the windows, pull the shades, and unplug every appliance.

There's a rumble from the west and then another and another, as if some giant is shaking the ground as he lumbers toward us. Tree leaves begin a slow rustle, and limbs scratch against the side of the house as if pleading to get in. Then comes the tip-tap of a few raindrops, fat and hesitant.

I peek outside, and the sky is boiling. Black clouds are fast approaching, and beyond them, a curtain of tormented gray. A sudden flash drives me back until I feel the reassurance of an inside wall behind me. I slide down it, close my eyes, and hug my knees to my chest.

The rain intensifies, and the lightning and thunder become inseparable. Sometimes I feel the actual sizzle of the bolts and imagine it crisping my body like bacon. I cover my ears and whisper the Act of Contrition, a prayer that is supposed to cleanse the soul and prepare you to meet God.

Even though there is a sturdy house around me, I feel vulnerable. Even though I've folded myself into a tiny ball, I feel exposed. Life has suddenly become tenuous. Death, imminent. Accomplishments, ridiculously impertinent.

The storm continues to build, shaking the room now, as if that giant has finally arrived and wants me out. I scrunch myself up tighter—hiding, praying—until I feel a hand upon my shoulder.

"Pappajack. Pappajack. Are you okay? Don't be scared. It's all right," says my 6-year-old daughter, Claire. And she sits next to me on the floor and hugs me. I'm ashamed I've let her see me this way, embarrassed that I've shown her my fear.

Fathers are supposed to be invincible. We're supposed to be walls that surround and protect. But I crumble whenever a thunderstorm rumbles, and my children have witnessed it. I worry that every time I cower, I lose some of my power over them. It's just not possible to look up to someone who's hiding down below.

Dr. Mario slowly opens his eyes and nods but says nothing. The room gradually brightens. The din has subsided, and it is mercifully quiet. We awaken, both of us. Water drips in the distance.

"These fears. Tell me some more about them," he says, drawing a long, deep breath before closing his eyes and preparing to see as I do, again.

And we're outside now, on a single-track trail in the mountains of Colorado, riding bicycles. The air is so crisp and thin at this altitude that it feels sharp against the back of the throat, almost as if we're inhaling icicles. We're sweating and grinning, watching the aspen leaves dancing daintily in the morning breeze and trying to be just as light upon our pedals. We've been climbing for hours, not realizing how far above the valley floor we've risen.

Then, without warning, we turn a corner and the world opens

up before us. We are suddenly on a cliff edge. To my right is secure woodsy underbrush, to my left is a sheer thousand-foot drop-off. The ribbon of trail we've been following has become a tightrope pulled taut across an abyss.

My legs instantly turn to jelly. I carefully get off my bike and back away. *I can't do this.* Other riders shoot past me, whooping. I pretend I've merely stopped to take a drink and enjoy the spectacular view, but the hands that hold my water bottle are trembling. From feeling so strong to feeling so weak—the plunge has almost sickened me.

The magic touch of balance is a trick of which I'm no longer capable. So I carefully position the bike between myself and the rim, move as far to the right of the trail as possible, and begin walking. Although the way is clear, it feels like I'm slogging through swamp mud. Each step must be measured and willed. Fear knows but one speed, and that is agonizingly slow.

Halfway across, my energy runs out. Too far along to turn back and not quite far enough to sense relief, I am trapped in the limbo of my own cowardice. Other riders are still streaming by, some weaving toward the edge, yelling "Whoa!" and faking a plunge. But I've stopped looking at them, stopped pretending. My whole body is shaking.

"Dear. Dear. Are you okay? Don't be scared. It's all right," says my wife, Maria, who's finally caught up to me. She places a steadying hand on my back and gently guides me past the precipice. As composure leaks back into me, a blush of humiliation replaces my paleness.

Husbands are supposed to be strong. We're supposed to hold our wives in our burly arms until their tremors subside, not vice versa. But heights give me an inexplicable fright, and my wife has witnessed this. I worry that every time I step back, I become less of a man to her. She sees my retreat in one thing as a likelihood that I'll flee from others. What kind of husband is that?

Dr. Mario slowly opens his eyes and nods, but still says nothing.

The trail has disappeared, replaced by a mercifully flat expanse of floorboard and carpeting. We come back to reality, both of us. Dirt flecks my sneakers.

"What does the fear feel like?" he asks, after a while. "Describe it for me. Make *me* feel it."

Without hesitating, I tell him it is bone. Not goosebumps that can be rubbed away, not muscle tenseness that eventually fades, not adrenaline that temporarily torrents through the veins, not a heart beating explosively, not even a scream from the center of the lungs—but something much deeper down.

It is bone.

That's where I feel it. That's where I go weak.

When you're scared by a sound in the middle of the night or a near-miss in rush-hour traffic, the fright sweeps over you like a wave. It is suddenly there, shocking you, knocking the breath out of you, but then it breaks and tapers away, leaving you wide-eyed but safe. True fear is different. It doesn't ebb and flow. It's always within you. You know it's there, and what's worse, you know when it's coming.

Fear is different from fright. Fear is not Halloween dress-up. Fear is not a movie stalker. Fear is not the word boo. These things make a mockery of it. True fear goes to the core of you, sickens you, paralyzes you. It reaches way down inside and makes the soul cold. It is bone.

Dr. Mario furrows his high brow, considering, understanding. I think he knows.

We all know.

"Can you tell me where these fears might have originated?" he asks in a slow, sleepy voice, as if encouraging a trance. "Can you re-member anything about the first time you experienced either of them?"

It was an August Sunday, hot and thick. I was 15 or 16, pitching beanbags with my father and a neighbor by our backyard swim-ming pool. The sky was darkening and there were a few grumbles of thunder, but nothing to hint of any immediate danger. Until the explosion. A flash, brighter than any strobe. Heat, on the skin, palpable. A boom, like a bass drum we were within. All simultaneous.

I ran to my father and embraced him for the first time since I was a toddler, momentarily forgetting that I was a proud, emotionless teenager. I pressed my face against his soft white chest, my eyes wide with terror. Lightning had struck somewhere very near. And in that instant—illuminated—I had seen that I wasn't invincible. I had felt the diameter of the thread that makes life tenuous. I had glimpsed death's fingertip upon the switch. That quickly, I had grown up. And that swiftly, I had regressed.

Although my father and I relived this experience many times, we never discussed what that lightning bolt really struck inside us. But I believe he was changed as much as I was, only in a different way. While I was hugging him, he felt the need inside me. And he cherished that instant. So much so that in the years afterward, he began acting stupidly brave during thunderstorms. In all but the worst ones, he'd be in his garden picking weeds or even, unbelievably, cleaning the pool with a 12-foot aluminum pole. My mother and I would yell at him to come in, but he'd ignore us and grin. Perhaps it was his small, foolish way of proving that he was braver than me, that he was in control, that he was a man. And since I'm incapable of exhibiting such bravado to my family, maybe that's why my fear is so bothersome. No doubt, there is the raw memory of that lightning bolt, a scene seared into my subconscious like a negative. But maybe the fear also stems from my inability to act like him, to stand tall in dangerous situations, to reassure my children, to make them forever need me in some tiny way.

Dr. Mario does not respond. He looks at me, placid as a summer pond. Nonjudgmental. Calm.

"And the other one?"

I don't know. When I was a boy, I loved heights. Trees, ladders, tiptoes, sturdy drain pipes. Sometimes Mark Kovaleski and I would spend all afternoon shoveling dirt into a big mound just so we could launch our bikes from it. I remember those few seconds of soaring flight as authentic delight.

One summer, my parents took me to an amusement park near San Diego called Magic Mountain. It had the world's tallest skyride, or so it seemed to me, rising thousands of feet into the air and disappearing out to sea. As we stood in line to ride it, my father kept asking if I really wanted to do this. Even he was apprehensive. But I insisted, pulled the bar down decisively across our laps, and rode away with legs dangling above the Pacific. It was magnificent.

But with age has come tentativeness. The older I get, the greater my dread of being anywhere without a safety net. I prefer to stay securely grounded. Maybe it's because I'm increasingly aware of my mortality and all the people who depend on me. My fear is a warning not to be foolish, to weigh the potential penalty, to be mindful of my responsibility.

But there's another possibility, one that's more uncomfortable to consider. Perhaps as I've gotten older and attained a suitable height, both in stature and vantage point, I've lost the drive to climb, to reach, to fly. I'm content with where I am; I've reached my cruising altitude in life. And although I realize I could head higher, I also see how far I could fall. It's a compromise of ideals.

Dr. Mario shifts in his chair, intently aware. "You realize, of course, that fear is a rational emotion," he says. "Everything you've told me is logical. It makes perfect sense. Although fear may seem otherwise, it exists to protect us. There is even evidence that it's hereditary, that there's a fear gene. It's there for the survival of our species, for the survival of you and your family. Your fear of lightning and heights has a purpose. There is nothing crazy about it."

He's right. It's true. In fact, sometimes I'm even thankful for my fear. It keeps me humble and respectful. It reminds me how small and insignificant I am. It keeps me honest. It keeps me human. When the storm subsides or the earth comes back into sight, I appreciate life more. The closer you think you are to death, the more tenaciously you experience reality. I breathe in and thank God for every summer afternoon that isn't clouded. Every guardrail along the path is not a sign of man's meddling but evidence of someone caring. And to me, that's reassuring.

If fear is a rational emotion, then to be fearless is to be stupid. It is to be dead already—to the world, to your own smallness, to a method for improvement. In my fear are my flaws, and if I look closely enough, perhaps I'll be able to overcome them.

"Let me suggest something," says Dr. Mario, raising a single finger. "Let me make not a diagnosis, but a guess. Because that's all I can really do; the rest is up to you. Maybe your fear of lightning and heights isn't a fear of those things at all. Perhaps what you really fear is your own weakness."

There's no doubt I am a perfectionist. My desk is dotted with neat paper stacks. My stories are all spell-checked and superbly punctuated. To me, the greatest satisfaction lies not in the doing but in the polishing. That's where I separate myself from the rest. I take that extra step. If life is a knob on a car radio, then I am a fiddler, an incessant fine-tuner. The fidelity is always highest when you're right on the frequency. I've never understood why more people don't realize this.

Control is what I crave. It makes me feel whole. It's what leaves me sated after any process, no matter how trivial. And control is what I lose when the sky blackens and the valley gapes. Although I take all the necessary precautions, they're never enough. I am still powerless. And that's what's so difficult. That is why I'm here, in this room, this private tomb. Such is my fear, and yes, my weakness.

The most out-of-control time in my life was immediately after my father died. It was another lightning bolt, only this one hit me. He had a heart attack in his sleep and never woke up. It was that painless for him and that painful for us. It shattered my world and my mother's. In retrospect, my response was totally predictable. Instead of letting myself be consoled by friends and relatives, I fled to the solitude of my office and started making phone calls—to insurance companies, banks, leasing agents, funeral parlors, caterers. I was trying to regain control by organizing his end. If there could be no immediate grasp of why, then I could at least find solace in the who, the what, the where, and the when.

I eventually organized his death, even used it as inspiration to write an entire book about fatherhood. It took me 7 years to come to grips with it, to digest it, to control it. I finally know what it means, or at least I think I do. It remains a hurt, but it is no longer a weakness.

Come to think of it, the whole journey of this book, the one in your hands right now, is toward perfection. Every one of these regrets, every lament I've tried to reenact, has stemmed from some perceived failure or weakness. The man with no regrets is the ideal man, the perfect man. And perhaps what I really fear is something my mind won't yet accept but my soul already knows—that I'll never become him, that such a goal, for me at least, is unattainable.

"Here's another guess," says Dr. Mario, after pausing, pondering. "*Closure.* What does that word mean to you?"

It means a train with no caboose. It means waiting at the railroad crossing in town every day, feigning patience. I look down the line, trying to see the end, but I never can. For some reason, in my part of the country, cabooses have become obsolete. All our trains end abruptly with open boxcars. And the incompleteness of it gripes me. It represents the lack of closure in our lives. We are all hanging, waiting, without a clue as to what's coming or going.

Remember the test pattern that television stations used to broadcast? How an appreciative announcer came on at 2:00 A.M., played the national anthem, and declared the viewing day over? Remember how grocery clerks used to end every transaction? How they said "thank you," acknowledged your presence, and even bagged your purchase? These were cues, however small, that something was finished, it was done right, and only now was it time to move on. This was closure.

But now, everything spills into everything else. The world is one long continuum. No wonder life is stressful. Instead of completing things and feeling the satisfaction in that, we're forgetting to sign off, make eye contact, attach cabooses.

Maybe I'm becoming obsessive, but I need these pseudochapters. In fact, this is probably the driving force in my life, to finish what I start, to reflect back at the end of the day on what I've accomplished. But with these fears I've made no progress. They've been with me, smoldering for years. That is another reason I'm here, to finally understand them, to defeat them, or if that's not possible, then at least to achieve some semblance of closure.

Dr. Mario shakes his head, as if I have abruptly veered onto a path that dead ends up ahead. It is the first time he's been the least bit animated. "Maybe the reason you're plagued by these fears," he gently corrects, "is simply because you haven't *accepted* them."

Now I am the one who pauses, ponders. Up until this point, I've been feeling like an onion, with layer after layer being peeled away in a slow, methodical progression toward whatever is at the core. But now that I'm almost there and the inside is looking just like the outside—firm and white and capable of provoking just as many tears—I am starting to feel frustrated and disappointed. There is no evident solution. No closure. Except, perhaps as he is suggesting, to accept its existence, its continuance, the permanence of my weakness.

"It might help to think of our discussions as a quilt with many different sections," says Dr. Mario. "Instead of working toward the core, you work outward, gradually discovering interconnected patches you never knew existed. That is the process."

He lets that settle into me, as if he's spoon-feeding a baby. Then, as an afterthought, he adds: "Copernicus preached that the Earth revolved around the sun, but it wasn't until 200 years later that this was accepted as fact. He experienced no closure in his lifetime. He was even ridiculed for his theory. But he kept it open, accepted the criticism, continued thinking, and refined what he believed in."

For some reason, I'm reminded of a veteran marathon runner, a friend of mine, who once mentioned that the best way to cope with pain is to envision it as fire in the pit of your stomach. Not a raging blaze, but a candle flame—intense but contained. By acknowledging its presence by permitting it a small part of you on which to feed, you become better at managing it.

Perhaps fear must be dealt with similarly. Not as an enemy but as a grudging ally. We all feel it, but it's only when we fight that we lose. To accept it is to contain it. Maybe it's that simple.

Dr. Mario nods, rocks in his chair, and says one word: *Opportunity*.

That's it, isn't it? These episodes of fear and weakness, imperfection and dissonance, are not inherently negative. They are what I perceive them to be. Suppose I start viewing them, like he suggests, as opportunities?

Dr. Mario rocks more quickly, looking at me, into me.

Suppose I decide to leave here with no solution, to deliberately keep these wounds open? Suppose the next time a thunderstorm hits or I'm perched on a cliff, I imagine my fear to be a flame? Suppose I hold out my finger, permitting it to tremble, and touch it to the fire? Suppose I feel how hot and hungry it is? Suppose I decide to keep it there?

There are things feeding my fears that I may never completely understand. Some of them have been unveiled here, but our pasts are too complex, our influences too convoluted, to ever find the true source. The flame has fuel—always has, always will. I can't extinguish it. But I can regulate the wick. Feeding out just enough to feel like I'm in control, while still permitting it plenty of open air to lick.

And before long, maybe it will burn a new hole in me. After all, fire feeds best on dead wood. Once that's all gone, it'll be time for regrowth. And in the process, I'll have learned.

Dr. Mario gives no evidence of satisfaction. He offers no congratulations. Instead he merely says our time is up.

I put on my coat. He opens the door. We don't even shake hands.

"Same time next week," he says.

"I'll see you then."

CHAPTER 15

never winning the big prize at a carnival

t's the giant stuffed gorilla that catches my eye and, next to it, the sign ONE WIN PICKS PRIZE. So I slap a $5 bill on the counter, and the girl working the booth slowly counts out 50 dimes. All I have to do is pitch one coin onto any of the red dots painted on the floor of the stand, and I win. But NO LEANING! and NO EDGES TOUCHING! and ALL DECISIONS BY OPERATOR ARE FINAL!

It seems pretty simple until I start tossing dimes. The first $2 worth skitter across the board, absolutely hopeless. I raise the arc on the next couple of bucks, but they all bounce off. Next, I go with a gentle thumb flip, and on the very last one, I get close.

"Almost," says the girl, snapping her gum. "Wanna try again?"

I slap down another $5, and she counts out 50 more, even lets me have a few extra because she says I'm a good "cussomer." I continue flipping, employing all sorts of bizarre body English to coax them in, but nothing works. Frustrated, I wait until the girl turns her back, then lean way out. But I still can't put a dime inside one of those damn dots! Finally, I launch a fistful, thinking that the law of averages will somehow be beneficial. They look like silver raindrops falling from the sky, but after a few hopeful seconds of sliding and spinning, they settle to Earth. Not one is in the red.

The stuffed gorilla, I swear, is grinning at me.

The only carnival prize I've ever won was a goldfish in a plastic bag that died before I got it home. I've never scored a giant stuffed animal for an adoring child or girlfriend. I've never gotten to parade my plush winnings down the midway, making all the other fathers and boyfriends jealous. In fact, barkers make me nervous, taunting me from their little stands, daring me to put my ego on the line, pointing at me with their chewed toothpicks. It's worse than walking past the dunking tank.

But since I'm in the process of reliving regrets, no matter how incidental or ridiculous, I decide to chase this one down as well. Make of it what you will. A guy, a ball, a milk can. A guy, a dart, a balloon. On one level, it's simple-minded good fun. On another, it's the very essence of manhood. You don't see many women rearing back and chucking baseballs at stacks of plastic bottles. Nor do you see any ladies pleading, "C'mon, honey, just one more try!" while being led forcefully away by fed-up husbands.

Carnival games aim directly at where men are most vulnerable: our anthropological middle. Deep inside, we are still providers. That's our instinctive job. So when our hungry tribe is waiting for us to bring home the prize, we naturally get obsessive about it. We see those stuffed animals as trophies for our caves, testaments to ourselves as hunters and gatherers. And when other guys, other providers, other potential tribe leaders, are watching, it becomes even more competitive.

My neighbor came over the other day. He's moving to Chicago and is in the process of packing everything in boxes. "I must have a dozen of those big stuffed animals in my basement," he says. "I won 'em playing SkeeBall at the amusement park. Do your kids want them?"

Tight-lipped, I say no.

Of course, the cruel twist in all this is that the minute you win one of those things, the instant you put it under your arm and head for the car, you no longer want it. It only looks good hanging in the carnival booth. It's only valuable in a crowd. When you're driving it home, it's already become a stuffed albatross.

Nevertheless, on a sultry summer evening, I decide to settle this regret once and for all. I drive my family to the Schnecksville Fair—wife in a halter top, kids all grimed up, me wearing a pocket tee and a This Old House cap. This is the standard carnival look, minus the tattoos and missing front tooth.

In southeastern Pennsylvania, where we live, summer fairs are big. Just about every community has one. There are amusement rides, sideshows, food stands, crafts, livestock judging, and my perennial favorites: Masters of the Chainsaw and the Pig Races. The former involves burly men in coveralls sculpting bears, eagles, and busts of Elvis from giant logs, using an assortment of chainsaws. It's loud. It's dusty. It's high bubba art. In the stands, hushed kids with baseball mitts wait for their heroes to toss out a thumb. The Pig Races, by comparison, are pure hootenanny. Six little hogs blast out of the gate, propelled by the promise of an Oreo at the finish. They wear numbers, not jockeys, and it takes about 10 seconds for them to race around the tiny oval. (See Chet in the 4-H tent, and he'll lay you some good odds on the daily double.)

But I'm sorry—I digress. Fairs tend to distract you like that. More to my immediate purpose are rows and rows of carnival games. All the classics are here: SkeeBall, Down the Clown, Spin the Wheel, Milk Can Pitch, Frog Bog, Hoop Shoot, and, of course, that damn Dime Toss. And the prizes are fabulous.

As I survey the midway, planning my strategy, I ask my wife and kids what they want most.

"One of those giant inflatable baseball bats," says my son without hesitation.

"No way," I say. "You'll hit your sister with it."

"Okay, then I'll take one of those big Winnie-the-Poohs so I can practice my wrestling moves."

After much deliberation, my daughter inexplicably decides on a six-foot stuffed snake, and I do believe I'm partial to the giant Tazmanian Devil. Either him or Yosemite Sam. I've always liked them.

Maria, continuing to play the role of trailer park wife, bats her eyelashes, clutches my biceps, and says loudly enough so people stare: "Honey, do yuh think yuh could win me a Tweety Bird? Pretty please. It'd make me *so* hot, I wouldn't be able to control myself."

Suddenly, I am focused. She has delivered the ultimate pep talk. For what she is promising, most men would willfully try to pick up a Volkswagen Bug. I am no different.

Ignoring the tantalizing aroma of funnel cake, striding boldly past the barbecued beef pit, refusing to pause even at the Dangler's Sausage Stand, I hitch up my pants, adjust my cap, and swagger onto the midway. I've noticed when I'm alone, the barkers don't pay as much attention to me as when I have my kids or wife in tow. They're not stupid. They know. Like hunters in a blind, they're adept at spotting ducks in their sights.

"Step right up, buddy!" a skinny, pimply one yells my way. "This could be your lucky day."

"You better believe it, fella," I say, peeling off a single from the thick wad of bills I've brought (just in case).

The game is Dart Balloons, two tries for a dollar, couldn't be more straightforward. I tell my kids to give me some room, take aim, and throw. But no pop punctuates either shot. Instead, my last dart hits the balloon, point-first, bounces off, and falls to the ground.

"Hey, did you see that?!" I ask, incredulous.

"Unbelievable," says the barker with a smirk. "Never saw anything like it. I'll give you three tries for a buck to make up for it."

I miss with my first two, but on the third shot, the same thing happens.

"Man, Lady Luck just ain't smilin' on you. Tell you what. I'll give you four darts for two bucks this time. My best deal. You're bound to break one."

As I'm reaching into my pocket again, my son pulls me aside. "Dad, this game is fixed," he says. "Those balloons hardly have any air in them, and the darts are dull."

"You think so? Maybe I'm just not throwing them hard enough. . . ."

"*Dad!* C'mon."

So this duck moves on.

Bushel Basket Pitch: The idea is to loft a softball just high enough so it lands in an angled peach basket and doesn't bounce out. I drop $8 here because it looks so simple, and because Amber Dawn, the buxom booth operator, is having just as much trouble keeping her own softballs from bouncing out. Eventually, though, I recognize the odds are stacked against me in more ways than one. The booth isn't tall enough to allow the appropriate loft, and the promise of Amber Dawn bending over to pick up my missed shots is more of an incentive than the top prize itself. This time, my wife yanks me out of there.

Whack the Weasel: This is an arcade game. The object is to hit furry fake weasels over the head with a foam mallet as they pop up from various holes in the playfield. Fifty cents gets you 20 frantic seconds. The machine awards tickets, which can then be swapped for prizes, based on your score (5,000 gets you the toaster oven). The game is great fun (I annihilate the little brown buggers), but after pumping in $6 worth of quarters, all I have to show for it is a handful of plastic spider rings, some x-ray specs, and a sore wrist.

Frog Bog: This just might be the most brilliant, irresistible carnival game ever invented. Two bucks gets you three giant rubber frogs, which you position on a special frog launcher that's bolted to the counter. In the middle of the booth is a pond with revolving lily pads. The object is to hit the launcher with a hammer so the frog flies through the air and lands on a lily pad. It takes strength. It takes timing. And it takes a keen understanding of frog aerodynamics. None of which I apparently have. My first shot is way too strong, hitting an old lady walking by with a custard cone. Successive attempts are equally erratic. In fact, I eventually begin to suspect my launcher is defective. Another $8 here.

Rope Ladder: Since I'm not having much luck in the games of skill, I decide to try something more athletic. I figure if my finesse is failing, why not try something physical? This game looks as if it were lifted from an Indiana Jones movie. A rope ladder, 20 feet long and 6 feet wide, is suspended over a foam pad. The challenge is to crawl from one end to the other and ring a bell. I pay the required $5, slip off my shoes, and venture out. As suspected, the ladder is highly unstable, and I splay myself out trying to keep it from swaying. I advance tentatively, like a spider approaching something unfamiliar in its web. I'm two-thirds of the way to the bell when my foot slips and I suddenly lose control. All the change falls out of my pockets as I spin wildly around until I'm completely upside down. I have no choice but to let go. I land in something sticky.

Knock 'em Over: If I'm going to hit it big, I figure this is the game that will allow me to do it. I used to pitch in high school—7-0 my junior year. Mowed 'em down like grass blades beneath a John Deere. So knocking over a pyramid of plastic milk bottles from 30 feet away should hardly be challenging. After all, I'm a natural.

With my family cheering me on, I wind up and let one hum. *Ball one.*

Well, it's been a few years. I probably just need to loosen up. . . . *Ball two.*

Maybe if I try it from the stretch. . . . *Ball three.*

Perhaps sidearm will do it. . . . *Ball four.*

While I'm shaking my head, a punk with a nose ring, huge pants, and a purple-haired girlfriend steps up. He looks at me, cigarette in mouth, as if to say, "Watch this, Pops." He rears back, barely managing to keep his pants up. But I'll be damned if he doesn't sail one over the counter and directly into the stack. "We have a winner!" the carny yells. "Look at how easy that was!"

"Dad?" my daughter fortuitously interrupts. "Can I play some games now?"

"No."

"But why not? You're not winning anything."

"No. I have to do this."

"But why?"

"Because it's what daddies do."

"Oh."

Horse Race: One dollar buys me a seat at a counter with nine other eager contestants. We all have high-powered squirt guns mounted in front of us, which must be aimed at tiny holes in targets about 6 feet away. The more water I pump into the hole, the farther my little horse and jockey advance on the overhead board.

"A-a-a-a-a-and, they're off!"

I get out of the gate slowly, as do most of the others. But soon, I find my aim and start gaining on the number five and number seven horses, which had sprinted to an early lead. Halfway around, I'm in fourth position and looking strong. Coming out of the third turn, I start to close, and as the pack heads into the homestretch, I'm neck-and-neck with the leaders. My trigger finger whitens, and my teeth clench. At the wire, it's my horse by a nose!

I punch the air and whoop, my family dancing around me like we'd just hit the trifecta at Saratoga. I immediately start scanning the menagerie of stuffed creatures hanging from the ceiling, trying to decide which one I want, when the operator reaches under the counter and hands me a puny red bulldog.

"What's this?" I ask.

"Your prize," he says. "Win again, and you can trade up. Four wins in the same day gets a big one. Who wants to play next?"

I stare at my puny red bulldog, dumbfounded. The label, which reads MADE IN CHINA. KEEP OUT CHILD MOUTH is almost as big as the toy itself.

Trapped, I play six more times but win only once and retire dejectedly with a 4- by 8-inch mirrored picture of Aerosmith.

As I'm walking down the midway, shaking my head and thumbing my thinning billfold, I see a young father walking toward me in cutoffs and a muscle shirt. He has a giant Pink Panther on his shoulders and his boy and girl, each holding one of his hands, are smiling and looking proudly up at him. It's an idyllic scene.

I fight the urge to go over and trip him.

Still hopeful, I try the Hoop Shoot, Football Throw, Speed Pitch, Ring Toss, Spin-the-Wheel, SkeeBall, and halfway through, just to shake up my equilibrium, the Tilt-a-Whirl. But 2 hours later, there is nothing riding atop my shoulders except disappointment. I'm still virtually empty-handed, despite having dropped an embarrassing $76. I could have bought a half-dozen stuffed animals for that. Dejected, I sit on a picnic table and buy my family a plate of fried dough.

"Don't worry," consoles my daughter, her face dusted with powdered sugar. "It's all just junk anyway."

"Yeah, darlin'," drawls my wife. "I still luv you anyhow."

Nevertheless, I can't quit now.

As I feared, this has advanced beyond a simple stunt. This is no longer about having fun on a summer evening with my wife and kids; it's about proving to them and to myself that when I set my mind to something, I get it done. I'm providing an example, a life lesson that my children will undoubtedly tell their children about. It's important, I'm sure. I just can't immediately explain why.

Hoping to channel all my accumulated frustration into a single awesome display of power and victory, I roll up my sleeves and head for the Hi Striker. This is the classic carnival game—the supreme test of manly brute strength. Whoever brings the sledgehammer down with enough force to rocket a weight up the tower and ring the bell is a god. And as if that isn't incentive enough, on the prize table is a giant Tweety Bird.

I give my bride a long kiss, hand over a couple of singles to the operator, and pick up the sledge. It's quite a bit heavier than I expect, but I don't let on. I rest the handle against my stomach, smile at the crowd, and spit on my hands for effect. Then I rear back.

As I'm doing so, though, I feel a shooting pain between my shoulder blades, like something other than my pride has just snapped. The hammer arcs slowly through the air, driven by barely more than its own momentum. It hits the launch with a *thimp* instead of a THUMP and sends the counterweight struggling upward. It just barely eclipses the "Weakling" level.

"You okay, buddy?" asks the operator when I don't immediately straighten up.

I nod and limp stiffly off, feeling no stronger than Tweety.

"What happened, honey bumpkins?" asks Maria, hustling to my side. "Did yuh hurt yurself?"

"Yeah, I think I pulled a muscle in my back."

"That's it," she says, dropping her act. "We're leaving now before you kill yourself."

"Not yet," I insist. "There's one more game I have to play. I've been saving it for last. It's a lock, I promise."

My daughter and I are hunched over the Duck Pond, surrounded by at least a dozen screaming toddlers waving miniature fishing rods. I spread out my elbows to secure us some room. And although it hurts my back to bend over like this, I'm focused.

"Get number 22," she says, pointing with her rod, "and I'll go for number 12. They look like good ones!"

So we both dangle our plastic hooks into the kiddie pool, simultaneously biting our lips as we try to snag two rubber ducks from the bobbing throng.

"I got one!" she screams, yanking it from the stream.

"I got one, too," I yell an instant later. "Somebody grab the net!"

The guy running the game, who isn't amused by my joke, checks the bottom of our ducks to determine the exact prize. Then he hands my daughter a glow-in-the-dark necklace and me, an official marching band kazoo. They're two of the best toys.

All the other kids around the Duck Pond are envious. They resume fishing, intensely.

"See?" says my daughter. "It's easy!"

And as we walk slowly toward the exit gate, she proudly wearing her necklace and I stooped over with my kazoo (playing the "Battle Hymn of the Republic" seems strangely appropriate), I realize you don't always have to bring home the biggest prize to earn respect and deliver happiness. And sometimes it helps to share the responsibility, too.

Despite the frustration, the $80, the indigestion from the fried dough, and the possible herniated disc, I'm satisfied. Together with my family on a star-tossed summer night, another regret erased—that is reward enough. Yes, I'm finally over this.

"Hey, Dad," whispers my daughter. "I have 60 cents left. Wanna sneak over to the Dime Toss and try one last time to win that gorilla?" A S

CHAPTER 16

not being a real man

There's not much time before the sun sets, so I clear a camp-site from the rubble, gather some old juniper branches, and lay out my fire-starting tools. Here in the Utah desert, this is done with the reverence and precision of an infantryman cleaning his rifle. Without a weapon in the battle against cold and fear, you are exposed, alone—maybe even dead.

I pick up my bow, a pliable willow branch as long as my arm, and tighten the string that connects the ends. When properly tuned, it's not unlike what you put to a fiddle, always ready to smoke a few notes and chase the blues.

My drill stick is 8 inches long, a sturdy piece of weathered sage that I've whittled to a point at each end. The sharper of these fits into a notched rock that I cup in my left hand, while the other slips into a hole in a flat fire board that I brace with my foot on the ground.

With the drill twisted into the string, I move the bow back and forth in long, steady strokes. This makes the drill spin in the board and eventually smoke. With whitened knuckles, I work and pray until a delicate ember is born. Carefully, I nudge it into a nest of tinder, hold it skyward, and blow.

At first there's nothing, and I fear I've lost the spark. But then, with my next few breaths, I see a growing glow, smell smoke, and feel the heat building between my palms. I blow harder, the furnace quivers, and with one last blast of oxygen, the bundle ignites. *Fire!*

I pound the ground and grunt, just like a Neanderthal. Flicking a Bic or striking a match was never this magical. I fan my new friend into a giant blaze. Since I have little to feed myself, I feed him with armfuls of gray kindling. As the night deepens, I imagine animal eyes, as prevalent as the stars in the sky, looking out at me from caves in the canyon walls. I lay my blanket as close to the fire as I dare, rest a hand upon my knife, and doze through an all-night watch.

I never played high school football, never joined the military, never shot anything, never learned to fix cars, never got a tattoo, never rode a Harley, never worked construction, never bench-pressed my body weight, never got in a bar brawl, never grew any chest hair, never developed a taste for whiskey, never drove a truck, never hung drywall, never chewed tobacco, never gambled away a paycheck, never broke a bone, never owned a gun, never got arrested, never let anything get infected, never saved a life, never had a firm handshake, never defended my country, never dared someone bigger than me to do that again. In short, I guess, I never became a "real man."

Rationally, I know that these markers are outdated and stupid, that character is not built of testosterone, aggression, and crudeness. But viscerally, these things touch something dark and brutish inside me. Most are grunt behaviors and caveman traits that, although stereotypical, are difficult for me to shake. In some unfathomable way, they appeal to me.

Unlike my father and his male ancestors, I never had an opportunity to definitively prove my manhood. In my 40 years, there have been no depressions, no world wars, no new Americas to pioneer. The hardships I've faced have largely been self-inflicted—the intense but transient effects of contact sports and late-night excesses. As a result, I have no idea if I'm half the man they were—if I'm even a fraction as brave or stalwart. I played paintball once and had but one thought as I lay in the dirt with pellets whistling overhead: I'd never be able to do this if these were real bullets. And I was embarrassed.

Even though I know it takes more than piss and vinegar to be a real man, I still want to know how I compare. I suspect every guy does. We all need our tests, our yardsticks. We need to know how we'd react and whether or not we have the guts. So once and for all, I decide to find out—to immerse myself in a week of macho, to finally erase the doubt.

And that's how I ended up in the desert of south-central Utah, trying to start a fire while squatting in the dust. It's the headquarters of a small organization, fittingly called BOSS (Boulder Outdoor Survival School), that stages survival camps. Its instructors escort you into the wilderness and show you how to live by your wits. I figure it'll give me a sampling of the traditional manly behavior I'm so curious about. And maybe, if I'm lucky, it'll also give me proof. Or failing that, at least some newfound confidence in myself.

BOSS isn't a military training camp. Guns, fatigues, and Rambo snarls are discouraged. Any forewarned day of reckoning is personal rather than global.

What BOSS teaches, during guided desert treks ranging from 7 to 27 days, is how to cooperate with the land rather than how to subdue it. You learn to navigate by the sun, build a shelter out of forest debris, catch fish with your hands, weave string from plant stems, and create fire from friction. It's an unforgettable lesson in primitive living, a refresher course for your savage soul.

Men rarely have to worry about survival nowadays. Food, water, and shelter are in such abundance that they're taken for granted. Self-preservation has become more a case of not getting caught in the wrong part of town, always wearing a seat belt, and not eating too much fried food. As a result, we've grown fat and vulnerable on our own self-assurance.

But survival is more than living long enough to tap your 401(k). It's using your wits, the vast buried knowledge of your animal ancestors, to live but another minute, then another minute more. Survival is awakening to the dawn, not with complaints of an aching back or an early appointment, but with elation that the night has passed and you have not.

There are 15 of us enrolled in this course. We range in years from 18 to 48, in hometowns from Omaha to Mexico City, and in occupations from student to law enforcement officer. Our seven-day, $725 trip is divided into three parts: two days of rigorous hiking and acclimatizing called impact, three days of intensive group travel and skills instruction, and two days alone in the desert. We will hike almost 40 miles, from high forest to barren wasteland, through cactus thickets and chest-high swamp, on just 1,500 calories per day. That's less than you'd get from eight large fig bars.

Since this is an exercise in self-reliance, tents, sleeping bags, and flashlights aren't allowed. Before leaving BOSS's base camp in Boulder, Utah, we're stripped of watches, Walkmans, and even sunglasses. ("We need to see your eyes out there.") We carry only knives, jackets, and blue enamel cups. Our blankets and ponchos, which we've learned to roll into makeshift backpacks, remain behind for now. There's no food, no water, no visible means of dialing 911.

A van deposits us at the trailhead near Hell's Backbone, and we stand there pawing the dust like anxious mules. Another instructor, Beata Kubiak, delivers last-minute directions, including how to shit in the woods. Since the BOSS wilderness credo is to leave a positive impact on the land (even campfire coals must be pulverized), this becomes a challenging maneuver. For 10 minutes she discusses the options and the relative effectiveness of various natural "tissues." (Hint: Sagebrush and maple leaves are the backwoods equivalent of Charmin.)

Already, the actual experience of survival camp isn't sounding so romantic. Going from modern life to real life is, as BOSS field instructor Scott van Den Bergh says, "like a bug hitting a windshield at 60 miles per hour." But that's what makes the program work. If your plane crashes in the Andes or your spouse runs off with someone else, you'll be unprepared. In such a situation, it's natural to panic, to drift toward despair. But if you are to survive, you must shake off the psychological paralysis and adapt. That's what impact is all about—having the false confidence knocked out of you but still finding the strength to prevail.

It is night in the Dixie National Forest. Sand Creek splashes and gurgles nearby, while the surrounding pines rustle in the breeze. For warmth some of us strangers are huddled together like pups in a whelping box, while others are burrowed into makeshift beds of pine needles and boughs. But no one is comfortable. Without covers, we are trembling like spiderwebs in the 43-degree air, drifting in and out of sleep as if it were a warm cavern we could approach but never enter. I'm trying to recall the warning signs of hypothermia, wiggling my fingers and toes to prevent numbness. The guy next to me has frost on his sleeve.

Then comes light in the east, a dim glow, toward which 15 sets of hoot-owl eyes turn in private anticipation. It grows, as does our collective confidence that we will survive this first night in the wilderness and live to scoff at it. But when our savior peeks over the horizon, its brow is pale yellow instead of reddish orange. In silent despair we watch as a full moon rises. The shivers return, even stronger now, and though we are but a single day into the course, some of us are already wondering why we've come.

Breakfast the following morning is scrambled thoughts of bacon and eggs. Gathered around a pinecone fire, which Scott sparked around 3:00 A.M. after one of us chattered for mercy, we wonder when he'll start the coffee and what a *full* day of impact might bring. Cold, hungry, and eventually frustrated when neither beans nor schemes materialize, we dine instead on the scent of a

Jeffrey pine, the sap of which smells like warm butterscotch.

Throughout this week, questions you'd expect to have answered—How much farther? Where are we? When do we eat?—would be deftly avoided as if they were rattlesnakes sunning on the trail. The six instructors would simply shrug. At times, even *they* appear lost. The net effect, whether by design or by simple circumstance, is of our being adrift on the land, never knowing what to expect. Slowly, we realize that the guides are here only as safety nets—someone to start that fire when hypothermia threatens or splint a fracture should a ledge crumble. For the rest, we are on our own.

We trudge all day into the desert, a thin line of soldier ants with neither crumbs nor a destination to sustain us. Ten, 15, maybe 50 miles—who can tell? We are offered no food, and what little water we have is scooped from putrid potholes teeming with tadpoles.

Dan, a 48-year-old ex-drill sergeant, coughs, gags, then rolls over in the dust to vomit green slime. His 18-year-old son, Nathan, a behemoth of a boy, groans along with him, their intestines sharing the same waterborne plague.

We console them as best we can; our leaders are off trying to scout a way, or so they say, and we've been left alone in the withering afternoon to rest. But after hours pass, we get nervous. Federico, a concert promoter from Mexico, paces in circles. Naomi, a paling student from Brown University, covers her ears against the retching. And the rest of us stand like cigar store Indians on a hill, our hands shading our eyes while we look for some sign of help.

We've all heard that survival camps are dangerous. The night before we left Provo, a local TV station broadcast a story about a 16-year-old boy who died during a 9-week wilderness therapy program for troubled teens (not BOSS) in this same area. He reportedly went 11 days without food and succumbed to a bleeding ulcer.

We consider this as Dan and Nathan spill their guts. Our fear is exaggerated by our hunger, dehydration, and fatigue. Suppose Dan, who's not in the best of shape, loses consciousness or has a heart attack? Suppose our guides don't return? Suppose this is the first test of our survival skills?

Just in case, we look for a campsite that fulfills the five Ws, as Scott taught us: water, wood, weather (shelter), wigglies (no snakes or creatures), and widowmakers (nothing big that could fall on you). Our panic subsides amid the planning, but before we decide to go it alone, we fan out one final time and scan the canyons. That's when we spot Beata trekking back, and in the distance behind her, another guide named Josh Bernstein.

The whole week would be like this: little trials and little reliefs. "You have to push your comfort zone to learn how to survive under these conditions," Josh would explain later. "As long as it's not life-threatening, it builds character."

To bolster our spirits, Scott unveils our destination, a distant mesa called McGrath Point. We feast upon this single scrap of knowledge as if it were a chocolate bar and draw enough energy from it to continue.

Eventually, in the purple twilight, we stumble onto its summit and discover the reward left there for us: bunches of bananas and gas cans filled with Gatorade. Beside them lie ponchos and blankets for the night ahead. Surprisingly, there is no feeding frenzy. Instead, we sit contentedly immobile, savoring and sipping. Normally, a banana isn't something to love, and warm Gatorade would be spat upon the ground, but under these skies, after this day, the two go together like champagne and caviar.

The next morning, the alarm clock sounds: A hummingbird is buzzing by our heads. We awake energized, certainly by the nourishment, but to an equal degree by this bizarre game we're playing. Survival is the ultimate amphetamine, a jousting match with death, however disguised. Ours is a staged battle, of course, but some of the raw elation from winning still filters through. And it's addictive.

Spirits are high as we set off, heading who knows where. Without hunger and thirst to blind us, we notice the land. Everyone calls this a desert but that's only accurate from afar. Down here, in its washes and slot canyons, there's a jungle of life. Fat with sweet spring rain, the cacti have burst into bloom. Patches of silver-blue sagebrush perfume the air. And down by the still-trickling creeks, cottonwood trees and cattails elbow each other for shore space.

To a survivalist, it's an all-you-can-eat buffet. As Beata points out, the nuts from those pinecones and even the dethorned flesh of that prickly pear cactus are edible. She encourages us to graze as we go and drops wild onions and peppermint into her pack for later.

The perfect mindset out here is that of a wandering opportunist. When you find food, eat it; when there's shade, bathe in it; when there's material for fire-starting, stockpile it; and when you're lucky enough to discover a water hole, ignore the tadpoles playing there (in fact, water swarming with life may not be germ-free, but it *is* probably safe) and drink deeply. You do this because there's no guarantee you'll find these things later.

Swallowed by this country and its towering sandstone shelves, we begin to understand why life passes so quickly. No one back home studies the cactus flowers or drops a single pine nut upon his tongue. No one pauses amid all the planning and anticipating to live in the present.

"Be careful where you step," says Scott, calling us around a crusty, blackened patch of earth. "This is cryptogamic soil. It's the desert's way of preventing erosion. Looks like miniature sand castles, doesn't it?"

More than ever before, we begin to notice what is underfoot. When you whittle life down to its simplest forms, you're humbled by the richness and complexity of everything you see.

The beauty of this country is not all that's breathtaking. There are moments of real fear today, like when I'm edging along a cliff and watch a pebble fall away into the abyss. Or when we wade through a stinking swamp and realize that quicksand is real.

Exhausted and filthy by nightfall, we collapse into Cowboy Cave. In a moment of proud delirium, we catch some frogs, but the instructors tell us they're too skinny to eat. Instead, we roast cattail stalks and bubble rice and beans in billy pots, scouring our cups with spoons that we've carved.

Toward morning, a few of us awake to loud grunts and snuffles.

For one long, sweaty moment, we think a bear is loose in the cave, and we reach for our knives. But it's just a neighbor snoring. I never thought I'd find that reassuring.

A few hours later, Scott is thigh-deep in the creek, teaching us how to catch fish with our hands. *Yeah, right*, we think. First, he says, you crash down the middle of the stream, scaring the fish into their hiding places under the banks. Then, once they're secure, like ostriches with heads in the sand, you sneak up and feel for their bellies. As he explains this, he roots under the bank as if he's frisking an old sofa for change. Suddenly, he stops talking, pauses, and then with one primal yell pulls out a squirming 16-inch trout, its gills and tail neatly speared between his fingers. He immediately wraps it in moist grass and stows it for later.

Our journey resumes under a featureless sky. No clouds, no variance of blue, just the sun marching ever onward as we do. Besides the fishing lesson, we're learning navigation—how to pick our way across this emptiness using the sun, buttes, and topographical maps. Gazing at all the contour lines, I find it both amazing and depressing how even the middle of nowhere is so finely delineated. Fifty years from now, will it even be possible to escape civilization?

There's a waterfall somewhere around here. It plunges, as you can too, 25 feet into a shimmering green pool. The water is so cold that it steals your breath, and you surface bug-eyed and gasping. Then you bake on the rocks, settle your heart, and scramble back up to do it again. This place isn't on the map, and the guides won't divulge its name. But we're coming to accept secrets like this and demand far fewer answers.

Cool and momentarily clean, we lounge in an oasis of shade. Mike Ryan, another instructor, squats before us with treasures in his hand. They're arrowheads, tiny jewels of red, gold, and black, from a distant age when the Anasazi Indians lived here. To hold one is to touch their legend, to see them patiently chipping away under this very tree, and to feel their pleasure at such finished perfection.

As evidenced by their elaborate cliff dwellings and rock carvings, they didn't only survive here, they thrived.

When the noonday sun subsides, we press on, still plotting our own route but aided now by the hint of a game trail whispering through the brush. We head toward the confluence of Sand Creek and the Escalante River, where we'll camp for the night. Our progress, though, is painstakingly slow. We must wade some two dozen creeks and bushwhack through thorny thickets that cat-scratch our arms and legs.

It is Steve's misfortune to be sick today. A Chicago cop, he tries to shrug it off like a flesh wound, but his pale complexion and stooped gait belie his intestinal pain. Later, after the virus passes, Steve confesses to a worrisome trait. His job, he said, is infecting him with a basic mistrust of man. "But I couldn't believe how many of you asked if I need help," he added. "It reminded me that all people aren't bad."

Indeed, it's tough for evil and deceit to thrive here. There are no riches to covet, no power to manipulate for, not even any face worth saving. Simple living is honest living. That's why survival camps, when expertly conducted, can be therapeutic, not only for drug-troubled teens but also for wayward adults like us.

At dusk Scott bakes his fish on a flat rock in the fire. It's the first meat we've seen or smelled in days. It's passed around the group as if it were lobster, each of us respectfully pulling off a shred of buttery white flesh. The head, the skeleton, even the eyes are eaten. Nature wastes nothing, so what right have we?

It's one thing to survive in a group, but it's another thing to make it on your own. And that's the real challenge. Among the Anasazi and other primitive tribes, you couldn't become a man without first having a vision quest. Within a remote circle drawn in the sand, you meditated and fasted for days or even weeks until your path in life became clear. Whether this vision was heaven-sent or hallucinated didn't matter. Denial and survival made the boy a man.

Our course would end with an abbreviated vision quest. The

instructors would string us out along the muddy Escalante, "iso-lating" us every quarter-mile or so. We'd be told not to wander and left with some raisins and a plastic bag of blue-corn flour. Then, for two days and nights, we'd be alone with ourselves and the land.

Think for a minute. Can you recall the last time you were com-pletely alone for more than the drive home? No radio, no televi-sion, no phone. None of us can. And although this is a part of the course we had once anticipated as a restful escape, now that it is at hand, we're no longer so sure.

We break camp and hike downriver, dropping off our compa-triots one by lonely one. I'm left in a stunning red-rock canyon, a private parlor for my game of desert solitaire. I sit in the dust and try to take it all in. Across the river, over the tops of the cotton-woods, is a delicate sandstone arch. An eye of blue sky, opened by the wind, peeks out from beneath it. If this fragile bridge can sur-vive, suspended for centuries, then maybe so can I.

Despite my nervousness, I spark a fire on my first try. To cele-brate, I decide to make ash cakes for dinner. Scott said you take the bag of flour, add some water and knead it into dough. Then you fold a small piece over a few raisins and roast it. It sounds good, but my water is dirty, the dough absorbs the crud from my hands, and my baked cakes disintegrate into gritty crumbs. Dis-gusted, I break down and unwrap a mocha Power Bar—one that I had smuggled for just such an emergency. It tastes better than Godiva chocolate.

It's amazing how satisfied you can be on just a comparative morsel. My stomach has shrunk, but I'm not weak with malnutri-tion. Instead, I feel strong, invigorated, and embarrassed by all the times I've complained of black specks in restaurant ice cubes or left food on my plate.

Beyond thinking and tending the fire, there's utterly nothing to do. All the next day, I watch birds flit through the canyon and think that if there's reincarnation, I'd like to be so blessed. I stare at a boulder's shadow and futilely try to see it move across the ground. I check if my silty brown bottle of river water has settled any. And

I inspect my arms and legs, breaded a pale orange by the sandstone particles that bombard everything around here.

I come to the conclusion that man is incapable of doing nothing. To just sit here, even in this remarkable cathedral, is incredibly difficult and frustrating. Each of my muscles is drunk with adrenaline, poised for the unexpected, but nothing happens. Every time I look at the sun and see its lack of progress, I want to scream. My only epiphany is that I have it so much better back home than I thought, and that I want this to end.

There's a road nearby, I know. I saw it on the map. Just follow the river for 3 to 4 miles and look for the power lines. Someone had asked Mike if anyone had ever fled, and he had laughed quietly. "Some do," he'd said. "But they usually come back, because around here finding the nearest road doesn't mean you'll find anyone anytime soon."

It's the last day of survival camp, and the plan is this: At dawn the first person upriver gathers his belongings and wakes up the next, then they hike along to the third, and so on down the line.

I'm waiting, all damp and impatient, as if this is the senior prom and my limo is late. I've been waiting for hours—hell, since I got here—for this moment. I'm standing atop a rock in the brilliant morning sunshine, looking up the trail for my friends, my heart beating fast with the promise of escape.

When I eventually spot them, I'm overcome with emotion, as if I'm being rescued. There's Dan, Nathan, Federico! We shake hands and slap backs like battle comrades, and then move on, stirring the rest. One by one, they emerge from the thickets and makeshift shelters in which they've lived—faces drawn, mosquito-bitten, and dirty, but smiling nonetheless.

During the next hour, our gritty group swells to its original 15 members, but we are hard-shell beetles now instead of crushable ants. We no longer trudge with chins on our chests but walk with heads held high, full of confidence and determination. Our guides have left us to find our own way out. No problem. We look for broken twigs and sandal prints whenever we doubt our way. And when we ford the river, we do so not as wobbly individuals but as a sturdy, hand-linked team.

Policeman Steve turns and jokes about his "vacation" being over. Laura, a registered nurse, shakes her head at having chosen this over a luxury bicycling trip. And someone else computes that BOSS rang up around $10,000 from this course, so there should be a tremendous brunch awaiting us in Boulder.

When the power lines finally come into view, our mood becomes electric. The talk turns to pizza (with bubbling cheese), steak (medium rare), showers (steamy enough to wilt wallpaper), and clean sheets (all white and warm from the dryer).

We cross the river one final time and clamber up to a trailhead parking lot. We exchange congratulatory hugs with our guides, and for a moment stare like spotlit deer at the cars, the bathrooms, the posted trail rules . . . all this civilization.

There is a feeling of accomplishment, but it is not cocky triumph. There is collective relief, but it does not stem from any lucky deliverance. We all survived something this week, if only a journey into ourselves.

"You know, I hated every minute of this," admits Steve, sitting in the van that would ferry us back. "I never thought it would end. But now that it has, I know I'm a better man because of it."

Most of us nod our heads in weary agreement. I can't, with a clear conscience, urge anyone to do this. It would be the most difficult and disturbing week of their lives, and they would curse me for it. But at the same time, with honest conviction, I want everyone to do this. It would be the most educational and empowering week of their lives, and it would forever change them.

It did me. Now, whenever life gets tough, I have a baseline. If I can survive *that*, then how bad can *this* really be? Such an experience bestows an enduring and satisfying amount of confidence and control. It helps put life in perspective. And I suspect that is all that men in today's soft and indistinct world really need. Something to assure them that they are men, if only in a different context.

CHAPTER 17

not taking better care of myself

t happened during a game of knucklehead football—so named because you don't wear any protective gear even though it's tackle. I caught a knee in the balls and crumpled instantly to the ground. The pain was sharp and sickening, but I eventually picked myself up and actually played for the rest of the afternoon. The next morning, however, I had to crawl from the bed to the bathroom because my scrotum was the size and color of an eggplant. Being a typical guy, I did the manly thing: swallowed a few aspirin, sucked it up, and went to work.

But I couldn't complete my shift. The pain became unbearable. Finally, I drove to the emergency room, where a doctor diagnosed a fractured testicle and said that he had to operate immediately. He ended up removing a third of it. Despite how gruesome it sounds, I was fortunate. It could have been much worse.

This experience is indicative of my youth: *reckless.* Like most young men and women, I thought I was invincible and acted accordingly. I was excelling at a game of knucklehead life. Consider:

• *My favorite foods included rye bread heavily buttered and salted; potato pancakes fried in Crisco and dipped in sour cream; chili dogs topped with cheese (five at one sitting); midnight pizzas with extra pepperoni; grilled T-bones with all the fat; gallons of presweetened iced tea; any kind of fast food. . . . Believe me, I could go on.*

• *One of my best buddies in high school went 83 consecutive days without reporting for homeroom sober. He was either drunk or stoned, and since we regularly commuted together, I was right there with him. His streak was halted by graduation.*

• *I played varsity baseball in high school and dabbled in other sports, but I never exercised like you're supposed to. I couldn't run more than a couple of miles or even do 10 pushups. Physically, I was pathetic.*

• *Every weekend at college there was a different fraternity party. Cases of Genny Cream Ale stacked to the ceiling, metal trash cans filled with grain-alcohol punch, nubile coeds with full cups. There are entire stretches of freshman year I can't recall. Brain cells?*

• *After I graduated from college, I became a sportswriter for the local newspaper. I worked four to midnight, fueled myself with takeout food, went drinking until dawn, slept late, then did it all again.*

• *Heart disease runs in my family. My cholesterol has been well into the 200s ever since I started getting it tested. Researchers now say the foundation for future illness is laid in childhood.*

I probably would have continued this lifestyle had my father not died of a heart attack at age 61. He hadn't taken very good care of himself either, and his sudden death hit me hard. It was like once again being kneed in the groin. For the first time in my life, I became aware of my mortality. And since no man expects to live longer than his father did, I started calculating the number of years I had left.

As a result, I took up running and cycling, revamped my diet, lost some weight, and generally turned my life around. Or at least that's what I keep telling myself. Because no matter how good the report from my annual physical, I still worry about the damage those first three decades of life may have caused, what permanent scars the excesses of my youth might have left. Now that I'm 40 years old, it's a nagging regret.

But suppose there was a way to look inside your body and inspect all the blood vessels and organs there as clearly as if you were viewing them on TV. Suppose there was a way to see exactly what kind of shape they're in and how badly they've been damaged. Suppose there was a way to find out how close you really are to death. Would you take a number? Would you wait in line? Would you dare to know?

I first learned about "electron beam computer tomography scanning" from an article in the *Wall Street Journal*. It described a new, potentially revolutionary way to spot disease and arrest it while it's still formative. Instead of waiting for acute symptoms or monitoring vague markers like cholesterol, this new procedure allows anyone to take a computerized 3-D journey through his body and inspect all of its vital parts. It sounds like science fiction, but it's not. It's based on the same technology used in CAT scan machines, and it costs as little as $695.

This time I wasn't going to be a knucklehead. I signed up for it.

The waiting room at the HealthView Center for Preventive Medicine in Newport Beach, California, is futuristic and serene. I sit facing a Japanese wall fountain, water trickling across bromeliads. At its base is a pool, the bottom of which is spotted with pennies. Like the patients before me, I pitch one in for good luck.

The video playing on the miniature monitor attached to my

chair is explaining the upcoming procedure, how the scanning machine will take hundreds of picture-slices of my body in less than 15 minutes. A computer will then assemble them into remarkably clear and accurate images of my heart, lungs, spine, stomach, prostate, colon, and every other internal organ. It all seems so pleasant, like I have absolutely nothing to worry about.

But I'm both excited and scared. Suppose they find something? Cancer, heart disease, an aneurysm . . . anything is possible.

When it's time for my exam, a white-coated technician named Nancy shakes my hand. There is no nurse to take my blood pressure, check my weight, or press a cold stethoscope to my chest. No one even asks to examine the results of my last blood test. At this facility, such things are obsolete.

Nancy ushers me into a beige, sterile-looking room and asks me to remove my belt and empty my pockets. There's no embarrassing, open-back gown I have to don. All my clothes stay on. The only prep work required is not eating or drinking for 6 hours before, having three electrodes taped to my chest, and swallowing a cup of supercarbonated fluid to inflate my stomach.

Then I lie back on the scanner's tabletop surface and extend both arms above my head. Since small amounts of radiation will be emitted as the machine takes its snapshots, Nancy goes into another room and communicates via intercom. The tabletop slides slowly backward through a large ring. It's an open unit with a perfect forest scene on the ceiling for me to gaze at. I feel like I'm looking up at heaven, which is not at all reassuring.

"Take a deep breath," says Nancy. "Blow it out. Now inhale again and hold."

The scanner screens my torso in three parts. I hold my breath for approximately 30 seconds during each. Then it takes two more slightly longer scans, this time stuttering its way back down my body. And that's it. I sit up, put my belt back on, and shake Nancy's hand once more. Then she escorts me through another door, into the office of Harvey Eisenberg, M.D., for the typical hour-long consultation.

Dr. Eisenberg is the pilot of this operation and fittingly, his office looks like an air traffic control center, only without the view. Computers and printers clutter a wing-shaped desk, and behind them is a wall of video monitors. The doctor is 60 years old but looks about 10 years younger. That's a good sign.

A specialist in radiology, Dr. Eisenberg has been doing these physical exam/scans since 1986. HealthView is one of the country's largest providers, seeing 30 to 40 patients per day. Tens of thousands of people have had this procedure done, and many are alive today because of what was found. And there's something hiding in everyone.

"I joke that I have a box of gold stars, and I'll put one on the forehead of the first person who gets through this without my finding something significant," he says. "I've yet to open the box."

Dr. Eisenberg insists, however, that this is as much a preventive procedure as it is a diagnostic one. Any abnormalities uncovered are likely to be in the formative stages, when they can be easily managed and eliminated. In fact, he claims someone of my age who is scanned annually and follows recommendations could live into his 90s or 100s. That's 20 to 30 years longer than the average man's lifespan. With better scanning equipment, which he says he's on the brink of introducing, the images will be even clearer and diagnoses more exact.

"The way medicine is practiced today is flat-out wrong," says Dr. Eisenberg. "Doctors are trained to wait for people to develop symptoms and then react. Yet what person would conduct business by sitting and waiting for catastrophes to happen? That's called crisis management, and everybody knows that that doesn't work.

"Your body isn't an early-warning system," he continues. "It's not this wonderful machine with whistles and bells that go off the minute something is wrong. With major killers like heart attacks and strokes, in most people, the first symptom of disease is the heart attack or the stroke, and a third of them die from it."

Dr. Eisenberg has scanned more than 350 physicians—cardiologists, family practitioners, surgeons, deans of medical schools—and he says that every one got excited about the process. Those in the medical world who remain skeptical argue that too much knowledge can be dangerous, especially for younger patients. For example, a small growth uncovered in a lung could remain small and asymptomatic for life, or even disappear on its own. Yet once you're aware of it, you'll risk life-threatening surgery to remove it.

This argument agitates the normally subdued Dr. Eisenberg. "You tell *me* what disease you don't want to know about," he says. "The answer to cancer isn't in the billions we spend on new forms of radiation treatment or exotic surgeries. The answer to cancer is finding it very early, when you can effectively deal with it in any number of ways. Let me show you something. . . ."

And with that, he begins tapping at his keyboard, summoning to his computer screen a succession of virtual body parts. Each is an actual internal image, startling in its clarity, from a severely diseased patient who was supposedly perfectly healthy.

"This is a 53-year-old male who looks like Mr. America," he explains. "He'd just come from a major teaching hospital, where he had a stress EKG, and the chief of cardiology gave him a clean bill of health. Yet look at all this plaque in his arteries. This is the kind of guy who just keels over, and everybody is amazed because he was so healthy."

"Here's another guy, a member of the National Academy of Sciences, who'd just had an annual physical that he passed with flying colors. Yet look at this gigantic mass in his pancreas. He didn't have any symptoms. This turned out to be a benign tumor with a core of malignancy."

"And here's a woman, the wife of the head of one of the top cancer centers in the world. She came in for a routine exam, and we found this mass in her breast. She immediately went back to the center for a mammogram, and it didn't see this. Mammograms miss malignancy 12 to 20 percent of the time. These are the kinds of stories we see here every day."

"Now," says Dr. Eisenberg, shifting in his chair. "Let's take a look at you."

On the computer screen is a picture of me, only I can't believe it. A portal has been opened in my chest, exposing my ribs, heart, lungs, and intestines. I have become the frog in biology class. Dissected.

Dr. Eisenberg gives the image a quick once-over to see if there are any obvious problems. Then we crawl in, like spelunkers into a never-explored cavern. Using increasingly higher levels of magnification, we begin to inspect what's there.

One of the doctor's first observations is that I have very little internal body fat. That's good for overall health, but it makes his job more difficult. Fat appears as darkish areas on the scan, surrounding the light-colored organs and helping to define them. "But it's still a good visualization," he assures me.

He asks if I have any particular health concerns, and I mention my family history of heart disease and my total cholesterol count of 230. But he appears unfazed. "We look at our parents and figure we're going down the same path," he says. "But that simply isn't true. No matter what we find, it can be readily dealt with, even if there's a bad genetic drive. So let's start there. Let's examine your cardiovascular system."

Dr. Eisenberg navigates the blood vessels of my body, steering through them like a veteran river guide. As he does so, he points out areas of interest while warning of upcoming trouble spots. ("At the undersurface of the aortic arch is an area of high turbulence, where the blood swirls around a corner; it's typically where we first see plaque formation.") But I don't have any there, thank God.

He inspects my heart more closely, examining it now in 1-millimeter slices, just like he's flipping the pages in a book. And there, right at the origin of the circumflex artery running between the heart's left atrium and its right ventricle, is a small white dot. It's instantly visible against the black-and-gray backdrop. The white is calcified plaque, an actual bit of formative bone. It represents an artery that's begun to harden.

"Plaque is made up of fat, collagen, muscle fiber, and bone," explains Dr. Eisenberg. "Once the calcium gets into the plaque, it anchors it. And the anchoring, together with the mechanical stress of blood flowing against it, can cause a fissure. Blood then clots around this crack, rises up to plug the artery, and causes a heart attack."

At one time, it was thought that only large plaques behave this way. "But two-thirds of the time the plaque causing a heart attack is less than a 50 percent blockage," he says. "So the real risk predictor is not how big your plaques are, but how many plaques you have. The more surface area they cover, the higher the probability that one will rupture."

Dr. Eisenberg scores each of his patients based on how much plaque he finds. I have two lesions—this one near my heart and another of similar size in an artery leading to my pelvis. (Thankfully, there is none in the vessels feeding my penis, which would be a sign of impending impotence.) Their combined volume gives me a "score" of 1.1 on a scale of 1,000. But before I can rejoice, he looks me squarely in the eye and says I am now carrying a disease that I have to take seriously.

At first, I find this difficult to accept. I mean, my score was pretty damn close to perfect. But the doctor explains that disease isn't something you measure by degrees. You either have it or you don't. What's present in me is the beginning of a deadly process. In fact, my score is exactly average for a 40-year-old guy. And while my risk of heart attack is low, Dr. Eisenberg stresses that I want to have a score of zero. "*That's* normal," he says.

The most striking part of this analysis for me is how crude and undependable it makes the standard cholesterol test seem. "Cholesterol only has a 7 to 10 percent predictor value," says Dr. Eisenberg. "It's not very good. Two-thirds of people with high cholesterol don't get heart disease, and most heart attacks occur in people with normal-range cholesterol."

The second eye-opener is that despite all the time I now spend exercising, it doesn't completely protect me. I've entered the risk game at age 40, just like every other guy. I have developed a disease. "That's the great male misconception," says Dr. Eisenberg. "Physical fitness does not protect you from this disease. While there's no question that going from sedentary to some reasonable level of activity changes your cardiovascular risk, it just takes you part of the way. Proper nutrition and stress control play even bigger roles. I've seen a lot of professional athletes in here, guys at the absolute peak of fitness, who are just loaded with plaque."

"So this speck could kill me?" I ask, pointing to it on his computer screen, still incredulous.

"This little dot right here could kill you, yes," says Dr. Eisenberg.

And with that, he taps at his keyboard some more and electronically pulls the plaque out of the vessel, enlarges it, and enhances it three dimensionally. The tiny deposit, which had been no bigger than a pinhead, is now looming on the screen, rotating under the doctor's inspection.

"Your job," he deadpans, "is to get rid of that."

In order to do so, Dr. Eisenberg suggests a multipronged attack: 1) Eat a low-fat, whole-food diet replete with antioxidant-rich fruits and vegetables, 2) Keep my immune system strong by learning to better manage stress, 3) Take a baby aspirin every other day to thin my blood so additional platelets won't aggregate around my lesions, 4) Have my blood examined by a lipidologist to determine exactly how my body metabolizes fat and whether I should be taking medication to combat it, and 5) Continue to exercise but regard it as a stress reducer rather than disease armor.

"Untreated, we watch plaques like yours grow at a rate of 20 percent to 250 percent per year," says Dr. Eisenberg. "But treated, we watch them grow minimally, not at all, or even disappear. Now, let's take a look at your lungs."

I have never smoked a cigarette, and I am suddenly thankful for that. Dr. Eisenberg is scrolling through my lung fields, one of the most complex structures in the body. The job is tedious, simply because there is so much of it. If you were to spread out its entire anatomy, it would cover a tennis court.

But what really makes this process painstaking, at least for me, is that he's searching for cancer. Yes, cancer, inside *me*. "I'm looking for a little blip," he explains. "I can see it right down to a half-millimeter in size. On a chest x-ray, a tumor would have to be the size of my fist to produce a bulge in the border of the heart big enough to notice. So we're talking a 2,000 to 3,000 percent increase in sensitivity to lung cancer with this technology. The chest x-ray fundamentally belongs in the Smithsonian, along with the stethoscope."

I can't help but hold my breath as he performs this virtual bronchoscopy. The lungs actually comprise three intertwined trees: the airway tree, the artery tree, and the vein tree. Using sophisticated software, the doctor separates one from the other. On the screen is my air tree. He inspects its individual branches, cuts them open, and even examines the surrounding airfields at a cellular level. This last component resembles a fresh, moist sponge. He terms mine "beautiful" and congratulates me for taking such good care of my lungs. To give me some perspective, he calls up the same section from a patient of similar age who's been smoking for years. His sponge is in black tatters.

"That's the result of inhaling 4,000 substances, including cyanide and carbon monoxide," he explains. "Secondary smoke can do that, too. It's a real thing; we see it all the time. If you want to get somebody to stop smoking, this is how you do it. You show them their own lungs."

But with nothing to focus on in mine, Dr. Eisenberg moves on. "Now we're in the abdomen," he explains, continuing his surreal play-by-play. "This is your liver, and this sack hanging off the bottom is the gall bladder. That looks okay, as does your spleen. These V-shaped structures are your adrenal glands. I can tell by their size and appearance that they're functioning normally. Now here is the pancreas, which is a deadly organ (he pauses to inspect it, as I pray silently), but I see no signs of tumors.

"In this area, I'm also searching for abdominal aneurysms," he goes on. "About 15 percent of men over 50 get them, and they're lethal. None here, though. Now I'm looking at your prostate gland, which is a little enlarged. It's in the upper limits of normal, but it bears watching. I don't need to put my finger in your rectum to feel that. I can see it. You should continue getting prostate-specific antigen tests.

"Moving on to the colon, you can see how difficult it becomes to trace the intestine through this area. That's because there's a lot of residue in your bowel—feces. (He looks at me accusingly, but I swear I don't have to go.) If it were clearer, I'd be able to get right in there and do a virtual colonoscopy."

Next, Dr. Eisenberg summons my stomach to the screen. Fortunately, it's emptier than other parts of me, and he is able to slice it in half and search for ulcers, cancer, and polyps. He finds nothing worrisome, not even any remains from that Whopper I ate a day ago. But again, to show me what's possible, he calls up another stomach, this one belonging to a supposedly healthy guy. When he opens it up, there's a grotesque, golf-ball–size tumor growing inside it.

Finally, he zeroes in on my kidneys. They look good, except that toward the bottom of the left one, there's a bright white spot, similar to the plaque I saw near my heart. "That's a kidney stone," he points out. "It's still small enough (less than a millimeter in diameter) that it should pass. But you'll need to drink a lot of fluid. If it grows larger and gets stuck, you'll think you've been kicked by a mule."

Without thinking, I reach for a cup of water and swallow hard.

The last stop on my fantastic voyage is the spine, and the detail here is unbelievable. After examining my spinal column from the outside and pronouncing it "healthy," Dr. Eisenberg splits it lengthwise and looks inside. Not only can he measure the size of the canal, but he can also visually check for osteoporosis, which he says he finds just as often in men as in women.

"You're lucky," he says. "You were born with a really good spinal canal. These holes are gigantic, and there's nothing compromising the nerves. Your bones are solid blocks. There's no hollowing out. This is a healthy spine, and I don't see many of them."

But when he moves to a higher resolution and begins inspecting each vertebra, he detects some early signs of degeneration.

Specifically, he notices a slight bulging in my bottom two disks. He enlarges the area for a closer look, views it in black and white to better differentiate bone from ligament, and finally puts it alongside a healthy disk to give me some perspective. The problem is suddenly obvious. My lower spinal column is starting to get pinched.

"Despite the fact that your joints are normal, the ligaments around the joints are thickened," he explains. "This little bulging in here isn't normal. It's quite minor, and most people would say that's fine, but it isn't fine. It's the beginning of a process that could take you down when you're older. The time to deal with it is right now."

Dr. Eisenberg guesses that I'm a runner, and he's right, usually 20 to 25 miles per week on pavement for the last 6 years. That pounding is what's probably causing this compression. To alleviate it, he suggests that I switch to power walking or trail running, or have my stride biomechanically analyzed by an exercise physiologist.

"So that's it," he says, turning away from the computer for one of the few times today. "We'll give you follow-up materials and send referrals, but before you leave, you need to understand one thing: The most important physician you'll ever have in your life is you. The things you do on a daily basis will mean far more to how long or how well you live than anything any physician will ever do. Hopefully, this visual imagery will be the motivation. *You* are in charge of your disease."

Four weeks later, my desk is littered with empty water bottles, and every time I pee, I pay way too much attention to the stream. Any twinge in my chest reminds me of that piece of plaque, and my low back has seemed a bit crankier lately, even though I've curtailed my running on hard surfaces. I fear such intimate knowledge might turn me into a hypochondriac. It's going to be a long year before I go back, get re-scanned, and see if I've made any progress.

But such worries don't concern Dr. Eisenberg. "It's important for you to be aware of your disease on a daily basis," he says, "because that's when you're making decisions about diet, exercise, and stress control that will ultimately affect it. I used to tell patients they need to do x or else y is going to happen, but they rarely followed my advice. Now, with this technology, I supply a different kind of motivation. Yes, it can be disturbing, but that's what makes it so effective."

And he's right. I just have to learn to keep things in perspective.

One unquestionable benefit, though, is the deep sense of relief and satisfaction that comes from knowing my misspent youth didn't cause any lasting damage, and I won't be dying of natural causes anytime soon. I was right to opt for the extended warranties on those new appliances.

Finally, I have a thorough, accurate assessment of the state of my health. The doctor and I have stood shoulder to shoulder and looked under my hood. I may be coming up on 100,000 miles and showing a few signs of wear, but otherwise, things are looking good.

Not bad for an old knucklehead like me.

CHAPTER 18

mistreating a dog

When I was a boy, the first thing I did every winter morning was peek through our small, rectangular bathroom window, hoping for snow and school cancellation. Many days it was like looking into a freezer, with thick frost creeping in around the edges, indistinguishable white mounds in the distance, and the whir of the wind sounding like a just-opened refrigerator.

But no matter how white it got outside, there was always one dependable black spot. That was my dog, Inky, a German shepherd–beagle mix, peeking out of his doghouse. Somehow, he survived for 12 years in a plywood box with a plastic roof and a hay-strewn floor connected to a 20- by 8-foot caged pen. That was it—nothing more.

In January, sometimes the snowdrifts got so deep that they would close the entrance to his house. We'd see him after the storm, digging out just like one of our diligent neighbors. In April, when it turned wet and muddy, he'd pace in his cage, all dank and matted, often sliding in his own dung when he'd turn and pivot.

And on thick, humid August afternoons, he'd disappear into the deepest corner of his home, hiding from the thunderstorms he knew would soon boom through.

Whenever I'd let him out to play or take him for walks, his joy was palpable. A few times he escaped by dodging the leash or slipping out of his collar, and when he did, the freedom instantly intoxicated him. He'd forget everything, including me. My father and I would chase after him, driving in the car, hunting for a streak of fur in suburban backyards. Sometimes he'd run so far that we couldn't immediately find him. Amid my worry, I'd tell myself he was having fun, he was free. But part of me also knew that part of him was trying to run away.

When we'd finally corner him, hours later, it was like apprehending an escaped convict. He'd put his belly to the ground, look up with doleful eyes, and surrender. I'd scold him, but there was no regret in his brown eyes—just a mixture of fatigue, wildness, and resignation that it was time to go back to the cage.

The reason Inky lived outside was that my mother wouldn't permit a dog in her house. In fact, she'd barely acquiesced to getting one in the first place. She was obsessed with cleanliness, wearing out one vacuum cleaner every year and actually making my father and me take off our shoes and change pants in the garage before coming inside. To permit a shaggy, drooling mutt in this surgical ward of a home was unthinkable. He was an animal first and my pet second.

Although it sounds cruel, Inky had never known better. I adopted him as a pup from the local animal shelter, where he was one of a large, abandoned litter. I paid $7, and I like to believe he was forever thankful.

Since I was an only child, he was the brother, the companion, I'd always wanted. And for a while, I played with him endlessly. But each evening, I had to put him in his cage, and each morning, there were a thousand new things to distract me from immediately taking him out. After a while, he became just another one of my chores. Feeding every day, pen-cleaning every Saturday. As I got older, took a part-time job, and eventually entered college, our daily interaction was reduced to a food delivery and a head pat. Often it seemed he was happier to see dinner than me. Once, when I hadn't quite gotten all the food into his bowl and I tried to take it away, he growled at me ferociously.

One cold winter morning when I was home from school and I looked out our bathroom window, I didn't see a black spot. When my father went to feed Inky later that day (for it was his chore now), there was no tail-wagging to greet the delivery. Inky was cold and stiff in his doghouse, and my father resolutely chipped a hole in the frozen earth and buried him. He didn't ask for my help, because burying is a job from which fathers instinctively protect their sons.

At the dinner table that night, after the usual grace, he added, " . . . and God bless Inky; he was a good dog." His voiced cracked, and my mother started to cry, and surprisingly, so did I.

I've always regretted how we treated that dog—how I didn't fight hard enough to get my mother to elevate him from animal to pet. I owed him that. I made him spend a lifetime waiting, when I couldn't tolerate waiting myself. I was caged inside, and he, outside. But when I finally did break free and leave home, I didn't think to take him along.

People want dogs for selfish reasons. I was guilty of that. But objects don't fill voids; only understanding does. I was searching for an antidote to loneliness, when in fact what I really needed was to become comfortable with myself.

More than 20 years have passed and I now have two children of my own, but until recently we didn't have a dog. My wife, like my mother, wouldn't allow an animal in the house. And knowing all about sad compromises, I refused to adopt one just to put it outside. But my kids are more persistent than ants around a graham cracker, and they eventually wore me down. One rainy Sunday, they carried me off.

While their mother was working, we visited a puppy farm and returned with a 3-pound, 8-week-old Jack Russell terrier. My wife had long threatened that "the day we bring a dog into this house is the day I leave." So as a warning and a joke, my daughter left her mother's suitcase in the hallway.

Even though we were all asleep when my wife came home, both she and the puppy were still there the next morning. In fact, in the months since, this dog has burrowed into her heart the deepest. I've seen it happen before. It's almost as if dogs can sense when someone is uncomfortable or hesitant around them. And it becomes a challenge. They concentrate their nuzzles and licks, as if they know that a person who cannot love animals is a person who needs love most.

My kids creatively named her D.O.G. (pronounced *dee-oh-jee*). Her name is what she is. If only everyone's signature were so clear. In a year, she has matured into a 12-pound adult with a 20-pound heart and more snap than a string of Fourth of July firecrackers. She's lying on my lap, one-eye dozing, as I write this.

D.O.G. sleeps in a cage, but this one is under the stairs in our kitchen, and she goes there each evening voluntarily. The rest of the day, she pads around the house, auditing every family member and every errant crumb. She is queen of a vibrant kingdom that exists from the baseboard molding down.

Since moving in, she's changed our lives in subtle yet striking ways. We are somehow more of a family now, more traditionally complete, more of a Norman Rockwell painting. And in the evening, just being together and doing nothing is somehow less boring. With a dog to pet, wherever you are, you are immediately more content.

But the thing that has affected me most is seeing how much love is in my kids. Even my teenage boy, who rarely expressed love previously, now routinely does. With people and especially parents, there are too many risks and undercurrents. It's so difficult to be genuine. But with a dog, love's intensity is measured simply by tail-wag velocity. If only everyone's intentions were so plain.

Each morning when my children come down from bed, hair tousled and eyes red, they cuddle this white ball of fur as if it were a reincarnation of their long-outgrown security blankets. And D.O.G. soaks it up and sighs, then somehow reflects it until it warms us all inside.

What my mother didn't realize is that when you open your door to a pet, however mangy, you are inviting in love. And that is an opportunity, in whatever form, that no person should be deprived of. Nowadays, anything that makes us feel, anything that cracks our stoic façades, should be welcomed. Even if that anything is a muddy, smelly, erratically housebroken animal.

Sometimes I wonder why Jesus never had a dog. Although it's a bit dangerous to second-guess God, I think it would have helped him get his point across, maybe enabled him to talk less in parables. After all, a dog is plainly faithful, instinctively good. It is a worthy example, a good place to begin, an excellent first lesson in the power of love. If we were to swap psychologists and doctors for dogs, and replace sermons with 10 minutes of vigorous ball-playing or scratching behind the ears, I suspect more people would be touched and changed and cured in 1 week than in all the centuries past.

There's actual medical evidence to support this. Researchers have found that dog owners generally have lower blood pressures, lower cholesterol levels, fewer illnesses, less stress, fewer heart attacks, more friends, and even happier marriages. This is because a dog facilitates relationships, not only between people but also between us and the strangers inside us. A dog imparts worth and confidence and health by administering a daily dose of unconditional love.

No matter how crummy my day has been, I open the door to this quivering little mass who's so excited to see me, my mood immediately lifts. My children may not rise from the couch, nor my wife greet me with a passionate hug and a kiss, but to this dog, I am the godhead that's been missed.

But I'm getting too grand. Suffice it to say that I've been watching D.O.G., and I'm trying to get on her program. Living this closely with an animal is helping me remember what I'd forgotten.

The few tricks I've managed to teach her are circus antics by comparison. She has already been expertly trained by instinct and evolution. Dogs possess what most people sorely lack, what our so-called intelligence obscures from us. If we let them, they can show us how to fetch back peace and happiness.

Here's a list of things D.O.G. has taught me about life so far. It's not that she's smarter than other dogs. It's just that because of the pet I once exiled, I pay more attention to her. At first, she was my work in progress, another youngster to shape and make good. Now I see that I had things backward, that I'm the one who needs the disciplining. So I'm trying to act more like my dog (stopping just short of squatting in the yard and sniffing the FedEx gal). It's an experiment that, so far, has brought great benefits. Now I challenge you to imitate her habits.

Stretch: Every morning, immediately after waking up.

Visit the vet regularly: The best way to protect your health is with an annual checkup.

Live in the present: It helps slow time and ease stress.

Sleep on the floor: An extra-firm mattress is best for your back.

Play: The opposite of work, it provides balance.

Nap: Even a few minutes are restorative.

Learn one trick to delight people: It works magic.

Run: No reason, as fast as you can.

Be good: Or at least try.

Yawn widely: It briefly lowers blood pressure and relieves anxiety.

Have a treat: Reward yourself, occasionally and guiltlessly.

Drink lots of water: The body needs 48 ounces daily; the trick is keeping it handy.

Be loyal: Give every person a second chance.

Circle before lying down: Feng shui masters say that sleeping with your head facing north (which most dogs do) increases circulation, slows heart rate, and improves metabolism.

Love unconditionally: Expect nothing in return.

Heed your instincts: Don't overintellectualize your impulses.

Live simply: Shelter, food, love—is there really anything else?

Have a master: Find a mentor.

Keep yourself well-groomed: Both for the image you project and for your self-respect.

Get excited about going for a walk: It's still the simplest, safest, and most effective form of exercise.

Bask in praise: Don't humbly deflect what you've earned.

Let yourself be petted: Periodically surrender to a massage therapist.

Be affectionate: It's unhealthy to hide your emotions.

Chew: A stick of gum after eating cleans teeth and aids digestion.

Wear a collar: Dress shirts command respect.

Be wary of pussy: Woof!

It's early on another winter morning, and I'm walking D.O.G. across the frozen athletic fields of our local community college. There's no one around, and the space is vast, so I decide to conduct an impromptu experiment. I reach down and unclip her from the leash. In other words, I set her free.

It takes a moment for her to recognize the absence of restraint. When she exceeds her usual boundaries, she looks at me briefly in puzzlement. But then she's off! She runs full speed across the field, all four legs simultaneously off the ground like a thoroughbred. As the gap between us widens and my nervousness grows, she suddenly stops, sits, and looks back. Her tongue lolls out the side of her mouth and her ears prick to attention. It's a moment of decision.

But with just as much joy as she ran away with, D.O.G. accelerates again and sprints back to me. I praise her tail into a blur, then together we head into the adjoining woods, following a deer trail through abandoned apple orchards. She insists on scouting the way, but whenever she gets too far ahead, she diligently turns and waits for me.

We spend an hour like this, and it is bliss. In fact, I've experienced few things more comforting and contemplative. This dog just made a choice. She picked me over being free.

There's a horribly tacky plaque sold in 99-cent stores and inspirational boutiques that bears a picture of a soaring bird and the words "If you love something, set it free. If it loves you, it'll come back." No doubt, you've seen it. But this was the first time I had ever worked up enough courage to try it.

Girlfriends, wives, children, dogs—I should have been doing it all along. It's a gauge of personal worthiness. Although it's risky to unsnap that leash and invite something to run away, it's ultimately more perilous to tighten the harness and make it stay. We are all meant to be independent, uncaged, and free. And it's the choices we make when in this state that are the most sincere, enduring, and meaningful.

We're approaching the end of the trail, and I call D.O.G. back. She comes immediately. "Good girl," I say, rubbing her neck.

How I wish I had done this with my other dog. But there's no way for me to right that regret, no way to get Inky back. It's one of those forever laments you learn to live with, because there is no possible recompense. But there's a key word in the sentence you just read that harbors some solace and redemption. The only way to eventually accept a regret is to open your mind and *learn* from it. The moment you recognize the mistake in whatever it is you fouled up, you've made good. You can move on. You've cleared your conscience.

This is all that the wronged desire: an unspoken apology, a realization, a change, a choice. This is all that's needed to put them (and you) at peace. I may have failed one pet and many people along the way, but I can continue to live with myself because I do better with their successors.

CHAPTER 19

not having a hero

I almost puked in Jack La Lanne's bedroom.

All over his flowery bedspread, right on his plush carpet, in plain view of his sweet wife, Elaine, who was finishing her makeup.

But I'm getting ahead of myself.

It's not yet 7:00 A.M., and I'm trying to match Jack in his everyday series of gut-busting, good-morning exercises. Never mind that's he's 85 and I'm 40. The old man is snarling and cussing and methodically humbling my ass.

"This is not pussy stuff, boy," he barks, as I hang from a chin-up bar in his sprawling California home. "Come on, make it hurt! Once more! *Harder!* Outta my way, kid. Watch this."

And he grabs the bar, locks his knees, and proceeds to slowly swing his legs forward and upward until his toes nearly touch the ceiling. Then he does it again and again and again. While doing so, he taunts his muscles as if they were street thugs surrounding him in an alley.

"C'mon, you bastards!" he yells. "See, you gotta talk to 'em

These muscles are saying, 'I can't do it anymore.' The hell you can't! I won't feed you! You sons of bitches work for me, Jack La Lanne! These muscles are my servants."

Finally, he drops to the floor, not even winded. "Feel these mothers," he says proudly, slapping his gut. "Go ahead, hit me. *Hit me!*"

And when I do (although somewhat hesitantly), his stomach is as flat and hard as a cinder block.

"Now come over here. I'm going to give you a little something I want you to do for a month. It's called the Hindu jump. I invented this exercise way back when I was in my teens, damn near."

Jack pushes me down into a squat, then orders me to jump as high as I can. "Drop your butt almost to the floor! Now jump high, *higher!*" After a series of these, he has me do splits—front leg bent 90 degrees, back leg extended, dip down, then quickly alternate. Finally, he raises his arm to chest level and tells me to march in place, goading me to touch my knees to his hand.

"I do six sets of these three exercises," he growls when I collapse after one.

And that's when I feel like I'm going to be sick.

Jack La Lanne is to inactivity what Jonas Salk is to polio—its scourge, its antidote. His TV exercise show debuted in 1951, and 8 years later, when it was syndicated nationally, he became America's first personal trainer. Dressed in what would become his trademark one-piece jumpsuit and ballet slippers, the former Mr. Professional America charmed housewives everywhere.

"I have never seen an ugly woman in my life," he said on that first show, "because I see what she can be. We're going to do this together. I'm going to come into your home each day. Let's be friends."

And using nothing more than an ordinary kitchen chair, he'd get them bending and panting and perspiring. He'd talk candidly about their inner thighs, butts, and bustlines. He'd even sing to them when he was done. This daily 30-minute affair left aproned America flushed in more ways than one.

And in case any husbands considered him a namby-pamby, he performed incredible feats of strength, such as doing 1,033 pushups in 23 minutes, swimming from Alcatraz to Fisherman's Wharf in San Francisco while handcuffed and shackled, and paddling the 6½-mile length of the Golden Gate Channel towing a 2,500-pound cabin cruiser.

No stunt was more audacious, though, than his offering a $10,000 bounty to anyone who could keep pace with him in his regular morning workout. Lots of guys took this challenge, but no one ever collected. He beat all comers, including a young Arnold Schwarzenegger. Although Jack no longer publicly offers such a reward, I'd convinced him to let me try for an article that would appear in *Men's Health* magazine. And that's why I'm in his bedroom doing twisting crunches and Hindu jumps before the sun is even up. I'm going after that 10 grand.

But there's another, more personal, reason why I'm here—a subtle regret that has gnawed at me for years. Prior to this, I wrote a book called *The Father's Guide to the Meaning of Life.* The most difficult part was choosing five men to spotlight in a brief chapter called "A Father's Heroes." No matter how introspective I forced myself to be, there was really no one in my 40 years who meant that much to me.

As a boy, I had the usual sports heroes: Manny Sanguillen, the wild-swinging catcher for the Pittsburgh Pirates; Julius Erving, the notorious Dr. J in his ABA days; and just about any member of Vince Lombardi's Green Bay Packers, football's greatest dynasty.

But these faded when I realized that they were all just ordinary men in valorous uniforms. What changed my opinion was a job in the sports department at the local newspaper. Occasionally, I assisted the beat reporter for the Philadelphia Phillies, which meant I went into the locker room after games and actually met some of these "role models." But Pete Rose turned out to have the foulest mouth of anyone I'd ever heard speak, and Tommy Lasorda sprayed food at us across his buffet-laden desk during interviews. They were both just pinstriped pigs.

As a teenager, I had the usual war heroes: Harry Truman, because I'd read his autobiography for school; General George Patton, because I liked the opening scene to his movie; and "Desert Fox" Erwin Rommel, the German field marshal, because I'd built a plastic model of his combat vehicle.

But these faded, too, when I realized that they were all pretty ruthless individuals who had killed thousands of people. Good guys, bad guys, it didn't matter. Growing up in the wake of Vietnam, I came to regard all war as murder and the behavior that commands it reprehensible.

As an adult, I idolized my father after he died. But as the shock of that subsided, I came to see that my reaction was mostly reflex. He was a worthy but simple man who left no legacy except a son with aspirations. Even now, almost a decade later, it's difficult to separate the obligation I feel to make him my hero from the reality of how he actually inspired me.

So when it came time to write that chapter, to list the heroes I have as a typical middle-age man, husband, and father, I was empty. In the end, I chose a few guys who are certainly laudable but are really far from Ulyssian. I think that this is a weakness of my generation. There aren't any heroes left. The media has torn down the veil of mystery that heroism requires. There isn't anyone worth emulating because there are no more enigmas. The more we know about people, the more ordinary they become.

Predictably, after having so many near-heroes dashed by the press, we've become cynical and independent. But although we may have stopped following, we have not yet ceased hoping. Part of us still craves inspiration and covets strength, leadership, and conviction. It's not necessarily perfection that we're after, just someone slightly above our present condition to give us some direction.

Too many people today are lost, navigating without instruments in a fog. And that's why stress has become our nation's biggest killer, the underlying cause of most major illnesses. We need someone to look up to besides God, someone closer to earth and the reality of our 9-to-5 existence. We need someone human whom we can identify with and admire. Someone to say, quite simply, "This is the way."

A child grows by digesting his heroes, his ongoing succession of role models. He consumes their best traits like milk, and from them, builds himself a skeleton, a foundation. Adults need to keep doing this, too, especially middle-age men like me adrift in their second adolescence.

So I have this unspoken hope for Jack, that he just might turn out to be the mentor I've never found. Part of me says I'm foolish, that the man is a nut, a maniac, capable of nothing more than out-landish publicity stunts. But the more I train my body in prepara-tion for his $10,000 challenge, the more I come to appreciate the conditioning of the 85-year-old man who's delivering it. And the deeper I delve into his background, the more awestruck, expectant, and intimidated I become.

Jack was a skinny weakling who built his body up, then appar-ently never let it go to pot. On his 70th birthday, he towed 70 boats bearing 70 people 1½ miles across Long Beach Harbor while hand-cuffed and shackled. When a car accident banged up his knees later in life, he had a chinup bar installed over his hospital bed the day after surgery. His typical breakfast has long consisted of 400 dif-ferent vitamin and mineral supplements, for a while chased with fresh blood from a slaughterhouse. Occasionally, he has even com-pared himself to Jesus—a preacher of rebirth, an invincible being, a genuine miracle worker.

But it's this magazine quote that scared me most: *I believe in vig-orous, violent, daily, systematic exercise to the point of muscle failure.* Ev-idently, this has been Jack's credo ever since he was 15. In the same article, he claimed to have never missed a workout during that time and presented a 49-inch chest, 27-inch waist, and 17-inch biceps as proof.

So it is with a mixture of trepidation and expectation that I sidestep barking dogs and barbell topiary to ring Jack's doorbell at 6:45 A.M. The evening before, when I'd called to confirm, he said he'd decided to cut me a break and push back his typical 4:00 A.M. workout until 7:00 so I could sleep in. Brenda, his publicist, had also taken some last-minute pity on me, recommending that I bring a wetsuit since the January temperature in his outdoor training pool is a crisp 55 degrees.

"You're early," Jack snaps as he opens the door and squints at me, my photographer, and our two assistants. "You brought a damn army! I thought you were coming alone. Elaine! Let's get this thing going!"

And with only a perfunctory greeting, he hustles us into his bedroom, lies down on an upholstered bench, and immediately begins to exercise—*hard*. At such proximity, the legend is still impressively large, but my hope for victory is buoyed by some noticeable dents in the armor. There are a few small holes in Jack's blue velour jumpsuit. I have to speak loudly and clearly in order for him to hear me. He alludes to a recent shoulder injury. He's just 5½ feet tall, not a centimeter more. And he can't instantly recall the names of his two watchdogs, Nicki and Princess.

He seems like the quintessential grandpa—cute, absentminded, and delightfully ornery—until you notice those impressive muscles and his remarkable flexibility. He boasts that a recent computer analysis pegged his physiological age at 29. Indeed, with his tousled red hair and bright eyes, he looks no more than 55.

As he grunts out 10-rep sets of various types of crunches, Jack gradually warms into his stage persona. When it's my turn to duplicate what's been done, he's pumped up and ready to go on. Stop. Look. Listen. It's time for the *Jack La Lanne Show* from Hollywood. . . . But unlike those housewife workouts he did on TV, this one flirts with agony. My gut burns as he hovers over me.

"Contract everything as hard as you can!" he raves. "C'mon!"

I keep pace on this part of the challenge, then follow him to the narrow doorway separating bedroom from bathroom. He pushes mightily against the frame with the outsides of both arms, while stepping first forward and then back again. When I try, I feel contractions that must rival childbirth. But I grimace and keep doing it.

Next we're in the lavatory, where on the floor in front of the bathtub is a small device that looks like it came from the 1940s. Called the Mini-Gym, it resembles a bathroom scale except that the needle specifies not weight but the amount of force generated when you pull on a foot-long handle. We take turns standing on the thing, doing overhead presses, bent-over rows, and pull-up presses. When he finishes his set, he starts singing, "*To dream the impossible dream. . . .*" Although these exercises hurt like hell, I'm proud to notice that I'm yanking more forcefully than Jack. Despite his bravado, maybe he'll crack.

But any hopes I had for pocketing the cash quickly disintegrate when he touches his toes to the ceiling and has me do those Hindu jumps. I had lasted all of 20 minutes. "See why I had that $10,000 challenge?" asks Jack, as I gradually fight back my nausea. "These exercises would wipe them out. Plus, when I work out alone, I never rest more than 10 seconds between sets. . . . That's it for the warmup. Let's go to the gym."

Jack actually has two gyms in his home, one that's a daily workout room and another that's a sort of museum. The latter is stuffed with memorabilia, photographs, and trophies, but most notably the exercise devices he invented and used in his original Oakland health club in 1936. He calls these his babies, the crude predecessors of what eventually evolved into sleek, chromed weight selectors, cable pulleys, leg extensions, and Smith machines. He never patented any of them, claiming that he just wanted to help people, not make money. Whether it was philanthropy or foolishness is tough to tell, but he explains it with such characteristic intensity that I want to believe him.

Jack's gym and certain niches of his home have a mad-scientist feel to them. He's constantly pointing to various contraptions. "That one over there fits in a corner, and you can do over 200 exercises with it," he explains with a pitchman's fervor. "You want to market it? A guy could take this and be a millionaire in a year, no doubt about it. It's terrific."

Such inventiveness is fueled by an almost manic desire for new challenges and diversity. "Fitness starts between your ears," Jack says, poking himself there. "Your muscles, what the hell do they know? Nothing. It's brains. If you had to eat carrots for the rest of your life, you'd go nuts. It's variety, see? That's why I change my workout completely every 30 days, and that's why when I had my gym, I'd invent a new piece of equipment every month or two to keep my students' interest up. *Variety!*"

By now, we're well into the second third of the workout, and even though his $10,000 is secure, Jack isn't letting up. Lat pulldowns, seated rows, dumbbell circles, and swings—on every one, he lifts at least 50 more pounds than I do. Inevitably, he does his set, watches me struggling with mine, then yells, "Hold on, kiddo, that's too heavy for you!" It's a thoroughly humbling thing.

What's worse, while I'm sweating under the iron, Jack is coming on to my wife, whom I'd introduced as an anonymous note-taking assistant. "You're looking really great. You have a good butt. I thought you'd be topless! Are you married or are you happy?" Fortunately, these comments aren't dropped in a lecherous way but in the style of a guy who's brimming with life and lust and has reached the age when he can finally say anything he wants. Publicist Brenda, dressed in a bright green miniskirt, arrives for work and kisses him full on the lips. Elaine, who's in her mid-seventies and still carries the nickname Iron Buns, is obviously used to it. She and Jack have been married for nearly half a century.

"You getting any help from Viagra?" I ask, in an effort to reassert my manliness.

"Are you kidding?" he scoffs. "I wake up every morning with an erection a cat can't scratch. Trouble is, I don't know what the hell to do with it. Let me tell you something, kid. I never think of age. Never, ever. And I never think of dying. I think of *living*. Any stupid ass can die. That's the easiest thing there is. But living, boy, you have to work at it."

And Jack certainly does. His diligence with his exercise and especially his diet is admittedly obsessive. "If man makes it, I don't eat it," he says. "And I don't eat anything that comes from a cow—butter, cream, milk. I'm no suckling calf. That goes for chicken, too. They're filthy creatures."

Breakfast, his biggest meal of the day, consists of a blended concoction of juice, wheat germ, brewer's yeast, bone meal, protein powder, and handfuls of vitamins and minerals. He drinks it immediately after his workout, when he's too thirsty to mind the wretched taste. Lunch is five pieces of fresh fruit. Dinner is a salad with 10 raw vegetables and fresh fish. The total is 2,000 daily calories. If he and Elaine are at a restaurant, he'll call out the chef and make sure "he doesn't give me any crap." Some sashimi, an occasional glass of wine, a few spoonfuls of frozen yogurt—these are the extremes of his culinary indulgence.

"Look at my Corvette, a '98—one of the finest sports cars I've ever had. Would I put water in the gas tank? Well, think about the crap people put in their bodies—white flour, sugar, all this processed food. It's just like using water for fuel. With every bite I take, I'm thinking, 'Jack, this is helping your hair, your teeth, your sex life. You're going to feel better, have more energy.' I love it! Everyone should eat this way. They should be thinking, 'This is going to give me a big fat ass or make me constipated.' Then they wouldn't eat it. We're combustion engines, just like my Corvette."

And with that, he abruptly tells me it's time to get wet.

"Strangers in the Night" is playing softly in the poolyard when I step outside dressed in my new wetsuit. Jack is already in the adjacent hot tub, suspiciously absent of any insulation except swim trunks. Only his head is visible, and he's grimacing as he tries to quickly move a pair of Hydro-tones back and forth through the water. Aqua aerobics is another area of invention for Jack; in this case, he's using what look like oversize plastic pool toys to do dumbbell flies.

"I pretend I have a walnut between my shoulder blades, and I'm trying to squash it as I pull back," he explains, grunting. "Then I pretend I have a nut in the middle of my chest that I'm trying to crack as I push forward. It's a bitch. Now get in the pool."

I toe the icy water, then follow orders. He drill-sergeants me through another series of bizarre exercises. While floating on my stomach and gripping the side of the pool, he has me kick as fast as I can without bending my knees. ("C'mon, get your legs out of the water! Harder, harder, harder, harder, *harder!*") Then he throws me a pair of neoprene mitts (another creation) and has me do a bunch of arm exercises against the increased water resistance. ("How about those babies? Tougher than weights, am I right?") Next, he tells me to tread water like a drowning man, as quickly as possible. ("Keep going, don't stop, *breathe!*") Finally, he waves toward a white strap lying on the sidewalk and says, "Put that on."

It's the crudest device yet. It looks like a seat belt that's been ripped from an old Buick. It's attached to a thick, braided rope that's bolted to the concrete pool edge. "Now buckle it around your waist and start butterflying," says Jack, his cheeks infuriatingly pink from all that hot water.

Despite its primitive appearance, the harness works surprisingly well, allowing me to swim in place relatively unencumbered, yet with noticeable resistance. But I'm no butterflier, and my thrashing prompts Nicki and Princess to start barking. They sense that someone's in trouble.

After just a few minutes, I start to tire and thank God for the extra buoyancy my wetsuit provides. When Jack yells at me to switch over to freestyle, it gets only marginally easier. "How does it feel?" he taunts, finally telling me to halt. "I used to do that for an hour when I was training for my boat pulls."

The genius behind Jack's training style is intensity. Every exercise is done as hard as possible. There's no squandering of effort, no wasting of time. He rolls his eyes at step aerobics, lambasts Suzanne

Somers and her ThighMaster, and shakes his head at those guys reading newspapers on Lifecycles. If you're going to make the effort to work out, then go *all out*. Even when you're lifting weights, it'll raise your heart rate enough to simultaneously supply a cardiovascular workout.

Completeness is Jack's other fitness caveat. He claims that he works every one of the 640 muscles in his body every day. This includes goofy facial contortions to discourage wrinkling (don't laugh—he's had no cosmetic surgery) and picking up marbles with his toes while watching TV.

After the challenge is finished and all 640 of my muscles are sufficiently aggravated, Jack leads me through a hallway hung with photos of him and Hope and Streisand and Tormé, and up the stairs into what he terms his little escape. I brace for another torture chamber. But it's a room, above and beyond all the rest, decorated in strong earth tones—the obvious lair of the man of the house. There's a deck with a marvelous view of the surrounding hills, an aquarium with tropical fish that Jack talks to, a big-screen TV on which he likes to watch sports, and a luxurious leather recliner that swallows him when he sinks into it. For the first time today, he is motionless.

I have been thoroughly impressed by this man—his ability, his spirit, his gutter wisdom. But watching him here, there's another feeling I start to have. It's sadness (or dare I say pity?) because I can tell that he's clinging. When I tried to put a tape measure around his famous physique, he balked, conceding that his chest is a less-impressive 46, waist 30, and biceps 15 only because he's no longer competing. But I think he's exaggerating. He doesn't want the world to see that he's slipped, that Jack La Lanne isn't invincible, that ultimately death *will* ruin his image. Sitting here in his easy chair, reading me jokes from a list he keeps by the phone for radio interviews, he seems tired, and not from the exercise.

For everything he's accomplished, for all the millions he's made, in this room, at this moment, he seems forgotten and remarkably hidden away. Although he still does lecture tours, produces exercise videos, talks of returning to television, and helps Elaine run BeFit Enterprises, most people are surprised to learn he's still alive.

For a generation of baby boomers who are doing everything possible to ensure that they'll never die, it seems ironic that we've overlooked the poster boy. Exercise, nutrition, all our healthful disciplines have already been extrapolated out in him. There's living proof for the beneficial hell we subject ourselves to, and it's the man in the blue velour jumpsuit. He is me. He is you. If we're smart. If we take care of ourselves.

Not that we won't die. Not that we won't age. Just that we will do both with vibrancy, grace, and dignity. That's the last exercise in Jack's show, the one he's teaching us now.

After all these years, I've found my hero.

CHAPTER 20

missing our wedding

Maria and I had been pronounced man and wife just 10 hours earlier. Now we were sitting in a booth at Salvatore's Pizza, our eyes entwined over a large cheese-and-onion pie.

"It's over," I say sadly.

"That's it," my bride agrees.

"I really wanted it to last," I insist.

"So did I," she admits.

"Maybe next time," I joke.

"Yeah, maybe next time," she laughs.

That was 15 years, two children, five jobs, and three mortgages ago. Despite what you may have concluded from that conversation, Maria and I are still together. Rather than discussing annulment, we had been commiserating about our wedding. Somehow, it had gotten away from us. Parents, caterers, photographers, relatives . . . despite their good intentions, they had quietly transformed *our* day into *their* day and left us feeling a little lost.

Don't get me wrong, ours was a great wedding. From the char-tered bus that brought all my relatives to tiny Forty Fort, Pennsyl-vania, to the pea brain in the wedding party who forgot to pick up my mother-in-law in time for the ceremony. From the angelic look on Maria's face when she lifted her veil, to the tremble in our youthful voices as we exchanged *I do's*. From the raucous reception with the live rock band to the earnest grandpa who collected al-most $500 from a simple bridal dance. From the stretch limo that whisked us home to a star-filled bottle of 1975 Dom Perignon. Everyone said our wedding was so much fun, we wished we had been guests instead of guests of honor.

To us, it was a blur. I was 25 and Maria was 22—neither of us was accustomed to so much attention. All the people we had ever known in our lives were present, and it was overwhelming. In every direction we turned was another familiar face, another hand we hadn't shaken, or another cheek we hadn't kissed since childhood. We were in love *and* in demand, and that is a totally stupefying combination.

Plus, we had this photographer named Sid Frackowitz. He had wild white hair and black, horn-rimmed glasses. All day long Sid kept motioning us here, positioning us there. To his lens, there was no such thing as the decisive moment. In fact, we missed most of the reception dinner because we were outside in search of the per-fect backdrop. Fittingly, ours was one of the last weddings Sid did. He became a door-to-door hearing-aid salesman shortly afterward.

So by the time we had fulfilled all our obligations and finally started to relax into the party, it was over. We had rented the hall from 1:00 to 5:00 P.M., but since there was another reception sched-uled for 7:00, we were efficiently hustled out. It seemed like we were waving goodbye before we'd even gotten to say some genuine hellos.

It was late September in the Pocono Mountains, and the col-orful leaves were smeared by our limousine's speed as we glided home. It was a fitting final scene to a day that had swept by and left us numb. Later in our condominium, having swapped wedding

dress and tuxedo for shorts and T-shirts, our exciting new life suddenly became routine. It was 9 o'clock on a Saturday night and we
were hungry, so like thousands of other married couples, we went
out for pizza.

It all seemed so anticlimactic. This was the biggest day of our
lives, the focus of our attentions for almost a year. Now we were in
its wake, the beneficiaries of four woks, two wooden salad sets, four
pairs of brass candlesticks, a crystal sugar dish, and nearly $7,000 in
personal checks. Sure, we were appreciative, but as with all wide-
eyed, expectant children, there's always a bit of a letdown the day
after Christmas.

That's why we decided to make one more vow to each other
before our wedding day was over, a private promise exchanged over
a linoleum altar with Salvatore himself as our witness: That some
day we'd do it all again and get remarried *our* way.

And now, a decade-and-a-half later, that time is at hand. While
everyone is trying to figure out a novel way to welcome the new
millennium, we know. On December 31, 1999, we'll get married
all over again.

Besides righting a mutual regret, there are deeper feelings at
work. Our love is no longer breathless. A soft touch from one does
not guarantee a quiver in the other. We have become familiar. So
accustomed are we that it's difficult to even tickle each other. But
this is not as mundane as it sounds. An enduring relationship supplies comfort, safety, and quiet reassurance. Our passion has become
strength; our former giddiness, resolve. We have survived our own
infatuation with each other, which few couples do. And while the
day-to-day romance may have ebbed, our love has grown. We have
matured into one another, becoming more alike yet still different,
but together nonetheless. And we are most thankful and proud of
that.

This is the perspective we bring to our second marriage. It's
not so much our future that has us starstruck this time, as it is our
past. In an age when 67 percent of first marriages end in divorce,
we managed to survive. We built this life and even created two

new ones. We found each other and seemingly got it right the first time.

It is truly a dream that we have lived (although usually only in retrospect do we awaken to it). We honestly never thought we had it in us to be a husband, a wife, a father, a mother, a breadwinner, a role model, and most sobering of all, a middle-age couple.

The thing I fear most as I get older is losing Maria, whether to death or to my own ignorance. I am not so good at maintenance. I stall over "I love you," and I've never seen the point to wasting money on cards or flowers. I assume she understands how I feel, realizing at the same time that love thrives on reminders. That's why I want to get married again. I want to say everything I should have been saying all along.

I want her to know.

Unfortunately, we can't renew our vows at the little mountain chapel where we were originally wed because it has been demolished. It's the first time I've ever witnessed an amen applied to a Catholic church. Like its parishioners, I thought each one had an eternal soul. But there's nothing left of this one now, except an empty parking lot. Good thing we're not superstitious.

So we broach the idea of a millennium wedding with our best friends, Sue and Bob. Like us, they've been married for 15 years. But unlike us, they own a huge, cathedral-like home. "Suppose we all get married?" we propose. And graciously, they accept—both the invitation and the job of host and hostess.

The plan is this: We'll invite a half-dozen couples—our best married friends—to participate in a New Year's Eve renewal of vows. We'll even fly in Maria's brother—Father John, a bona fide Catholic priest—to make the ceremony official. There will be no parents, no relatives, no caterers, no Sid Frackowitzes. Every husband will wear a tuxedo; every wife her original wedding dress. *(Inhale, honey! Inhale!)* The men will have white rose corsages; the women, a déjà-vu bouquet of their bridal flowers. We'll play all the traditional wedding hymns, including the special song that each couple first danced to as man and wife.

For the reception, we'll have an all-night buffet. Each person will be responsible for bringing the absolute best food or drink: chateaubriand, caviar, lobster, champagne, truffles. . . . And of course, we'll have a cake—multitiered and opulent—that we can slice and shove in each other's faces.

Sue promises to decorate her house to match the formality of the occasion. She'll drape garland off the second-floor balconies, set gold-plated utensils and Royal Daulton on the buffet table, and even add new wallpaper and fresh sheets to some of the honeymoon suites. That is, if anyone cares to sleep. This time, there will be no deadline on the celebration. It'll continue as long as there are people willing to continue it.

So we send out formal invitations and find five other couples who either are as enchanted with this idea as we are or are just looking for a cache of food in case of a Y2K disaster.

Like true middle-age men, we husbands talk mightily of organizing a bachelor party. Stag films, strippers, a half-keg. But in the end, we're all too busy and tired, and we never get around to it.

But there's one tradition I don't blow off. Since Maria and I will be getting married, I feel it's my duty to properly ask for her hand. In fact, I've always regretted the way I originally proposed. I was leaving on a month-long European bicycling trip, and frankly, I was afraid of losing her, even though we'd been dating for almost 4 years. She shared an apartment with this wild redhead named Dawn, and I knew Dawn would have Maria out dancing every night while I was gone. Maria said she loved me, but when you're 21, gorgeous, and lubed with alcohol, it doesn't take much temptation to make you forget your vacationing boyfriend. I realized it was a selfish thing to do, but I was that in love and that insecure. (Years later, I learned my ploy hadn't worked; Maria just threw the engagement ring on her dresser and slipped into a short skirt.)

To buy the ring, I cashed in my stock-savings trust at the newspaper where I worked. It was all the money I had ($3,500), and I exchanged it for a half-carat diamond at Bixler's Jewelers. It was the most agonizing purchase of my life, not because I was trying to win a woman's heart but because no matter how closely I looked through that damn "gemscope," I couldn't see any color or clarity differences. Just wanting it to end, I finally said, "I'll take that one" and saw my entire life savings reduced to a pebble in the palm of my hand. (Six months later, my newspaper was bought by Times-Mirror, and the three grand would have been worth seven.)

I took Maria to a country restaurant called the Weldon House. She was embarrassed because she had a cold sore on her lip, but I was too anxious to notice. She looked stunning nonetheless. After dinner, I had planned to ask the waiter to place the ring on his dessert tray, then casually mention that Maria could have the pecan pie, the ladyfingers, or, perhaps, *this*.

But I chickened out. The restaurant was busy, and our waiter was harried. So I merely slipped the ring from my pocket during dessert and asked her to marry me. Surprised and flustered, her hand subconsciously flew up to her lip. She blushed, got a little choked up, and quickly agreed. I was so naïve and self-conscious, I actually hushed her so no one around us would see. And they didn't. There was no congratulatory applause from the other diners, no complimentary bottle of champagne from the house proprietor. I simply paid the bill, and we left. We held hands all the way home in my Camaro.

Proposing a second time wasn't any easier. In fact, there was probably more pressure because I wanted it to be perfect. I took Maria to a country restaurant called the Glasbern Inn. (The Weldon House had burned years earlier and subsequently been demolished; is this some kind of trend?) She was embarrassed because another cold sore had bloomed on her lip, but once again, I was too anxious to notice. She still looked stunning to me. I'd had her original stone reset in an anniversary band containing six princess-cut diamonds. It was breathtaking, and this time, it wasn't just because of the price.

We sat by the fire, the best table in the house, chatting about all the things that married couples do—the small talk of households, children, and careers, but rarely focusing down to the two. That's what I wanted to bring back. That's what this evening was all about. Her and me, and nothing else. Was it still in us?

After dinner, I excused myself to seek out the maitre d'. He was aware of my plans and congratulated me profusely. I put the ring in his hand and joked that he shouldn't assume she'd say yes. After all, I was giving her an option, a choice, an honest chance to reconsider for the first time in 15 years.

Back at the table, I sat knotting the linen napkin in my lap, glancing for the waitress who would deliver our desserts. Finally, she placed my mousse in front of me and then unveiled Maria's crème brûlée from beneath a silver serving lid. The ring, in a green velvet box, was elegantly set on a single red leaf. But Maria didn't immediately notice it. In fact, she gazed right by, perhaps thinking it just an elaborate garnish.

"My, that certainly looks rich," I hinted, with a touch of panic.

And that's when she saw it, and she knew, and I asked her to marry me all over again. She was surprised and flustered; her hand subconsciously flew up to her lip. She blushed, got a little choked up, and to my relief, quickly agreed. The other patrons smiled upon us, and the maitre d' and waitress expressed their sincerest best wishes. The innkeeper even gave us a specially engraved ornament. After we had paid the check and left, we held hands all the way home in our Dodge Grand Caravan.

It's 2:00 P.M. on New Year's Eve—7 hours before the ceremony—but I'm already in my tuxedo. It's basic black this time, not satin gray (thankfully) like when I first got married. I intend to do everything possible to enjoy this day. I want to savor it, stretch it out, let its importance settle in. A little melodrama, but a lot of fun. That's my intention.

A lot of guys don't understand it, though. Whenever I mentioned what I was doing to male co-workers and friends, they thought it was unique but didn't seem to fully comprehend. They appeared a little surprised and puzzled as to why a man would want to do this. The male nature is to chase, conquer, and then procreate. Once this is accomplished, there's no evolutionary urge to repeat the process, at least not with the same woman. Even though men know it's romantic and sweet, when there's nothing left to win, there's no need to compete.

Conversely, the married women I told became instantly wistful. "How *nice*," they'd say, "I'd *love* to do that." But it's as if they'd already dismissed the possibility, accepting long ago that life is rarely a romance novel. "Maybe on our 50th anniversary. . . ." I wanted to shake them and say, "Why wait?" Why not repeat your vows every year, as a reminder of promises made and love felt? It can't hurt. Maybe churches, for all their lordly ranting about family and monogamy, should schedule such ceremonies regularly. Twice a year, right after Sunday service, for anyone who cares to participate. I bet it would touch more people than any sermon would.

Later, when the guests have all arrived, we conduct a brief rehearsal—where to stand, what the priest will say, when to take each other's hand. The women aren't in their wedding gowns just yet. We don't want to snub the drama of their grand entrance. The buffet and Sue and Bob's house are just as impressive as envisioned. All that's needed to complete the ambiance is a soloist and a pipe organ.

Each couple has brought their wedding album. The albums lay open on a coffee table—the pages becoming increasingly smudged by incredulous fingerprints. I am unanimously voted the person who has changed the most. I'm 40 pounds lighter now than I was then, but not all of this is due to exercise and better nutrition. Most of my thick, curly hair is gone. And I've taken to wearing glasses instead of contact lenses. The difference is startling. Physically, I am not the man Maria married. Yet she doesn't seem to notice. She still loves me. My wife, though, has hardly changed. In fact, she's much prettier than before. I wonder if my love, which has yet to be tested so dramatically by time, is just as true as hers. Or maybe she *has* changed, and I, too, am forever blind to it.

When the hour for the ceremony finally arrives, the grooms assemble in the hall at the base of the stairway. We pace stiffly like men do in formal situations, feeling awkward and pinched by our collars and cummerbunds. Our brides are upstairs, tittering like schoolgirls at a dress-up. As before, they make us wait.

Then the wedding march begins, and we all stand up straight with hands crossed—men this time, not boys. Instead of looking down the aisle, we gaze up at the second-floor landing, searching, just like we did from the altar years ago.

Whenever I attend a wedding, I always watch the face of the groom while the bride is walking toward him. His expression is usually a mixture of terror, stupidity, and pride. This time, though, I only see the latter. We all know what we're getting into.

With bouquet in hand, each born-again bride drifts down the staircase, takes the arm of her man, and disappears into the living room. When Maria finally appears on the landing, I feel a surprising amount of emotion well up inside me. I haven't seen her in this dress for 15 years, and she looks now just as she did. There are moments in life that you know you'll never forget, even while they're happening. Your mind temporarily disconnects, steps back, and marks this segment with an asterisk. This is one of those moments for me. She descends in slow-motion, eyes cast demurely down, the wave of brown hair on her forehead capped by a lacy white crown. When she puts her arm through mine, I feel strong. Like I know the way, and she trusts me to take her there.

Everyone forms a half-circle around the fire, and Father John says some introductory prayers. Pinch-hitting for Sid Frackowitz are our two kids. Fourteen-year-old Paul is capturing everything on video, and 11-year-old Claire is taking snapshots with a digital camera. I wonder what they'll record in their own memories of this. Whether they'll frame it as a corny stunt, or if at some point in their future lives they'll be genuinely touched. If it's true that the greatest thing parents can do for their children is to show them that they love each other, then we've just given ours a valuable gift. If not, then they'd better at least be keeping the cameras in focus.

Father John has brought 16 tall, ivory candles that he blesses and lights as symbols of the love that flickers inside each one of us. Then he says how impressed he is with us for giving our marriages priority on this eve of resolutions and fresh starts. He sprinkles our rings with holy water thrown from a balsam limb and repeats the vows that we heard so many years ago but have, sadly, not uttered since.

Maria and I add some of our own, preferring not to trust any priest or prophet to put the perfect words in our mouths. "I marry you again because . . ." is how we start, first Maria, then I, alternating back and forth:

"Because somewhere in the beginning of time, I believe we were meant for each other."

"Because you're more beautiful than you were 15 years ago—outside and inside."

"Because you make me think."

"Because you're positive, outgoing, and still one of the most fun people I know."

"Because you still think I'm beautiful."

"Because I'm curious about what you'll be like when you reach 40 and hit your sexual peak."

"Because you continue to surprise me."

"Because you're an incredible cook."

"Because you're not afraid to work on and improve our marriage."

"Because without you, I am half what I am."

"Because every day you try to be the best husband and parent that you can."

"Because even though I don't always say it or show it, I am still madly in love with you."

And so it ends with a kiss, somehow more tender than the first, and the swell of the wedding march, which buoys us up and out of the room. We flinch in anticipation of rice not thrown. (Sue, who'll ultimately have to clean up this mess, imposed a moratorium.)

There also aren't any tin cans or "Just Married" signs tied to our fenders, since none of us are going anywhere. We considered a group honeymoon, but decided it wasn't wise to fly on the first day of the new millennium.

And good thing. By the time this reception ends at 3:30 A.M., I am neither capable of carrying my bride across the threshold nor, pitifully, consummating. But neither of us is disappointed. We lie in bed, pleasantly exhausted.

"It's over," I whisper.

"That's it," my bride agrees.

"You know, I really wanted it to last," I say.

"So did I," she admits.

"Maybe next time," I joke.

"Yeah, maybe next time," she laughs.

conclusion

There you have it: 20 second chances, 20 regrets relived, 20 answers to questions I'd always wondered about and sometimes even feared. It has been the most entertaining year of my life, and it has taught me a great deal about myself. I am not the same middle-age guy I was before I started this journey. I am a bit more confident and slightly less baffled. But what you've read is just a portion of what I actually did. These are the 20 regrets that made good stories, the ones I learned the most from. There were others that didn't pan out so well:

Ballroom dancing: I've always wished I knew how to dance, so my wife and I took a course at the local community college in waltz, swing, polka, and fox-trot. Our big finish was supposed to be dinner and dancing at the fabled Rainbow Room in New York City, but after 10 weeks, the only steps I had down were the slow, dejected ones from classroom to parking lot. The instructor said I had "something," but he didn't specify what. I know now that it isn't rhythm or coordination.

Driving a truck: At the same college that offers ballroom dancing, there's a class called Professional Tractor-Trailer Driving. Although I'm not interested in a new career in trucking, I've always regretted never captaining anything bigger than a Ford Expedition. Unfortunately (or fortunately, depending on how much time you spend on the freeway), learning to drive a big rig is serious business. When I saw 158 hours of study and $3,650 of tuition looming in my rearview, I quickly pulled over.

Giving: There's an old man of meager means I know who over the last 25 years has given away $100,000 (usually in $1,000 increments) to needy people he hardly knows. I've always admired him and wanted to do the same. So I started scouring local newspapers for possible recipients of my charity. I planned to anonymously send $100 to whomever seemed worthy. But I never sent anything. For some reason, I found it incredibly difficult to be generous. No one ever seemed more deserving of my money than I did. Forgive me.

Taking a spontaneous vacation: I always travel by strict itinerary, and the pressure usually ends up driving me crazy. Once, just once, I'd like to walk into an airport terminal with no reservation, scan the departure board, and pick a random destination. In fact, that's the way I was planning to handle this year's family vacation, until I learned that walk-on fares can cost thousands of dollars. There is no last-minute discounting, no reward for the impulsive airport shopper. It's the exact opposite. So we ended up with four coach tickets, bought well in advance, to Denver.

Spending 24 uninterrupted hours with my kids: Every parent's chief regret is that they don't spend enough time with their children. I feel guilty about it every day. But when I told my 15- and 11-year-olds what I was planning to do, they weren't exactly overwhelmed. Sure, they enjoy having me around, but at their ages they don't need intensive one-on-one. "Dad," my son said. "Trust me. A couple of hours a day is more than enough."

Getting back all the valuable stuff my mother made me throw out: My baseball cards, my Creepy Crawler set, my Hector Heathcoat lunch pail, my Johnny Lightning Double-Loop Action Race Set, my G.I. Joe with Kung Fu Grip (in original package), my Daisy BB rifle, my Batman comic books, my little green army men, my Revell model cars and airplanes. . . . I remember it all. I have a list. I'm working on it.

And besides these regrets that I didn't quite relive, I have a bunch of others I haven't even started on yet. It seems that the more second chances I give myself, the more I think of. Someday, I still want to:

- *Buy something from an infomercial*
- *Apologize to my best man*
- *Move out of this little valley where I've spent my entire life*
- *Tell my boss to go to hell*
- *Build a treehouse for my kids*
- *Do something really artistic*
- *Buy a banjo*
- *Work as a waiter in a fancy restaurant*
- *Become fluent in a foreign language*
- *Skinny-dip*
- *Punch Jeffrey Gantzel right in the mouth*
- *Rip off my wife's clothes*
- *See the Packers at Lambeau Field*
- *Bench-press my body weight*
- *Ride a motorcycle*
- *Pledge a fraternity*
- *Own a Schwinn Stingray with a rear slick, sissy bar, and banana seat*
- *Learn how to defend myself*

There's 18 more of 'em, just that quick. You should try this. Start making your own list. We are all bound to some degree by the knots of our regret. I know, because whenever I explain the concept of this book to people, their reaction is always the same. First, there's a look of recognition, then a smile at the mere thought of getting another opportunity at whatever they're remembering. Regrets of love, fear, money, sport, career, guts, friendship. They confess. It's cathartic. But it's even more so if you take it to the next step.

I learned a number of things from this experiment, from tinkering with my own fate. Although there's a danger to putting life on hold as I did and going backward, ultimately, I made a lot of forward progress.

- *Reliving regrets made my life exciting again. It made me feel young and deliciously impulsive. It's freedom.*

- *Knowing once and for all is wonderful. I derived great satisfaction from finally confronting the uncertainties that had gnawed at me for decades. To bring something full circle, to feel its completeness, to finally get an answer, is to bury a worry forever. There is nothing that feels better.*

- *Believing in predestination won't get you anywhere. No matter how romantic and reassuring the notion sounds, it's just another way of shirking responsibility. The life I have is my doing, no one else's. I made these choices, and I don't necessarily have to live with them. I can take a mulligan. I can make my life different. Anyone can.*

- *Dreading what you're about to do is a sign that it's of great value. The regrets that made me most apprehensive were the ones that ultimately proved the most worthwhile to relive. The more difficult it was to go back, the more hesitant I was about picking up the phone, the more I needed to. And the more I learned.*

- *Having a regret-free life is impossible. I am sure of this now. Once I began writing this book and, most important, acting this way, a whole world of possibilities opened up. A man with no regrets is a man who lacks the guts to confront himself. I revisited*

20, but now I have 120. It has become an addictive lifestyle. But it's the pursuit, not always the result, that's most valuable.

So that's what I've learned. And honestly, I don't regret a single experience. To go back to the turning points of life, to stand no longer confused at its busy crossroads, is to truly be born again.

For 12 months, I was a driver instead of a passenger, and destiny was an actual place on the map. I was an ordinary middle-age guy with a crazy plan. And now that my trip is complete, I'm convinced that the secret to happiness, the key to feeling alive again, is to literally live again—to face those doubts you have of yourself, swallow hard, and give it another shot.